The Curious Case of Mike Lynch

ABOUT THE AUTHOR

Katie Prescott is the technology business editor of *The Times* and is a weekly columnist for the newspaper's award-winning business section. She is the co-host of *The Times Tech Podcast* and won Tech Commentator of the Year at the UK Tech Awards in 2024. A regular on Times Radio, she is a familiar voice to millions of listeners after a decade reporting for the BBC and presenting the business news on Radio 4's *Today*. Prescott studied Modern Languages at Pembroke College, Oxford, and now lives where she grew up in London with her two daughters.

The Curious Case of Mike Lynch

The Improbable Life & Death of a Tech Billionaire

KATIE PRESCOTT

First published 2025 by Macmillan Business
an imprint of Pan Macmillan
The Smithson, 6 Briset Street, London EC1M 5NR
EU representative: Macmillan Publishers Ireland Ltd, 1st Floor,
The Liffey Trust Centre, 117–126 Sheriff Street Upper,
Dublin 1 D01 YC43
Associated companies throughout the world

ISBN 978-1-0350-7423-5 HB
ISBN 978-1-0350-7424-2 TPB

3 5 7 9 8 6 4 2

A CIP catalogue record for this book is available from the British Library.

Typeset in Minion Pro by Six Red Marbles UK, Thetford, Norfolk
Printed and bound in India by Manipal Technologies Limited

To my beloved family

Contents

Dramatis Personae

Mike Lynch: Tech entrepreneur once dubbed 'Britain's answer to Bill Gates'. His flagship business was Autonomy, which he co-founded with **Richard Gaunt**. Sacked in 2012, in the wake of the Hewlett-Packard (HP) acquisition of Autonomy, and was later accused of fraud. Founded the investment firm Invoke Capital, which funded and shaped tech businesses like Darktrace, Luminance and Featurespace.

Leo Apotheker: CEO of HP from September 2010 who spearheaded the disastrous Autonomy deal.

Michele (formerly Anthony) Bettencourt: CEO of Verity at the time of its acquisition by Autonomy in 2005. Oversaw some of Autonomy's further acquisitions before leaving in 2009. Developed a strong relationship with Lynch and his family.

Jonathan Bloomer: Chairman of Morgan Stanley International and Hiscox. Joined Autonomy as non-executive director and chaired the internal audit committee from 2010 until the HP sale. Testified for Lynch in both the UK and US trials.

Charles (Chuck) Breyer: Judge who presided over the US trials of both **Sushovan Hussain** (2018), and Lynch and **Stephen Chamberlain** (2024).

Stephen Chamberlain: Autonomy Vice-President of Finance, 2005–2012. Tried alongside Lynch on fraud charges in the US.

Nicole Eagan: Chief Marketing Officer at Autonomy, 2005–2012. Co-founder and co-CEO of Darktrace (2014–21), where she remains as Strategic Advisor.

Christopher 'Stouffer' Egan: Joined Autonomy in 2001 as a Boston-based salesman, later given the (largely honorific) position of CEO of Autonomy US. Stayed on at HP after the acquisition.

Richard Gaunt: Initially hired by Lynch at his first company, Lynett Systems; went on to co-found Cambridge Neurodynamics (1990) and Autonomy (1996) with Lynch. Left Autonomy in 2003.

Mark Geall: Former City analyst who joined Autonomy in 2008 and became Director of Investor Relations; became concerned that the company was giving a misleading impression of its growth, and left in 2010.

Poppy Gustafsson: Former Autonomy accountant, chief executive of Darktrace and latterly Baroness Gustafsson, CBE, Labour Party life peer and Minister of State for Investment from 2024–25.

Mr Justice Hildyard: High Court Judge who presided over the UK civil trial brought by HP against Lynch and **Sushovan Hussain** in 2019.

Brent Hogenson: Head of Finance for Autonomy US, 2009–2010. Identified oddities in the company's accounts and voiced concerns to Lynch and senior management; fired soon after on dubious grounds.

Sushovan Hussain: Chief Financial Officer (CFO) of Autonomy, 2001–2012. Close friend and ally of Lynch, having attended Bancroft's and Christ's College, Cambridge at the same time. Along with Lynch, the target of HP's successful UK civil lawsuit. Jailed in the US after a jury found him guilty of fraud.

Rolo Igno: One of Lynch's bodyguards during his year-long house arrest in San Francisco (2023–24).

Andy Kanter: Joined Autonomy in 2000 and was appointed Chief Operating Officer (COO) in 2001, and more generally functioned as a right-hand man. Resigned in May 2012 amid the crumbling HP/Autonomy merger and soon afterwards joined Lynch's next venture, Invoke Capital, as a non-executive partner.

Daud Khan: City analyst based first at Merrill Lynch, then at Cazenove, covering Autonomy intermittently since 2001. First voiced scepticism about Autonomy's growth in early 2008.

Richard Knights: Senior Deloitte accountant who oversaw the firm's audits of Autonomy's books from 2005 to 2010. The Financial Reporting Council (FRC) judged him and his successor, Nigel Mercer, to have facilitated Autonomy's misleading presentation of its accounts.

Cathie Lesjak: CFO at HP from 2007 and then interim CEO after the forced resignation of the previous incumbent, Mark Hurd, in 2010. Sceptical of the deal with Autonomy, and clashed with her successor, **Leo Apotheker**, over it.

Angela Lynch, née Bacares: Born in the US to Colombian parents and educated at Brown and Dartmouth before starting a career in banking. Married Lynch in September 2001 and had two daughters with him, Esme and Hannah.

Peter Menell: Autonomy Chief Technical Officer (CTO) from 2004, replacing **Richard Gaunt**, and later involved in setting up Invoke Capital.

Christopher (Chris) Morvillo: Lawyer at Clifford Chance. Key member of the defence team that secured Lynch's acquittal in June 2024.

Frank Quattrone: Founder of Qatalyst Partners, an investment bank focusing on tech businesses. Contacted Lynch in 2010 about preparing Autonomy for a potential sale and helped market the company to potential US buyers.

Adam Reeves: Federal prosecutor of **Sushovan Hussain** and Lynch in their US trials.

Joel Scott: Joined Autonomy as General Counsel in 2005 and eventually became its Chief Operating Officer for the Americas.

Jack Stockdale: Joined Autonomy in its early days as a software developer; a key member of the tech team highly valued by Lynch.

Mike Sullivan: Senior Vice-President of Zantaz at the time of its acquisition by Autonomy and subsequently headed Autonomy's archiving and litigation division. Central to Autonomy's hardware sales in the US, which would become a focus of HP's accusations of fraud.

Robert (Rob) Webb, KC: Appointed Autonomy's first permanent chairman in 2009. Chair of Invoke Capital investee companies Darktrace (2014–21) and Luminance (2016–23).

Meg Whitman: Prominent tech executive who was CEO of eBay for a decade (1998–2008); member of HP's Board of Directors; appointed CEO of HP amid the Autonomy acquisition in September 2011 and stayed until 2018. Had a fractious relationship with Lynch and forced him out when Autonomy fell below its quarterly targets.

Author's Note

In June 2024, *The Times* held a summer party in the bucolic setting of Middle Temple Gardens in central London. The home of barristers is an elegant green space in the heart of the capital, surrounded by sixteenth-century buildings and sandwiched between the touristy Strand and The Thames. Suited and booted financiers and top lawyers have long replaced journalists in neighbouring Fleet Street, yet for one evening, we were back in the area and making the most of it. This legal setting is a very appropriate place for this very legal story to begin.

That evening, the perfectly manicured lawn was buzzing with reporters drinking wine and gossiping about stories and each other in the warm sunshine, when my phone started to flash with news from the other side of the Atlantic.

Over in San Francisco, it was only late morning, but another party was about to begin. In a pressure-cooker Californian court, Mike Lynch and his co-defendant Stephen Chamberlain had just been found not guilty of defrauding Hewlett-Packard (HP) during the $11 billion sale of his business Autonomy to the US firm.

The shadow of a life behind bars in America which had hung

over Lynch for more than a decade had been lifted. One of Britain's most controversial entrepreneurs, who had a mere 0.4 per cent chance of triumph in Silicon Valley's biggest fraud case, had won.

In London, amid the fray of the summer party, I ran to find Richard Fletcher, *The Times*' business editor, whose astounded eyebrows disappeared up his forehead. Having covered Lynch since his early days in business journalism, Richard was even more surprised than I was, and swore in a way only a South Londoner can at the shock news.

Ours was not an unfair reaction from cynical journalists – the situation was a bundle of contradictions. Lynch may have just won in the US, but he had previously been roundly criticized for fiddling Autonomy's accounts in the judgement from a very detailed British civil trial, filed by HP. The damages in that case were yet to be established, but HP wanted $4 billion.

In the years before Lynch's American trial, Sushovan Hussain, Autonomy's chief financial officer (CFO), had been sentenced to five years in prison in the US, following a criminal trial overseen by the very same judge who had just read out Lynch's not-guilty verdict in San Francisco. Furthermore, the British accountancy watchdog had also found evidence of fraud following a tribunal and fined Deloitte, Autonomy's auditor, £15 million over its work.

Lynch was an aficionado of Bayes' theorem which is a way of guessing an outcome based on probability, combining how likely something was to begin with and new evidence. In this context, with all the negative judgements which had come before, the odds really had been stacked against him.

I disappeared as quickly as possible to write the top of my story for the next morning. Like so many others, including Lynch, we had anticipated a very different outcome, and there was quite a lot of reworking to be done.

*

FOLLOWING MANY YEARS as a BBC business journalist, I joined *The Times* just shy of my fortieth birthday, in 2022, to cover the busy, exciting and often lurid technology beat.

In my first few months in the job there were some big stories emerging. Elon Musk started his serious foray into politics, driving a supertanker through the town square of the chattering classes by buying Twitter; crypto baron Sam Bankman-Fried turned out to be running a shambolic house of cards; and ChatGPT was launched on an unsuspecting public who were discovering the highs and lows of generative AI.

Despite the swirl of these various emerging dramatic narratives, I was always fascinated by the Autonomy vs HP saga: the clash between a Silicon Valley titan and a British tech startup success brought low. It had all the elements of a brilliant story: a cracking cast of colourful characters, a seismic culture clash between the UK and the US, and disputed fraud allegations.

In the months leading up to Lynch's criminal trial in San Francisco, I had cast around for a book to read or a film to watch about Lynch's extraordinary life and what really happened at Autonomy. Astonishingly, there was none.

I had wanted to understand how this unconventional man from a modest background in Essex had become Britain's first dotcom billionaire and gone on to build a business empire that had taken him to the heart of the British establishment. He'd started Autonomy in June 1996 in a small office in Cambridge, with only a handful of people. Just four years later, it would go on to become a FTSE 100 software business before he sold it to HP for $11bn in 2011, an astonishing figure, only for Lynch and others to be accused of cooking the company's books, something he always denied. It was an extraordinary rise and an extraordinary fall.

I decided to pitch a book, and combed through the many court documents to discern what had happened and to write a draft proposal. I even approached Lynch's team about the idea. He wanted to get the trial out of the way, they said, and then it might be considered. I persevered.

Why had no book been written about Lynch before I embarked on this one? I think the answer is twofold. First, writing such a story while legal cases in which he was a co-defendant were ongoing was complicated, to say the least. Second, Lynch had spectacularly fallen out with many of the technology journalists from the generation before mine who might have written it.

An irascible character, he felt the media was overly negative and did not give him a fair hearing. They in turn found him rude, abrasive and sometimes deceitful. It was a pattern in his relationships, repeated throughout his life.

Oddly, after his acquittal, publishers' interest in the project waned.

But then came another shock.

Just months later, in the middle of August 2024, Lynch took a special summer holiday aboard his yacht, *Bayesian*, to celebrate his court victory with his family and a small group who had supported him through his long, arduous legal battle. A freak storm hit and *Bayesian* sank off the coast of Sicily. Mike Lynch and his daughter Hannah died. So did five others: Lynch's warm and popular attorney Chris Morvillo and his wife, Neda; Jonathan Bloomer – the chair of Autonomy's audit committee and a well-known City figure; his wife, Judy; and the yacht's chef, Recaldo Thomas.

On that same weekend, Stephen Chamberlain, back in the heart of his family after so long living in San Francisco, was hit by a car while running in Cambridge and died in hospital.

What are the odds, people asked again and again, *that both men – the only two defendants in one of the biggest fraud trials in history – would both die in such unlikely circumstances on the exact same weekend?* Unable to deal with coincidence, minds flew to dramatic, unlikely conspiracy theories. But, above all, it was unfathomably sad.

Suddenly, interest in the story was huge – everyone wanted to know who this man was. To write this book in the short time frame I was given, I turned to Sarah Treanor, a friend and former BBC colleague. We'd worked on many documentaries together in the past, including in Tanzania, Rwanda and Arctic Norway. Picky about her projects, she didn't need much convincing with this one. She came on board quickly and worked tirelessly by my side as soon as the starting gun was fired.

Working systematically through the mountains of evidence and cutting through myriad conspiracy theories, we started to piece together the story. It meant lots of late-night conversations, interviews at all times of day and travel. We cast the initial net wide. In the trawl we started to find the treasure. A crackly tape of Lynch talking in the late 1980s in his student house, his story brought to life by the audio; another tape of him negotiating a legal dispute in the 1990s; and some astonishing corporate spoof videos which have to be seen to be believed.

As a creative audio editor, Sarah felt especially connected to these artefacts, finding more understanding in hearing a person than in reading their words. I am forever indebted to her diligence, enthusiasm and perspicacity.

There is no getting round the fact that Mike Lynch was a difficult, divisive character who often rubbed people up the wrong way. In the wake of his death, much of the coverage depicted him as a plucky British success story, brought low by the might of an American tech giant. The reality, as Lynch himself would so often say about life, was painted in shades of grey.

It was not an easy time to write this book. Initially, it felt like there was a collective omertà around everything to do with Lynch. People close to him were grieving and understandably unwilling to speak; those who disliked him were equally understandably sensitive and worried, they repeatedly said, about speaking ill of the dead.

At the same time, a message went round the network of former Autonomy staff that Katie Prescott was 'dangerous', a clear warning not to speak to me. Many who did agree to be interviewed expressed fear about what might happen to them if they were discovered, and did not want their names in print, especially at first. I could not understand it – we were discussing events from decades previously. Clearly Lynch inspired fear while he was alive, and it had not dissipated with his death.

Surprisingly, those who said they were 'scared' included some senior, mature and successful people at Autonomy. Slowly, attitudes to me thawed noticeably and people on all sides seemed to become more comfortable with sharing their experiences, but it took a lot of careful building of trust.

This book is compiled from interviews with almost one hundred people who knew Lynch. On top of that, we were given a slew of documentation and recordings from inside Autonomy and a rich cache of letters, pitches and emails which paint a picture of the atmosphere inside the business. Quotes within the book are directly taken from emails, court testimony, evidence submitted in trial, interviews or reconstructed from interviewees' memories. But, as Steve Chamberlain said in his diaries, extracts of which are contained within, it is very easy for false memories to be created. Drawing on all of this, I have endeavoured to build an accurate picture. Where there were gaps, I have used inference with care, always aiming to remain faithful to the spirit and substance of what occurred. Much of this story has been disputed over the years and I have done my best to make sense of it using the evidence. Any errors or misjudgements are mine alone.

Unpicking the truth was complex. I was told again and again that Lynch was a born storyteller, that he had the gift of the gab which marks out a successful entrepreneur. We quickly found that not all of his stories stood up to scrutiny. He would stretch and bend the truth to spin a better yarn. It gave everything a 'Lynch Premium', as one friend described it. This, I believe, is what sparked the fraud within Autonomy. His obsession with hitting financial targets, of making everything look rosy on the outside, drove the misrepresentations in

Autonomy's accounts: the undeclared hardware sales, for example, and sales which were recognized when they shouldn't have been.

Such behaviour started small, but it became like an addiction, senior Autonomy executives told me. It perhaps would not have been discovered – it may even have stopped – had the sale to HP not happened. Autonomy was caught with its clothes off when HP started digging into its accounts. It is most probable that this behaviour was led by Lynch; the evidence is overwhelming and he always admitted 'pushing the envelope' in private. But in public he fought with everything he had not to let that sully the reputation of his beloved business. Ever tenacious, Lynch doubled down, consistently denying any culpability. Instead, after the fraud accusations he continued to work on growing British tech companies, as he always had, even as he was increasingly shunned by the British establishment he had worked so hard to penetrate. It is a tragedy that this complex character never got to live out the next chapter of his life away from the shadow of the bitter fight with HP.

This book raises fundamental questions about trust in business: the relationships between companies and their professional advisers, the relationships between companies and the City and the veracity of the information companies disclose to the public. It also revives the age-old debate of why British tech businesses look to the US for growth and the issue of the extradition treaty between the UK and US. These themes of fifteen-odd years ago have not changed today.

This may be a business story, but it is a very human one at its heart. It is one of hubris, of a brilliant, difficult, indefatigable man who would never admit defeat and who fought right up until the bitter end.

Katie Prescott, July 2025

Prologue

SUNDAY, 18 AUGUST 2024. PORTICELLO, SICILY.

There is a rhythm to life in Porticello, a pace of existence set by the sea. Day after day, early in the morning, fishermen in the northern Sicilian village take their boats in and out, in and out, in and out, their trawls set by the tide.

Then they descend on the small market square, before dawn, to sell their catch, calling out their wares in a cacophony of Sicilian dialect, the singular language of the region, guttural and slurred. Some of it is snapped up by waterfront restaurants serving the influx of summer visitors, some by local matriarchs planning the day's meals. The bars fill up with old men taking their morning coffee, watching the daily ritual.

Porticello hides around the corner of the bay from the busy city of Palermo, sitting at the top left-hand edge of the football kicked by Italy's boot. The village has not been whitewashed by the tourist trade. The peeling facades of the buildings in its narrow streets are studded with satellite dishes, the streets hung with laundry, rickety mopeds weaving in and out. Modern cars somehow make it into spaces they were not built for and bravely take the sharp corners of the antiquated roads driving buttressed up against the walls.

It is beautiful here, but it can be a hard life in this very poor part of Italy. About half of Porticello's 12,000-strong population rely on fishing. Everyone understands how the waters can change from benign to vicious in a split second. Locals have long memories of tragedies in the waves, the names of those lost at sea are etched outside the fish market as a daily reminder. Each year in October, Catholic and fishing traditions merge when a procession of boats sets out into the water, dropping a laurel wreath into the sea in commemoration of the community's drowned loved ones.

Holidaymakers rarely see this darker side of Sicily; at sea, pleasure vessels play host to visitors basking in the Mediterranean sun, enjoying the famously warm and clear water.

It was here, at the height of holiday season in 2024, that the magnificent fifty-six-metre *Bayesian* headed late one evening, the sails of its mast – one of the tallest in the world – neatly furled.

On board the luxurious vessel, a group of family and friends stood together on the pale wooden deck as the yacht dropped anchor. One guest snapped a sunset picture on her phone and posted it on Instagram. Envious comments from followers at home flooded her feed. At the centre of this gathering was the host of the summer excursion, Michael Richard Lynch. Barefoot, dressed in his summer uniform of chinos, a brown leather belt and a pale linen shirt, he was a bald, heavy-set man with thick dark eyebrows framing his narrow eyes. His large, domed head housed a fierce intellect and an unwavering self-belief. A Marmite figure, he had been well-known in the business community for decades but was far from a household name, even in his own country. This holiday was a celebration of his freedom and of his partial redemption after the businessman had won his trial against the US Department of Justice, accused of a massive fraud. A couple of months before, a trip on board the *Bayesian* around the delights of the Mediterranean wouldn't have been possible for Lynch.

In fact, many times he had thought that such a voyage would never happen again.

The odds of the wealthy technology entrepreneur being acquitted were infinitesimally small, even with his almost limitless financial firepower. And yet he won the criminal case. He had worried about dying behind bars, but now here he was, back in Europe on his beloved superyacht, ready for a new chance at life.

The company on board the *Bayesian* was a convivial assortment of friends, professional connections and family; people who had helped him fight his legal battle, and those who never hesitated to remain loyal, even when others fell away. Lynch always liked to reward his supporters. By his side were his wife Angela and eighteen-year-old daughter Hannah, on the cusp of going to university. It was almost time for the holiday to end, and for a fresh start to begin in earnest – both professionally and personally.

But everything was about to change. The weather had started to turn. Looking across the calm seas, those on board the *Bayesian* could see occasional flashes of lightning. The sky in the distance was dark and cloudy, and the smell of rain was on the air.

A storm was brewing that would change their lives for ever.

PART ONE

The Outlier

ONE

Follow the Dog

An outlier refers to an individual or data point that significantly deviates from the norm or expected pattern within a particular group, dataset, or population. In the context of people, an outlier is someone whose characteristics, behaviour, or performance are notably different from the majority of the group.

– Definition generated by ChatGPT

East London in the early 1960s might not have been the land of milk and honey, but for Dolores O'Neill, it offered a damn sight more exciting opportunities than a life in the sleepy Irish town of Carrick-on-Suir. She was one of eleven children, nine sisters and two brothers. Some of her older siblings had moved over to London, sending back stories of an electrifying new life, and she couldn't wait to join them.

Life in the city was often busy, bleak and cut-throat. It could throw you in the gutter, but there was always the sliver of a chance, just the possibility, that the streets would be paved with gold. This was in sharp contrast to Ireland, where traditional industries were dying and the economy was struggling to modernize.

When she left school, Dolores bolted out of Tipperary, a county she'd barely left since her birth in 1939, as soon as she could. She joined her elder sister Nena in Walthamstow, where she had trained as a nurse at Whipps Cross Hospital.

With a sharp sense of humour and an Irish brogue which never left her, Dolores was the latest in a long line of strong women in the large family. More of a rebel than the others, she enjoyed the new life and independence she found in London, especially after the strictures put on women she'd experienced in Ireland. She suddenly had a foot in a cosmopolitan environment that was completely new to her, a melting pot of people from all over the world – and a familiar cohort of about 600,000 Irish-born residents.

She settled in Ilford, a popular destination for immigrants over the decades, where Irish social clubs would host the booming community until the early hours of the morning. On the city's eastern fringe, on the border with Essex, Ilford was a hotchpotch of hoity-toity areas and very rundown ones. It had parks with wide paths, duck ponds, and grand old trees, but the hum of traffic was never far away.

When Dolores fell in love, it was with a London-born Irishman also living in the area, Michael Lynch, whose family hailed from County Cork. He was a fireman, a dangerous and uncertain profession. Like Dolores's nursing job, it came with unpredictable and punishing hours. Holding down two such challenging occupations in a relationship was not a happy or easy combination. Yet they persevered, and married when Dolores was in her twenties, with Nena's son Gerard as their pageboy.

The couple settled in the Balfour Road area of Ilford, in the centre of the town. It wasn't the poorest area in the locality, but it wasn't far off. The streets had rough edges, there were gangs and criminals about, and rowdy houses with multiple occupants were starting to bloom. At home, money was always tight. Early on, the young couple turned to the bank for a £4 loan to get themselves established. It became an oft-told family joke that this early debt meant they began their life together on −£4. Their first son, Michael Jr, was born on 16 June 1965, when Dolores was twenty-six. Two years later, on 19 April 1967, Richard Lynch came along. Michael always looked after his younger brother, but the two boys could not have been more different.

From the start, Michael was an extraordinarily unusual baby, almost unique. For he arrived into the world without any fingerprints. The swirls and whorls which mark most of the population out as individuals were missing from his tiny hands, and they would never appear as he grew. You could ink up his fingertips and push them down, but they would not leave more than a smudge on the page. It is unclear exactly why – a rare genetic condition perhaps – but it was a great source of jokes for the man. 'I would make an excellent criminal!' he would say, laughing.

Lynch's arrival on the planet coincided with an auspicious year for technology. In 1965, in faraway California, Moore's Law was coined. The founder of Intel, Graham Moore, predicted that computers would become twice as powerful about every two years, while staying the same size and cost. It was a concept that would underpin the technological revolution that tracked baby Michael's lifetime.

LYNCH HAD FEW memories of these early years of his life, apart from watching trains hurtle in and out of London through a gap in the bricks on a nearby railway bridge. He could stay there, mesmerized by the machines, for hours.

While there was little money to go around, his parents always encouraged their sons to learn. Education could provide a better future, a chance of a new life. Dolores was a clever woman who read a lot of books and, as soon as the family was able to get their hands on a car, she would take her sons out every weekend to various museums, where Young Michael, as his parents called him, would be fascinated by aeroplanes and steam engines, just as he was by trains.

Michael was a curious child. Understanding how things worked always made his eyes light up. No mechanical item in the house was safe from his whirring brain, including his mother's alarm clock, the victim of an early experiment to see how things worked.

Scrawny and dark-haired, he didn't ever talk about wanting to be rich or wanting to be well-known, but he did always feel the need to fix things. The O'Neill cousins had a very early iteration of a computer games console – a prized possession. It broke one afternoon, and Lynch announced he would take it away and mend it, which is exactly what he did. He saw a problem and worked out a solution. It was obvious to his family even then that, somehow, he was going to get on in the world.

While London provided opportunities, it was a far from easy place for Irish families in the 1970s. This was the height of the Troubles, the brutal political violence which ripped Northern Ireland in two, and which the IRA brought to the British mainland. This backdrop of violence served to generate hostility against Irish people, who faced prejudice at work, problems finding housing, and difficulties being served in pubs.

For the young Lynch boys, this environment meant they had to learn to read the temperature of a room quickly. They learnt to duck and dive, to run fast to avoid getting caught up in retaliatory fights in the playground for something which had absolutely nothing to do with them. It bonded them to the local Irish community, where they found solace in a group of people who could understand what it was like not to fit in. It is striking that, throughout the rest of his life, Mike Lynch would consciously gravitate to outsiders.

The Irish were not the only arrivals who found themselves the target of hatred. Enoch Powell had made his infamous 'rivers of blood' speech in 1968, just a few years after Mike Lynch was born, criticizing the high rate of immigration and stirring up prejudice against new arrivals from across the former British Empire. Brawls, abusive language and spitting at immigrants were all common.

Having seen this kind of aggression over the years, it is perhaps no surprise that Lynch was always fiercely meritocratic, seeing through rank, money and status. He was only ever interested in how people thought and performed, not their background or even their politics. He may have banked vast sums of money and moved up several social rungs, but he had seen and understood other worlds along the way.

When he was about eight years old, at around the same time as the IRA launched its mainland bombing campaign, the family followed another well-trodden immigrant path and swapped their London suburb for cleaner air, a bigger house and more open space, in a new estate in Chelmsford in Essex. Dolores started work at the local Broomfield Hospital and Michael joined the Essex fire brigade. Friends and family report that they had a tense relationship, although Lynch's father disputes this version of events.

Lynch told people later in life that he quickly learnt that one way to avoid the fights was to 'follow the dog'. The family pet was so attuned to the moods of the humans around it that it could tell when Mike's parents were about to argue, and would promptly leave the room. He told friends that he would follow suit. It spurred his lifelong love of dogs.

Ultimately, Dolores and Michael Lynch finally separated when their sons had left home.

AWAY FROM ANY stresses within their core family, Mike and Richard's lives were softened by the experience of growing up in the noisy midst of a gaggle of first cousins in London – and even more in Ireland. There were fifty of them in total.

It meant the Lynch brothers were rarely alone. The O'Neill sisters were a community, and so their children all grew up together. It wasn't uncommon to pop round to an aunt or uncle's house and find several other family members already there. It was here, in the heart of his Irish family, that Lynch learnt an early love of storytelling, or spinning a good yarn.

Carrick-on-Suir might not have provided much in the way of adventure, or careers for his mother and her sisters, but it was a joyous location for summer holidays. The O'Neill children would all head over together and spend weeks in the idyllic Tipperary countryside, supervised by the family matriarch, 'Nan Ireland' (the maternal grandmother, Ellen O'Neill), and another auntie four doors down. It gave their parents back home in England a break from their offspring. One picture shows Lynch on a boat just off a riverbank there – he had the freedom to roam and plentiful company that life in Chelmsford rather lacked.

Michael Jr seemed happy enough with life, but something always troubled Dolores about her eldest boy. When he was still quite young, she realized that he was extraordinarily bright. It wasn't just because he pulled her alarm clock apart – he found schoolwork and problem-solving easy, and had a photographic memory.

Like a chess player, he could always see several moves ahead, but he was never solitary, strange or nerdy with it. He was good with other children, made friends and loved music. It sparked ambition within his parents to see him right, to make the most of his talents. There were brains in the O'Neill genes, the family would say, citing an auntie in Dublin who used to write speeches for the Taoiseach (the Irish prime minister).

Michael Sr always joked that he wanted to make sure his son avoided a job which involved running into burning buildings. It became part of Lynch-lore, a line that his son would often repeat, with a sardonic smile that revealed the truth behind the quip. Being a fireman was tough and risky. Michael Sr shared his wife's belief in the value of education, and he made sure that his sons always understood and appreciated the chances that were never available to him.

Dolores, in turn, swatted away the noises made by Lynch's primary school teachers, who told her imperiously that her boy had his hand up too much in class and was just too much of a know-it-all. She felt his work ethic was something to be encouraged, and she was not going to take their derogatory comments lying down.

One day, she was fretting about what to do with him, as usual, when one of his many aunts mentioned a scholarship scheme at Bancroft's, a well-established part-boarding and part-day private school in Woodford Green, six miles north of their old home in Ilford. No one knew much about the place, but it sounded intriguing, so in mid-1976 the Lynch family went for a grand day out to investigate. After marvelling at the sprawling nineteenth-century school buildings, which had echoes of a large country estate, young Mike was put forward for the entrance exam. When the results came in, Bancroft's made him an offer. He was just eleven years old.

The Lynch family could never have afforded to pay for schooling at Bancroft's. It was a world away from the education they had had themselves, but the well-funded bursary opened the imposing iron gates of the school and allowed young Mike access to an array of amenities, languages, sports and a rigorous academic tuition.

Bancroft's in the 1970s was not particularly smart, but it had the upright air that British private schools tend to exude. It boasted an active cadet corps, a strong musical tradition and even an armoury, where pupils could access a variety of guns to practise shooting. Old traditions, including corporal punishment, lingered on. It wasn't one of the big famous schools – it was no Eton or Harrow or Winchester – but, with its vast playing fields and russet neo-gothic building, it felt like a solid part of British establishment life.

And it was more meritocratic than it looked at first glance. Lynch was just one of the children who arrived at the school because of his brains rather than his bank account. A quarter of the boys were on scholarships and a further quarter of admissions were funded by Essex County Council. The result was that Lynch's year group featured an extremely bright cohort from a range of backgrounds.

They got in just in time. The direct grant scheme closed in 1977, the year after Lynch started. In one stroke, the healthy percentage of gifted attendees sponsored by the council was slashed. The change in policy caused uproar at Bancroft's and was derided as a political decision, and it led to other seismic changes to make up for the shortfall in enrolment – Lynch's year was the last to be all boys.

While the place he had won at Bancroft's afforded Lynch an educational opportunity that was clearly not to be missed, the school was a long way from home. In later years, he would recount tales of the onerous commute he would have to make from Chelmsford, forty miles east of London. He said that his travel to school involved waiting by the side of the road for an hour, until a friend of his father could pick him up and take him the rest of the way. Lynch's stories would often deviate from reality, but were just true enough to be believable.

In fact, things were a little more comfortable. Until he reached the sixth form, he regularly stayed in the attic room at his Aunt Nena's in Walthamstow, far closer to Bancroft's. This meant Lynch forged a strong relationship with his cousin Gerard Morris, seven years his senior. Theirs was a friendship which would last a lifetime. They used to walk the family dogs together in Epping Forest, behind the house, happily chatting the afternoons away.

LYNCH'S SCHOOLING WAS marked by the dawn of the computing age, a time when millions would cluster round television sets at home to watch programmes like BBC One's *Tomorrow's World*, featuring predictions and explorations of futuristic new inventions. Lynch was no different, fascinated by the advent and advances of technology.

Gants Hill, a neighbourhood some five miles from Bancroft's, was a Mecca for Lynch in his teenage years. There, he could pursue the two loves of his life – his girlfriend at the time, and computers. Gants Hill's high street boasted a Commodore computer shop, one of the only places accessible to him where he could gaze at a real-life personal computer.

Lynch's love of computing spilled into his academic life. During fifth form, he started an electronics club on Thursdays after school, in the physics lab. He even devised a beginner's course for other keen pupils, to equip them for what he rather earnestly referred to as the 'Age of the Microchip'. Lynch called on parents to donate surplus components and facilitated a system so the club's members could buy equipment through the school's supplier. He was practical, focused and made things happen, even as a teenager.

The electronics club ran in parallel to the computer club at Bancroft's, which had been founded by an enterprising mathematics teacher named Mr Hagedorn – this quickly became a centrepiece of Lynch's week too. Even though they weren't on the curriculum, there was a lot of interest in learning how to use computers, and by 1981 there were forty-eight club members, including the first girl. In the early days, when lunchtime came, Lynch and other members would excitedly plan out their next task for after school, when they'd be able to get their hands on the one computer the school had in its possession. They would type their program and then wait for the slow school printer to whir into action. Schools often only had basic terminals (like keyboards and screens) but no real 'computer' – just a way to connect remotely to a big machine somewhere else. Screeching static would sound as the computers got together and 'handshook'. It all took patience. After 3.30 p.m., they were able to dial up Imperial College's computer system and really get going.

Inevitably, leaving a group of young techies to their own devices meant mischief. For example, when you typed 'nuts' into that original computer, it would reply (much to the students' delight), 'And the same to you, sir.' They learnt how to send messages on the computer from someone else's name, another source of much hilarity. The club was extraordinarily influential on that generation of Bancroft children, sparking an interest which would turn into careers for many.

Later, Mr Hagedorn built the school its own computer – the Compukit UK 101 micro-computer – using one of the cheap and cheerful early home kits on the market, and the school allocated the club a dedicated little room of its own. This gave club members more time to play around with the machines, as they no longer had to wait until after home time.

Determined to be part of this new computer revolution, in his last year at school Lynch bought his own BBC Micro for a hefty £400, raising the money through a number of odd jobs, begging and borrowing. This was a formative moment, and not just for Lynch – ownership of a BBC Micro, specifically, shaped the careers of so many others who would later rise to prominence in the technology world.

Introduced in the UK in 1981, the Micro's development was a shrewd decision by the government of the time. Part of the BBC's Computer Literacy Project, and developed by Acorn in Cambridge for schools, the BBC Micro propelled technical understanding and software expertise. A decade later, it meant the UK had an enormous cohort of software developers at its disposal. Eventually, the Department of Industry aimed to install one of the subsidized machines in every secondary school in the country. By the end of 1982, as Lynch's time to depart Bancroft's approached, the school had a computer lab which featured no fewer than fifteen Micros.

At the same time, other affordable home devices were being unveiled in Britain, such as the popular ZX Spectrum, developed by Clive Sinclair. This system was instrumental both in teaching programming to enthusiastic amateurs and in making the UK a leader in the early computer games industry, as various bedroom experiments took off and became something more serious.

LYNCH AND HIS best friend from the Bancroft's computer club, an introverted young man named Richard Birkett, became bedroom tech tinkerers themselves.

During their sixth form, the pair started trying to work out how they could introduce a floppy disc drive to the Commodore 64 – a computer which used cassettes – and played around in the digital music scene with an early synthesizer, which allowed them to mix and sample various tracks. Birkett was always the software creator in the partnership, while Lynch focused on the hardware side, making use of his electronics expertise. The synthesizer was a magic machine for Lynch, who just loved the marriage between technology and music.

He had been a keen clarinet player from a young age and he also played the tenor saxophone. It came in useful – when a detention loomed, Lynch often pleaded a clarinet lesson, whether one existed or not. But clarinet practice was not a mere punishment-avoidance tactic – Lynch was absolutely passionate about the instrument. He liked to have fun with it at a time when the school would rather prod pupils down a rigid classical music route – so much so that, at the end of the fifth form, he started a band, called Blues Patrol at the suggestion of a teacher.

Lynch was a superb, if unorthodox, clarinettist. He would put the mouthpiece right into his mouth, with his cheeks puffed out, exactly as music teachers would tell you not to do, but with brilliant results. Blues Patrol's repertoire swiftly grew and grew from 1920s jazz and blues through swing and big band pieces – Glenn Miller's 'Pennsylvania 6-5000' was an early favourite – until it had four hours' worth of available material, which included 1950s rock and roll and even some 1960s pop.

It was all a bit too modern and funky for the school's music department, who tolerated the band by quietly giving it the space to practise, but the other students loved it. Blues Patrol's eleven members played a few times in the school, as well as at church dances, school parties and at the Chelmsford Working Men's Club. 'We enjoy an evening as much as an audience,' Lynch said. As the band's undisputed leader and founder, he would arrange all the music, writing

Blues Patrol, the Bancroft's band, featuring Mike Lynch.

down all the different parts while jiggling home on the bus. Later, the band started to play from jazz notation, working on an improv basis and lessening the pressure on Lynch.

As being a band leader might suggest, teenage Lynch was a far cry from the stereotype of an introverted tech pioneer. Indeed, he didn't really fit into a particular tribe or mould at Bancroft's – not a sports boy, not the most popular, not a bully, and not a clever but awkward nerd. Within his year group, he was not a particularly dominant or overbearing personality, but he always excelled in the classroom. Notably, when he didn't do well, it would make him even more competitive, and he would work harder to make sure he achieved the next time. One thing he always had was inner confidence which, as with the band, swept others along with him. He made a close group of loyal friends and, as he would go on to do throughout his life, collected smart people who impressed him; at Bancroft's these included two Richards – Anton and Birkett – who he would sweep into his businesses.

Away from school, the teenage Lynch learnt valuable life lessons working in his mother's hospital during the holidays. He served tea, bread and jam to the patients at three o'clock each afternoon, pushing a trolley laden with a big aluminium NHS tea urn around the wards. It was an early introduction to the realities of life, and to death as the great leveller. As Lynch saw it, once you're in hospital it does not matter who you are or how much money you have. People are just people.

By the time he reached sixth form, Lynch's teachers had him marked out as one of the most outstanding students in the school. He was a polymath, who excelled at everything from Classics to the scientific subjects he focused on in his final years. Bancroft's had developed a reputation for getting pupils into Oxbridge, and Lynch joined the classes that coached pupils for the entrance exams.

It was never a dead cert that anyone would win a place. To this day, nobody – no matter the privileges they've had – is guaranteed a place at Oxford or Cambridge. Admissions to both are notoriously competitive, and their rigorous interview processes are designed to test and even intimidate potential students.

After sitting A levels in Maths, Further Maths, Physics and Chemistry, the magic combination needed to carry on with scientific study, he won a place at the same Christ's College Cambridge where Charles Darwin had studied. By then, Lynch knew he was something special.

TWO

The Lynch Mob

In science and technology, Cambridge has a good shot at being the premier university in the world. Where else have you got? Stanford and MIT? It's certainly in that league. There is still a culture of excellence there that has been eroded in other places.

– *Mike Lynch*, Management Today, *1 June 2000*

The entrance to Christ's College Cambridge looks like that of a small castle. The gatehouse squats in the heart of the university city, its imposing tower topped with a flagpole and festooned with an enormous gilded coat of arms featuring two yales (mythical beasts), blood-red roses and a series of golden portcullis emblems.

At the heart of the Great Gate, as it is called, stands a small, brightly coloured statue of Lady Margaret Beaufort, the college's sixteenth-century founder. She was one of the most important ladies of her age, a powerful figure in the Wars of the Roses, the richest woman of the Medieval era and the mother of the first Tudor King, Henry VII.

From the outside, you cannot see what lies within. Pushing open the hefty oak door reveals a world that is closed off to most people; immaculate lawns are flanked by sandy-coloured stone buildings and there are a series of beautiful, interlinked squares known as 'courts'.

For Mike Lynch, though, from 1983 to the end of his life, the castle gate was always open. He could come and go as he pleased and nothing would ever be able to take that away.

At Christ's, tradition and innovation sit together in panelled rooms through semi-hidden doorways, some barely tall enough to admit a modern visitor. The student guide to Cambridge from the early 1980s ignored its striking architecture and gently mocked Christ's for its central location, lending it sardonic distinction for its 'easy access to the Wimpy, a hot dog stall, and Dorothy Perkins'. The college was renowned for its scientific prowess – perhaps one of the reasons Lynch picked it out from the many other colleges, each with their individual personalities and reputations.

His arrival in Cambridge in 1983 felt life-changing – even more so than it would have for most eighteen-year-olds leaving home for the first time. From the start, he felt a creeping feeling of belonging to the place. Christ's provided a calling card and a permanent badge of honour that translated around the world, marking out his extraordinary intelligence and giving him credibility. It brought him the recognition which he craved.

Christ's also gave him a room of his own, which was far more cossetted and privileged than his home life. There was no longer a need to bunk up with his cousin or travel a long distance to school. Here, everything was in one place. It was a sanctuary of academia and a social whirl. He was allocated a cleaner and his meals were provided in a grandiose hall under a soaring arched ceiling, dark wood panelling and stained-glass windows. For more informal meals, the Buttery, which also served as the bar and stayed open until 8 p.m., was available (behind the counter was Mrs NoButter, named for the question she would ask when making the students a sandwich). Looming over the Buttery was the college library, a constant reminder that any given student's time could be better spent elsewhere.

As bizarre and unfamiliar a world as it was to Mike Lynch, he loved Christ's for his whole life, and credited it with almost the entirety of his future success. Yet despite this, he always retained the sense of being an outsider in this cloistered place. Unlike some of the more privileged students, he had had a more worldly childhood – the pain and suffering he saw inside his mother's hospital, his experiences of being threatened as an Irish boy, seeing the poor eking out a living around the Balfour Road. There was never any attempt on Lynch's part to cover this part of himself up. He kept his strong Essex accent – and he often spoke about life back home.

LIKE CHRIST'S, CAMBRIDGE University in 1983 was a curious combination of rigid traditions and ripping up the rule book. Academic robes, ball gowns and black ties rubbed shoulder pads with neon, punk hairstyles, leather and studs. 'Blue Monday' by New Order was being played everywhere. Despite its privilege, the university was by no means isolated from the political tumult of the time. Margaret Thatcher was in power, having won a landslide second term for the Conservative party that year. In 1979, she had won the election pledging to bring down inflation and tackle the strikes which were ravaging Britain – yet come the early 1980s, Britain was enduring yet another deep recession with peaking unemployment. The Iron Lady, fresh from victory in the Falklands War, was battling striking miners on her home turf.

Brits were encouraged to be investors, many for the first time, and there was a growing public understanding of share ownership. Tenants received the right to buy their council house or flat, and the government's drive towards privatization meant shares in formerly state-owned companies like British Telecom were marketed to the ordinary person.

The big student activism issue of the day was ending apartheid in South Africa, especially prominent when 'Free Nelson Mandela' was released by the Specials in 1984. Racism more generally was under scrutiny and, in a night of mayhem, Enoch Powell took part in a debate at the Cambridge Union during Lynch's time. Globally, East and West were still at loggerheads, and fears of the Cold War turning hot remained real and very present. And away from the spiky geo-politics and mutually assured destruction, extraordinary advances in technology were rippling around the world, changing everything.

Lynch's time at the college was made easier by several familiar faces from Bancroft's, which made the city feel more like home. The Richards were there: Anton in the year below him at Christ's and Birkett at another college. Also at another college was Daniel Levy, a fellow Essex man who would become one of the earliest investors in Lynch's businesses – later, he also became the chairman of Tottenham Hotspur Football Club.

Aside from those he knew, Lynch was surrounded by stellar students, many of whom would go on to experience fame and fortune. Peers at Christ's included Rory Sutherland, the entertaining and vivacious future ad executive, and Richard Gnodde, the future vice-chairman of Goldman Sachs. A tall, suave visiting student from South Africa, Gnodde was a keen rugby player who made the British Christ's boys feel spotty and gawky in comparison.

Within his year, Lynch was far from the alpha male. He was well-liked and rubbed along happily with everyone, but he did not stand out as one to watch among his peers. He was never a huge, swaggering character on campus. Just as at school, Lynch was hard to pigeonhole at college, described as 'socially promiscuous', dabbling in a number of circles.

Those who studied scientific subjects at Cambridge were part of a singular and very distinct tribe with a language and humour all of their own. Lynch, studying natural sciences – known as 'natsci' – joined in. He was a skinny young man with long dark hair who often wore clashing colours, such as burgundy trousers with a bright green jumper – very much the garb of an academic who had more important and interesting things to worry about. While he wore the right uniform, again he was a bit of an outlier in the stereotypical science group in that he liked popular music, could talk to women (he even had *girlfriends*) and – most remarkably, perhaps – he could explain scientific concepts in plain English.

When it came to extracurricular activities, however, ever-present was the all-important and time-consuming question of money. University tuition was free in those days and there were generous living grants available too, but Lynch had to pay his own way for extras. During term time he eschewed the clichéd grubby bar job, instead doing computer work for other students. He also continued his business developing innovative music tech with Birkett, his school friend. Keeping the cash flowing was as important as keeping up with his studies, which, as his professors discovered, he could manage just fine without much effort.

He worked during the holidays as a researcher in an optical computing department at Marconi, the radio giant that was part of the General Electric Company (GEC). In the long-term, the prospect of a job with Marconi did not fill him with glee; he saw the idea of drifting into a technical career in the UK as a dead end. After his experience working there, he was forever scathing about the bureaucracy of large British businesses, which he felt killed experimentation and imagination. They just couldn't get things done – they were the opposite, he would say, of innovation. It was the last time the entrepreneur would ever work for anyone else until Hewlett-Packard came knocking well over a decade later.

He had one more passion project: his jazz band, the aptly named Lynch Mob. Just as he had at Bancroft's, Lynch created and led a musical group within Christ's, with songs such as 'Summertime' and 'Georgia on My Mind' being favourites to perform. The bulk of the band were pulled from the scientific tribe, and the college's two choral scholars were roped in as singers.

It was not a glamorous group. There were no fancy costumes or elegant lighting set-ups – just trainers and bare bulbs. Lynch did it for the love of playing music, and the band continued to thrive throughout his university career, driven by its tenacious founder. It was not easy to galvanize a group of students through rehearsals and performances, but he had a knack for inspiring others.

At their shows, he'd introduce the band with ironic and self-deprecating humour, but underneath that was inner strength, a sense he knew exactly what he was doing.

UNEXPECTEDLY, AS HE did not appear to do any work until at least quarter of an hour before his exams took place, Lynch achieved a first-class result in his first year's examinations.

This earnt him the privilege of living within the college for his second year, in a beautiful room in Second Court, which had the added draw of an enormous fireplace. It became a centre for social gatherings, especially for those who had not done as well academically and found themselves booted out of the hallowed college walls, living in housing dotted around Cambridge. Lynch would host lots of parties but was not a big drinker or ever into drugs. 'If you've got a brain like mine, you simply can't afford to do that sort of thing,' he said. But he always thoroughly enjoyed his food, even if his youthful metabolism meant he stayed slim for the time being.

His exam success was not to last into his second year, though, and *The Times* records him as having been awarded a lower second-class in 1985 for the second part of his natsci course – perhaps because he knew he planned to switch to engineering at this stage and had lost interest.

He certainly didn't seem to mind, and was content to amuse himself in other ways. He liked to mess with the people around him, sizing them up, probing and testing them. In his nasal tone and with his features showing little expression or movement, he would ask questions that were designed to catch people off-guard. Pointing to a random figure in a famous painting, he might ask, 'What do you think their name is?' He enjoyed seeing how different people would react, and the game could result in some very funny conversations.

At Cambridge, he was no longer always the most intelligent person in the room, but he was certainly up there and liked to assert the fact with his quirky conversation. 'If the world was ending,' he would ask, 'what would you do?' His own answer was always that he would take all the weapons he could, go to the top of the tallest building he could find, create a fortress and shoot.

He enjoyed probability games too, a characteristic which would only develop further as he got older. One of his favourites involved three closed doors – two hiding goats and the other a prize – a puzzle sometimes called the Monty Hall Problem after the host of the game show *Let's Make a Deal*. You pick one of the doors, and then the host (who knows where the prize is) opens one of the two remaining doors to reveal a goat. The central question of the puzzle is: should you then stick with your original pick, or twist?

The answer, somewhat counterintuitively, is to twist. Lynch relished seeing the panic in people's faces as they vacillated between the choices, when the answer to him and any of his mathematically minded friends was so completely obvious. (You can find any number of explanatory videos online, but in short, there was a 1 in 3 chance you picked the right door first time, but a 2 in 3 chance of getting the prize if you then switch.)

Every week during his final year, Lynch would weave through the narrow stone arch in First Court, stomp up the even narrower wooden staircase, enter one of the uneven-looking rooms facing the college's pristine grass and settle back into one of the squashy, weather-beaten chairs to face a grilling. His engineering tutor, the eminent Professor Peter Rayner – looking every inch the academic, with his snowy white beard – would peer over his glasses at the young man.

Rayner, a born-and-bred engineer, was a gentle man, but he did not suffer fools gladly. Lynch was no fool and Rayner was profoundly fond of his sparklingly bright student, but he would veer between gently exasperated and bemused by the lack of attention he seemed to pay to his studies. The weekly meeting between them was called a supervision – a regular test for Cambridge undergraduates which involved a lesson with a senior academic conducted one on one, or in a small group, once a week. Students were supposed to spend the week leading up to a supervision carefully preparing the work they'd been set in advance, so that they could explain their approach and tackle further questions in the meeting itself.

Lynch, though, would blag his way through and make up answers to mathematical problems on the hoof, yet Rayner would always be surprised at the considerable insight he brought to the sessions, apparently without any work. Lynch often proposed innovative solutions that weren't necessarily correct, but always interested his professor. He'd come at problems from a different angle than many others, thinking in a different way. Rayner had taught a revolving door of bright, talented students, but he had never seen anyone match Lynch's entrepreneurial ability and spark.

The reasons he was less than attentive were clear to Rayner from the outset: Lynch was far too distracted by the more entertaining side of life at Cambridge to prepare sufficiently – if at all – for his supervisions. It wasn't that he didn't want to be sitting with the professor in his cosy study each week; in fact, he had chosen to work with Rayner. He may have started college life as a natsci, but in his third year he switched to Rayner's specialism of engineering, more specifically with an interest in A/V (audio/visual) signal processing. He was fascinated by the subject, which mirrored the work he had done at school, exploring music technology with Richard Birkett.

Lynch and Rayner became close. They would sometimes share a

glass of sherry in Rayner's college room and the professor would later be paid as a technical advisor to Autonomy. Whenever there was a debate about something, Rayner would bet his students a pint of beer over the outcome. 'I'd like to be able to say that I never bought myself a beer, but the main reason for that was that I was always spending my money buying him beers, because he was always right,' Lynch said of his mentor.

Lynch enjoyed the intellectual sparring as much as Rayner, and respected the professor's opinions. There were a handful of others about whom he felt the same way, and they became a fiercely trusted and beloved cohort at university and beyond. For the most part, though, Lynch simply thought that people were stupider than he was.

Brainpower and dogged determination meant that he could – and often did – beat most people into submission during an argument, intellectually speaking. It did not, however, mean that he had always convinced them of his opinion, or that they ever forgot the scars of the fight. His was an attitude that would earn him many enemies over the years.

AS HIS UNDERGRADUATE student days drew to a close, a pressing question was what would come next. Companies circled Cambridge looking for bright young graduates. In those days, many of a mathematical or scientific bent were approached to join firms in the City of London, with its shiny new outpost under construction in Canary Wharf.

These companies were offering gargantuan salaries. Deregulation in London's financial sector in 1986, known as the Big Bang, saw the Square Mile quickly become one of the world's most important financial centres, a rival to New York. It was a complex hive of lawyers, auditors, consultants, bankers and investors, all of them feeding off one another and the big deals of the time.

The switch to electronic trading, replacing the old face-to-face dealing on the floor of the London Stock Exchange, increased the number and speed of sales at the same time as restrictions on sales commissions were relaxed. In short, it was an era of decadence which, it is rumoured, generated 1,500 millionaires as the old London firms, many of them partnerships, consolidated and changed hands. International firms from the US, Europe and Japan were allowed to own UK stockbrokers for the first time and to enter new financial markets. If you wanted to make money, this was the obvious place to go.

Lynch's somewhat laissez-faire approach to his studies led to him getting a disappointing second-class honours in his final exams. Rayner, though, remained resolutely confident in Lynch's potential, and persuaded him to stay on at Cambridge and pursue a PhD, a path normally reserved for first-class graduates. For Lynch, this route offered the chance of a continued life in Cambridge, another step further east from Chelmsford, and the chance to pursue his passion for entrepreneurship and engineering. It also gave him the chance to repay his tutor's faith – the person he would later describe as 'the man who made it all happen.'

THREE

Pattern Matching

Time is money. Most of all, time is dreams. And computers give you time for dreams . . . There's a New World coming again, looming on the desktop.

– *Roger Rosenblatt,* Time, *3 January 1983*

If there was ever any doubt that the 1980s was the age of the machine, in January 1983 – the year that Lynch started at Cambridge – *Time* magazine slapped a computer onto its famous front cover. Sitting on a bright-red desk with a white plaster man peering at it, the magazine proclaimed: 'Machine of the Year: The Computer Moves In'. 'By the millions,' the accompanying article said, 'it is beeping its way into offices, schools and homes'.

The most important personality of that year was a white plastic box, albeit one with unlimited potential. 'The enduring American love affairs with the automobile and the television set are now being transformed into a giddy passion for the personal computer,' *Time* magazine said.

The innovations came thick and fast: 1983 was also the year that the modern internet was born, as computers in a network could for the first time communicate with each other through the same set of rules, a standard protocol. Hewlett-Packard launched its HP-150 desktop computer, a compact and powerful machine, codenamed 'Magic'. Just a year later, Steve Jobs launched the Apple Macintosh.

The Santa Clara Valley in northern California was on the cusp of its transformation from a place of apple orchards and affordable homes, a refuge for hippies sick of San Francisco, into Silicon Valley – the beating heart of global technology. Bill Gates had founded Microsoft in 1975, and Microsoft Word, the world-beating word processing system, also landed in 1983.

Cambridge, too, had embraced the rapidly growing industry. Starting with the founding of Cambridge Science Park back in 1970, more and more high-tech businesses were founded or established outposts in the area. Big employers locally included Olivetti, a leading European manufacturer of personal computers, and by 1997, when Microsoft opened a research and development centre in the city to make the most of the talented students, the area was being called 'Silicon Fen'.

Yet it was a philosopher and statistician born more than three centuries earlier who Lynch always claimed had just as much influence on him as the generation of emergent tech bros in Silicon Valley: a quiet and studious Presbyterian minister, the Reverend Thomas Bayes.

At first glance, the theologian might seem an unlikely technological inspiration for a science-obsessed Cambridge student during the birth of the digital era. But the probability theorem that bears his name would become central to Lynch's personal philosophy and a cornerstone of the marketing around his companies.

The only known portrait of Bayes shows a serious, middle-aged man drawn in black and white, shadows across his face, with thin lips and a widow's peak, wearing a long dark robe, two thick white clerical bands dangling from his collar. But the authenticity of the portrait remains disputed, and not a huge amount of detailed biographical information remains about him.

What we do know is that Bayes came from a wealthy family in Sheffield who had made their fortune in cutlery. He presided over the wealthy parish of Tunbridge Wells in Kent, where the exceptional mathematician was utterly preoccupied by the concept of nailing down probability.

On his death in 1761 at the age of fifty-nine, Bayes left £100 and his papers to his friend Richard Price. In a notebook, as part of the unfinished 'Essay Towards Solving a Problem in the Doctrine of Chances', Price stumbled upon the now famous Bayes theorem of probability, later wrapped up in a neat mathematical formula:

$$\text{Posterior} = \frac{\text{Likelihood} \times \text{Prior}}{\text{Evidence}} = \frac{P(B \mid A)\,P(A)}{P(B)}$$

Start with a hunch (the prior), weigh it by how well today's clue fits that hunch (the likelihood), adjust for how common the clue is overall (the evidence), and you get a refreshed belief (the posterior).

The theorem is a mathematical way of doing what good detectives do naturally: updating beliefs based on new evidence. Combining prior knowledge with new data to calculate probability allows for more accurate predictions and decisions, which only increase in their accuracy as more new information becomes available. Far later, in the twentieth century, a group of statisticians used the theorem as the basis for a rethinking of statistical ideas.

Bayes' mathematical theorem is today used everywhere – in medical diagnoses, weather forecasting and betting. Simplistically, you start with a guess, then when new information comes in, you adjust that guess to be smarter and closer to the truth. Updating beliefs based on new evidence is right at the heart of many modern AI systems.

It was while sitting in an airless seminar room in Cambridge in the mid-1980s that Lynch said he had his eyes opened to the possibilities that Bayesian statistics and the new world of computing offered. The lecture was being delivered by Bill Fitzgerald, another of the small cohort of influential professors in this maverick, academic, higgledy-piggledy Cambridge world who would shape Lynch's life.

A warm and engaging man, with long white hair and a neatly trimmed beard, an easy laugh and an infectious enthusiasm for his subject, he was an eccentric Fellow and a fixture of college life. A conversation with him, Lynch recalled, could bounce from discussing a novel medical concept to a lecture about how to tell the age of a violin from tree rings. Like Lynch, he was passionate about music, his repertoire ranging from the violin to the flamenco guitar and the ukulele, the hurdy-gurdy and a number of different types of bagpipes.

Fitzgerald explained to the students in front of him how he was applying Bayesian inference to finding submarines underwater. The results he showed them were astonishingly accurate and this, Lynch said, struck him like a lightning bolt. It is a moment in his life he described again and again.

Lynch described the theorem in an Autonomy publicity film as 'a beautiful key to our minds', speaking over a track of woo-woo, hypnotic music. It was 'a rationally objective statement of uncertainty, where the answer depends on your own experience,' he said. Not everyone understood what he was talking about, but the high-flown language played well with the sales teams and made Autonomy's product sound clever.

When it came to his personal philosophy, he viewed everything through this lens of probability, weighing up the odds of something happening. In an uncertain, febrile world, Bayes, he said, gave him a solid foundation to help him in his decision-making, working out which step to take in which direction.

It helped in hiring decisions. 'What is that person like?' Lynch would ask when he met someone new. 'Who are they like that we know?' he would ask his team. He felt he could work out how somebody would fit in at the company and how they might behave, based on experience of similar personalities.

He would use probability to calculate the revenue for the end of each quarter, by working out the likelihood of a salesperson lying, or of a sale coming good.

It would also inform Lynch's management style, for good and bad. If someone who he did not like claimed to be going out for a cigarette, he might surmise that they were actually doing something they should not be. It was often wide of the mark.

Lynch would even later name his glamorous superyacht the *Bayesian* – a terrible irony given its improbable end.

A PICTURE FROM the late 1980s shows a small, rectangular room. It has parquet flooring, and students in jeans are lounging in chairs around boxy plastic computers. There is strip lighting and venetian blinds, and a bookshelf stacked with files runs the length of the far wall.

This was the Signal Processing and Communications Laboratory at Cambridge, where students would spend their time experimenting and putting their computer learning into practice.

The lab was founded by Rayner in 1969 and for a while he was the only one in it, with limited access to an old IBM with enormous plug-in disc drives. The whole machine was about three metres long and a metre wide and he was – frustratingly – only able to book ten- or fifteen-minute slots to use it. With the help of a Science Research Council grant, Rayner then bought a Data General computer and a fixed hard disc, with 256 kilobytes – at a cost of £5,000, it was a serious machine, for serious work, but cheaper than some alternatives. Later computers in the lab were the ubiquitous BBC Micros, with the major advantage being that everyone could have one to themselves.

Twenty years after Rayner's arrival, by the time Lynch was in the lab, it had about thirty PhD students, six staff members, six postdocs and six academics. It was a golden period for the close-knit, international group of students, where life revolved around two main pursuits: computing and cricket. While the sport was not one for Lynch, the lab always had a team it fielded against other departments. Rayner was at its heart and ran it with a pleasurable informality, bringing everyone together for a curry and trip to the pub on a Friday night when the lab shut.

Interesting work flowed in. The group was at the frontier of what was possible in the audiovisual field and was once taken on to clean up crackly old gramophone records by the National Sound Archive, a treasure trove of British historical audio. At one point, Rayner set Lynch the task of creating noise-cancelling headphones. The pair decided they did not have the computational power to make it work and – much to Rayner's regret – did not put a patent in for it.

As he worked for his PhD, Lynch switched uniforms. He dropped the jeans and trainers of the scientific student tribe, which he had previously favoured, and started wearing a suit which hung on him slightly uncomfortably, as if a gawky teenager were suddenly forced to dress up for a wedding.

It looked to the others in the lab like some sort of 'business disguise' – which indeed it was. For while he was researching his doctorate, Lynch was also running a music technology company that was starting to take off, and he was engaging in the world of business. He needed to look the part.

It was quite inspiring to his fellow students. His business attire and attitude showed a completely different way of thinking about the value of academic work, and made his peers realize that what they were doing could be useful and potentially very lucrative.

LYNCH LIVED A hectic life juggling his music business, his girlfriend at the time, his band and hosting house parties with university friends, but managed to submit his PhD thesis within four years, in 1990.

Dedicated to his parents, it was entitled *Adaptive Techniques in Signal Processing and Connectionist Models*; the Science and Engineering Research Council, Professor Bill Fitzgerald and the Marconi company helped to finance the research. Although the paper's title uses 'signal processing', it was really focused on pattern recognition – something which has now more or less been absorbed into machine learning. Lynch's research examined improving how machines recognize speech, images or written characters. The result was a new type of 'adaptive filter' that could recognize patterns more effectively, even in difficult environments – like a smart helper that can adjust itself to understand sounds or images better.

The thesis was about teaching computers to do tricky things: for example, if there's music and someone is talking at the same time, an adaptive filter can learn to block out the music, so it just hears the talking.

Lynch combined these filters with neural networks – computer systems that try to work like the human brain. His goal was to help computers recognize things like faces, voices, or letters – even if they look or sound a bit different each time. He wrote:

> *The beauty of adaptive systems for such problems is that it is no longer necessary to derive a set of explicit rules, as the system can be left to adapt itself 'on-the-job' to solve the problem without being explicitly programmed with sets of rules.*

In the end, the thesis showed how to create machines that can learn from experience, get better over time and deal with messiness – like blurry images, wrong sounds or missing pieces. Lynch put a lot of effort into maximizing the speed and efficiency of processing large volumes of information, an important process which has been made easier today with the huge increase in computing power. The thesis also referenced the application of Bayes' theorem, drawing on the ideas he had encountered in the mid-1980s. Lynch was very early to the practical exploitation of the idea, and continued research and the development of powerful cheap computation has now enabled the application of Bayesian methodology in artificial intelligence.

The thesis was accepted, and Young Michael from Ilford could now officially call himself Dr Lynch.

He wore his Cambridge doctorate like a medal. It gave him a status within the deeply hierarchical university, not to mention on the outside, proclaiming his intelligence and technical nous to the world.

FOUR

Early Ambitions

Things are changing in business on an amazing time scale and it's not predictable anymore, so you need people who realize there are no rules about what happens next.

– *Mike Lynch*, Management Today, *1 June 2000*

The flooring of the ordinary, scruffy student digs in Devonshire Road was taking another battering. Lynch scuffed absent-mindedly at the new blobs of solder on the carpet with his shoe, in a half-hearted effort to erase the evidence.

A messy mound of cables and a bare circuit board sticking out of a rough box were the start of a prototype of a digital sampler – an electronic instrument that could record, store and playback audio, which would give musicians enormous flexibility when they were laying down tracks. On the front of the box: LYNEX – the brand name he had chosen. The word incorporated the three letters from the start of his name. The swoop of the letters mimicked a signature. It is the image of Lynch everyone remembers from the time: a soldering iron in one hand, a keyboard in another. Dire Straits' 1985 album *Brothers in Arms* was playing on repeat.

Lynch's smart attire looked odd in the tiny house near Cambridge train station. He was thin, of medium height, with hair grown below his ears, and sporting a beard. The music sampler, he smirked, was all part of his attempts to become a popstar, knowing a rugby career wasn't going to work out. Decades later, a student told him there was still solder on the carpet of the little, slightly grubby, house.

Lynch's commercial career did not start with Autonomy. There were several companies before that which were formative in developing his business acumen. As he finished his PhD, he continued plugging away at Lynett Systems, the company he had started in his bedroom when he was just sixteen with his former school chum Richard Birkett. It was officially incorporated in 1986 when they were twenty-one; the company's name was an elision of their own.

Technology made the 1980s music scene sound different, with the chance to layer and repeat melodies and beats. The trouble was that the best samplers – made by Fairlight – cost thousands of pounds. The one Lynch and Birkett launched in 1988 was far cheaper and more accessible. They decided to dispense with the expensive bits, like the display, the bespoke knobs and buttons, and reduced the cost of the product by running everything via an Atari. It was a computer widely used by musicians because it had a socket on it for MIDI, the Musical Instrument Digital Interface, a technical standard that enables electronic instruments and computers to work with each other.

Getting the parts for the box had not been easy, he later said, in an elaborate story.

The special, and expensive, digital signal processing chip Lynch needed was only being produced for nuclear missiles at the time. Undeterred, he rang up the manufacturing company's sales rep, pretending to be a wealthy businessman, and asked him to send out a chip as a 'sample'. He only needed the one, he said.

The trick worked. The chip arrived. One day, there was a knock at the door of Lynch's Cambridge digs. Thinking they were onto a lucrative sales pipeline, the company had sent a delegation to Devonshire Road to meet their latest 'customer'. The hopeful group repeatedly banged the knocker. When the door finally opened, they asked the young man on the other side of it if they could meet a Mr Michael Lynch.

'Never heard of him,' Lynch said, and closed the door on the faces of the bewildered sales team. It is a good tale, but hard to verify.

Once the prototype was ready, Lynch travelled to some influential American trade shows to market the product, with a view to licensing it to a business who would then manufacture it. One frustration about these international gatherings was the language barrier. He would get extremely irritable as his friends spoke to, say, a German in German, because he could not follow the conversation and did not know what was being said. Knowing he could well be smarter than

Mike Lynch receiving a *Sound on Sound* award from music tech journalist Ian Gilby in 1989.

the people he was meeting, he could not help but patronize those he met while his friends, rolling their eyes, tried to rein him in.

The Lynex sampler was not the only product that Lynett Systems produced. There was also a smaller unit, known as the ADAS, and the company was exploring a standalone touch-sensitive piano keyboard, and other bits and bobs, such as adding one of those popular MIDI interfaces into computers that did not have one. The financial details of the business have now fallen off Companies House records, but Lynch was always proud that the pair never took any outside funding that required them to give away a stake. They had modest success with the licensing plan – some reviews of the products remain online even today.

Behind the scenes, Lynch and Birkett's relationship could be tense. Lynch, ever a perfectionist who wanted to be in control of every situation, used to get profoundly frustrated by Birkett's complex code, especially when he could not get it to work.

He started casting around for someone else to help him with the technology, when fortuitously there was a new arrival from South Africa.

'WANTED: FINANCIAL CONSULTANTS'. The job ad in the newspaper sounded tempting, smart and, most importantly, lucrative.

It was November 1990. Richard Gaunt, a young South African engineering graduate, had just arrived in England, a country he had not been to since he was a baby. He knew no one. His clipped English accent, inherited from a father who had spent time in the British army, was about all that he had kept from the country. Gaunt had grown up wanting to leave South Africa, to escape the horrendous political situation and an uncertain future, not to mention national service. He had no interest in ever spending two years in the South African Defence Force of the time, mainly used to repress the population.

With a pinstriped suit in his bag and an engineering degree in his pocket, he picked up a copy of the *Evening Standard* and set to work finding something to do. He replied to the advert and was delighted to be quickly offered the role. To his horror and later amusement, when he turned up for his first day, he had inadvertently become a life insurance salesman. It was not what he had escaped national service for and, after managing not to sell any policies, swerving ripping anyone off or mis-selling anything, he thought he had better put his degree to some use.

'Richard, you don't want to use the newspaper to find a job!' a friend rolled his eyes. 'Go to a proper person, you need a recruitment consultant.' This was all new and frustrating for Gaunt, but his luck was in. By happenstance, the recruiter he found was a friend of Lynch's, who was on the hunt for smart engineers. Lynch and Gaunt met for an interview.

On paper, Gaunt was not immediately Lynch's type. He went to a South African university and Lynch was always utterly snobbish about the superiority of Cambridge, with Oxford dismissed as 'OK'. However, Gaunt had won various prizes and had a Master's in physics, and Lynch dealt on intellectual merit. He would say the greatest people in technology were outsiders because they do not take anything for granted – 'they don't assume that tomorrow is going to be like today' – and he saw Gaunt as very much in this camp.

They got on well, both sharing a strong belief that tech was not valued enough in the UK at the time. Around March 1991, the twenty-five-year-old entrepreneur offered the twenty-three-year-old South African a job for £11,000 a year, 'doing whatever'.

By this point, Lynett Systems had taken a space in the St John's Innovation Centre, a co-working space for newly hatched businesses on the outskirts of Cambridge, set up in 1987. The company was still going when Gaunt joined, but his relationship with Birkett continued to drive Lynch to despair. Once, a contemporary recalled, the two school friends had to be physically separated as Lynch reached boiling point and lunged at Birkett. Shortly before, Lynch had taken one of their products, an eight-track recording system, to Akai, the Japanese stereo maker, and his demonstration didn't work. He had ended up in a hotel room with an electronic testing instrument – an oscilloscope – trying to work out why it wouldn't start, blaming Birkett from afar and cursing his complicated code.

As technology was moving fast, and better-funded people were cornering the vital US market, Lynch decided to move away from music and hardware. Musicians did not make enough money to buy expensive gear. The two men, with their differing ambitions, parted ways. Lynch was pushing harder than Birkett felt comfortable with.

Instead, Lynch and Gaunt kicked about with a new company based on the simple premise 'doing whatever' that Gaunt had been employed for. It even had a catch-all name: Cambridge Neurodynamics. Its business plan, such as it was, was simple: say yes to any offer of paid technology work whatsoever and work out the details of how to deliver it afterwards. Fake it till you make it, an ethos summed up by the officious sign reading 'Cambridge Neurodynamics Administration Department', which hung over the entrance to (the only department of) the company.

Not that many visitors ever came. If they did, staff would hurriedly stick a sign on the broom cupboard saying, 'Authorized Personnel Only'. It all helped to create a delightful air of scale and importance. 'For all they knew, there were five hundred engineers on the other side,' Lynch later joked.

The company's name – 'neurodynamics' – was picked because it was a buzzword in Cambridge at the time, linked to 'neural networks', a cornerstone of machine learning. It sounded clever and was suitably vague, which suited the business plan. Money was always tight, but Lynch was nothing if not resourceful, and he told a tale of spotting an opportunity that would become part of Lynch-lore.

Out in Soho in the 1990s, hanging around the music scene, Lynch met a drunk music promoter in a bar. The hard-living man would go to the same place night after night, starting at dusk and bringing the party to an end at four in the morning. Seizing his chance, Lynch managed to borrow £2,000 from him without being asked too many questions about his strategy for paying it back. It's an oft-told tale to journalists, with several iterations, mythologized over the years. No one who worked with him at the time remembers it happening. Lynch would later refer to this mysterious promotor as an 'English eccentric' who had made a lot of money in the music business, possibly linked to the band Genesis. Like many of Lynch's stories, the details and even the veracity are difficult to pin down.

'I'M SORRY, MR Bridges isn't here at the moment, but he will get back to you as soon as he can . . .'

Frank Bridges was the solid-sounding finance director at Cambridge Neurodynamics. He was a mysterious bloke, often rather hard to track down, who, strangely, never appeared to be at his desk, especially when being chased for invoices. He was such a key figure in the business that one bank even posted him a letter, inviting him to apply for a credit card. His elusiveness wasn't that surprising. Lynch never paid anyone until they threatened to close his account, which was a way of maintaining cash flow.

Also, Mr Bridges did not exist.

The invented finance director became a code within the company for sending someone up the garden path. If the phone rang for Frank, everyone would know what it meant and would obligingly 'take a message'. Entrepreneurship and bullshitting often go hand in glove, and nobody knew that better than Lynch. Throughout his career, it was par for the course; his businesses were always trying to appear bigger and better than they were.

Lynch had a keen understanding of the value of marketing. Think about it like a TV studio, he would say. Everything on set is beautiful and what is broadcast looks perfect, but then behind the scenes there is a whole load of mess, cardboard boxes and chaos. Business, like TV, was a show – the trick was to convince the client that you could deliver the goods without revealing too much about the inner workings of how you made it happen.

It was something that others begrudgingly admired him for. It was all well and good having great technology, but it was nothing without a show.

And there were plenty of inner workings that Lynch would definitely have preferred to keep in the background, not least his temperament towards his staff.

The office administrator at Neurodynamics learnt to kick the door shut when Lynch started on one of his rampages. He was intolerant and tempestuous, and the small cohort of employees were hit with a barrage of shouting when things went wrong which, in the world of a tech startup, they frequently did. Lynch would erupt without warning, and become red in the face when he exploded, ripping people to shreds, calling them out for their errors and stupidity. It was, one former staff member recalled, 'a horrible, horrible, horrible environment'. While he charmed the outside world, those inside the business witnessed an aggressive bully. He would describe people he didn't like as 'losers' and those he felt were beneath him were 'pond life'.

Perhaps it was being the boss which really brought Lynch's temper to the fore at this time. Employing people was more difficult than running a band and, for Lynch, his business was everything. Staff came and went with astonishing regularity, refusing to put up with his frequent rages, his unreasonable attitude. Lynch, in his turn, had a tendency to grow tired of people. He was so utterly focused on the success of their work, and frustrated when things did not go his way, he took it incredibly personally if people made mistakes and he sometimes acted as if they were purposefully out to destroy his company.

In an attempt to keep control of his staff and assuage his paranoia about how they were behaving, he would even ask colleagues to spy on one another and report into him with their findings. Some uncovered that this was going on and found it rather alarming. It might not have been pleasant, but being this ruthless got results. Success was far from assured, and it was the 'just get it done' attitude which drove the business forward.

The paradox was that Lynch could just as easily use his immense charm and vision to inspire people. Some chose to take the rough with the smooth. His charm was not the ostentatious flattery or obsequious platitudes associated with posh public schoolboys, or superficial enquiries about people's health or well-being. His self-deprecating sense of humour, wide-ranging interests, small quick smile and down-to-earth conversation genuinely won people over.

Despite his young age, Lynch appeared to have the experience of someone twenty years older, a remarkable business intuition. He could negotiate hard and smart like a man in his mid-forties. He developed a clever knack of partnering with other companies and making them shoulder superfluous costs, like travel. This was invaluable, as the fledgling business had little cash coming in and needed to blag all it could get.

The Innovation Centre at the time was home to many other scrappy startups whose employees would intersect while queueing for a lunchtime baked potato during a well-earnt break. It was a good source of business opportunities.

There was one which Gaunt found a real piece of work, in all senses of the phrase. At some point in those early years, Cambridge Neurodynamics was subcontracted for £30,000 to build, for a bank named Bradford & Bingley, a product which would encrypt signals between their mainframe computer and cashpoints. The original contract was worth ten times that, £300,000, and went to the contracting company which gave Neurodynamics the commission.

It was an early business lesson for Lynch about always doing a deal directly. Nonetheless, it was a job, and a job meant cash.

Turning up to Bradford & Bingley's offices to plug in the tech that his company had built, Gaunt found that it didn't work. He fumed to himself that he didn't know the correct protocol for the network, and he huffed and puffed over the mistake. This was not, he thought, how things were done properly; this was not how a business should be run. The client disliked Gaunt's aggrieved attitude and it all got a bit tetchy.

Later, Lynch would tell him that he should have been a little smarter in covering up the error, a little quicker on his feet. Just tell the client what they want to hear, Lynch said, something like, 'Oh, I've brought a different version. I'll go back and get the correct one.' Lynch could lie plausibly with fluidity. He had a hypnotic ability to make up realistic stories, talk up the company and exaggerate on his feet. Black was sometimes white and white was black: it could be a useful skill.

More curiously, he would also believe whatever he was saying wholeheartedly, even if it was a complete fabrication – Lynch-lore. Some who worked for him described it as gaslighting.

AS NEURODYNAMICS GREW, the business plan started to evolve and become less haphazard. Rather than picking up individual bespoke projects, Lynch and Gaunt realized, it would be more lucrative to build something that they could resell again and again.

They could use Lynch's signal processing background to develop technology that could recognize symbols, letters and patterns. Given Lynch's lack of fingerprints, their first hit product was totally improbable. An Oracle salesman had got in touch, wanting their help with a contract for the South Yorkshire Police for a new fingerprint-matching machine. For a force engaged on a murder enquiry, searching the whole database for an unknown print would take a whole detective bureau a week, presuming the officers knew the sort of person they were looking for.

Gaunt and Lynch said yes to the US giant immediately, and promptly spent the next five weeks working day and night to make it happen. Their technology took on the complex job of analysing the shape of a fingerprint pattern to detect its key parts. By using cheaper cameras and lenses, they cut the cost per fingerprint reader from £2,000 to £200 each. Only, Lynch could not be used to test the cutting-edge tech.

This led to contracts for national identification systems in Botswana and Jordan in 1995. High street banks started trialling the technology. Countries in the developing world used it to tackle welfare payment fraud, Lynch told reporters, while Neurodynamics' own literature said it was being tested by 'a worldwide passport and identity card supplier'.

While saying *yes* to projects from potential clients was easy, finding the funding before a British tech- or venture-capital ecosystem was fully established was less so, as the experience with the erstwhile Soho promoter showed. One day in 1995, the company was spotted by John McMonigall, one of the stars of an early British venture-capital fund, Apax Partners. He had heard about them through a friend of Lynch's from school and university, Richard Anton. 'You think it's worth it?' McMonigall asked. 'Yeah, I know this guy, and I think he's exceptional', came Anton's response. The pair got the train up to Cambridge to see what it was all about.

Lynch instantly stood out to McMonigall, in his mid-fifties at this point, for his brains, the tech and his ability to communicate. In turn, McMonigall proved a wise, smart and direct mentor to Lynch and Gaunt, someone who could guide them as and when they needed it. It was an association that would last Lynch's lifetime. McMonigall was so impressed by their makeshift outfit that Apax went on to put in almost £2 million for 49 per cent of the company, while Lynch retained the majority stake. Unusually, the money went directly to Lynch and Gaunt.

After searching criminals' fingerprints, Cambridge Neurodynamics turned to tracking down different kinds of rogues: speeding drivers. It partnered with Racal Electronics to launch a new camera system to read number plates for use in everything from security to traffic monitoring. It was also used to track containers at ports. Trained on a huge number of characters, to be able to deal with scratched and smudged lettering, the system claimed a success rate of 90 per cent, impressive in that kind of dirty, badly lit environment.

Lynch had realized that there was money to be made in recognizing patterns. But he was tired of number plates and fingerprints – as important as crime prevention is, it wasn't the most lucrative of markets. That honour belonged to the burgeoning giant that was the internet.

One particular company had already figured out how to recognize patterns in text – what all those web pages displayed – and they just happened to be headquartered in the very same building.

The young entrepreneur was about to cause a business fracas, the first of many.

FIVE

aut.on.omy

Our mission is to stop computers being stupid.

– *Autonomy website, 2000*

The St John's Innovation Centre – 'Cambridge's Innovation Destination' as it was advertised – was opened way before tech startups were cool and tech incubators were a thing. Its founder, Dr Christopher Johnson, had spent time in the US and had seen how the science parks in American universities were spawning interesting stuff, and he wanted to do the same for the UK. It was the first space for startups of its kind in Europe.

The building lacked any of the charm of the ancient architecture in the centre of Cambridge, but the buzz of people hustling to get their companies off the ground more than made up for the aesthetic. Within the co-working space, the atmosphere among the startups was intensely competitive, and Lynch, with his brains and innate business acumen, attracted a lot of jealousy. Lynch-lore held that in the early days, he could afford only one room with space for one desk, but he was employing about eight people. When the caretaker came round to see what was going on, Lynch explained away the numbers, saying the other seven were just visiting.

John Snyder, who had been in the year below Lynch at Christ's College, was also renting a space in the building, and he ended up subletting a desk to a developer contracting for Cambridge Neurodynamics, in the haphazard way that these things happen. A tall, broad-shouldered man with a warm laugh and a quizzical expression, one eyebrow always slightly cocked, Snyder had studied geography, social and political science, graduating in 1987. His choice of subject made Lynch sneer behind his back.

He had taken a roundabout route to the newly formed Cambridge co-working space, via the Sahara Desert. He and his new wife Sarah, consumed by their experience of volunteering in poor parts of Africa and with famine ongoing, had driven across Algeria to northern Mali. There, during the time of Live Aid, they lived with desert nomads, recording film and photographs of the people in the region for a project partly funded by the European Union, Apple Computers, Fujifilm and other sponsors. It aimed to tell the other side of the story than the patronizing one of Westerners rescuing starving people, which the media sometimes propagated.

Following a coup in Mali, with Sarah pregnant with their first child, the couple returned to the UK in 1990. Snyder went to see his old Cambridge professor, Alan Macfarlane, who was digitizing mountains of field notes and old books, using Muscat, the Museum Cataloguing Software, a technology that Snyder had not seen before.

The technology hit Snyder between the eyes. It looked for patterns, so context, rather than just words. Macfarlane was grabbing thirty or fifty words to find other relevant paragraphs across thousands of books, rather than one or two, without needing any pre-made link between them. The technology automatically found words and paragraphs that were related to each other. One paragraph, used as a search query, could easily find related material across the whole catalogue of book pages, pictures and video metadata. This was transformative to how information could be found.

Muscat had been developed by Dr Martin Porter, a search specialist from the Cambridge University Computer Laboratory where a host of influential academics were working on information retrieval, or search. Other innovators at the time included Huddersfield-born Karen Spärck-Jones, who believed 'computing is too important to be left to men' and helped to teach computers to understand language, combining statistics with linguistics to create the basis of modern search engines. She was a well-known character in the city, who would cycle around Cambridge with her dress pegged to her handlebars to stop it dragging along the ground or tangling up in the chain. Her husband was Roger Needham, who led the Cambridge Computer Laboratory and later set up Microsoft's research centre in Cambridge. There was also Stephen Robertson, based at City University in London, who worked extensively with Spärck-Jones and whose pioneering work with Stephen Walker led to the Okapi BM25 model, a sophisticated way of ranking information. This work was the start of search engines as we know them today.

Cambridge had let Porter keep the intellectual property rights to the Muscat system and, sniffing out an opportunity to free the tech from the university's dusty libraries and bring it to a global market, Snyder soon approached the initially suspicious academic.

With a bit of persuading, the two men became partners. There was some early interest. With Porter dressed like Sherlock Holmes and having packed his own tea, Microsoft flew them to its global headquarters near Seattle to find out more about their work.

It was only a matter of time before Mike Lynch, Snyder's new neighbour, heard about Muscat and came knocking. He was equally taken with the concept of probabilistic information search, a leap to looking for text-based information where he had been looking at images. Around 1993, he and Snyder started discussing how

Cambridge Neurodynamics could license Muscat's technology, in exchange for a royalty.

Lynch suggested that the best thing to do was put a pretty interface on the front, to make it more user-friendly and saleable. Snyder trusted him; they were fellow Christ's men after all.

They spent more and more time together. At Christmas in 1993, Snyder, Gaunt, Lynch and Porter sat down for chummy drinks in the Cambridge Neurodynamics offices late one evening. They were playing celebrity charades. Porter, ever the academic, wrote down the name of an obscure Russian philosopher no one else had heard of, which made the group roll their eyes and laugh. Lynch was trying to be an unlikely Madonna, miming cupping her famous pointed bra. The mood was jovial. The deal between the companies was almost done. A contract was being drawn up between the two.

Early documents show just how close they came to completing the deal. At one point, the US giant Oracle expressed an interest in the tiny company's software; a letter from Oracle dated 9 November 1993 thanked Lynch 'for organising our visit to see the Muscat and Oracle interface last week' and said, 'what you have is clearly interesting and commercially important in its own right'. Lynch was obviously involved, if not yet in charge; in an act of trust, Snyder had put his software source code onto a powerful Unix machine at the Cambridge Neurodynamics offices, because Muscat did not have one of its own that could run Oracle SQL.

As the idea for the partnership bloomed, to Snyder it never felt like they were equals. Lynch always liked to show that he was the top dog, pulling moves like making Snyder drive Lynch's new black Mercedes like a chauffeur to one London meeting.

In hindsight, Snyder was right about the imbalance.

AS A DRAFT of the terms went back and forth, Lynch pulled out of the deal. In April 1994, aged twenty-eight, he wrote a formal letter to Snyder which set out that Cambridge Neurodynamics had been 'unable to come to a practical and commercially reasonable arrangement' with him. An evaluation of the tech, Lynch wrote, had found that it was 'not suitable for our needs; consequently, I am returning to you the manuals that you provided. I have also instructed that the copies of the software are to be removed from the machines here'.

Snyder was upset and aggrieved, even more so when Cambridge Neurodynamics went off and built their own version of Muscat, which Lynch branded the Dynamic Reasoning Engine (DRE). It was a ruthless and cold move and left a litany of unanswered questions.

Lynch seemed to have swiped the idea from Muscat, which was infuriating for his erstwhile collaborators. Worse was the suspicion that he also swiped the code. Sarah Snyder urged her husband not to pursue the fight. She felt strongly that, with a family to think about, he needed to look forward and that any battle would be potentially ugly for them and their young children. He eventually agreed.

Things calmed down for a while. Muscat continued on its own and signed a prestigious deal with Reuters. But in 1997, tensions flared up after Snyder made comments to a niche computing magazine about how Lynch got the idea for Autonomy, stirring up questions among Lynch's investors. Lynch wanted to stop any further allegations leaking to the press.

The Snyders were so suspicious that they recorded the series of stilted conversations they had with Lynch, debating the issue. At one point Sarah Snyder even spoke to Lynch to try to resolve the dispute between the two men. As it came to a head, John Snyder said, 'I know what I'd have said, you'd have seen Muscat operating, you'd have seen some good ideas and you'd have gone off with those ideas.'

'You're right, we're getting close to the issue,' Lynch responded in his flat Essex vowels with a slow, deliberate tone. 'That statement on its own, I think, it would be unwise to make.' It is striking that Lynch sounds like a man who has been running a business for many years, confident, brief and firm, absolutely clear about what he is trying to achieve.

Snyder reluctantly agreed to sign a document in November 1997, absolving Lynch of breaching Muscat's IP, but although the relationship between Snyder and Lynch was legally severed early on, apprehensions about what really happened lingered. Lynch, always feeling intellectually superior, would forever sneeringly deride Snyder as a buzzing fly he had managed to swat away.

It should be said that Muscat did well on its own. In 1997, it was sold for an unspecified sum to UK- and NASDAQ-listed MAID, a supplier of online research for businesses, founded by Dan Wagner. Snyder and Porter then went on to found Grapeshot, which was later sold to Oracle for an undisclosed sum, thought to be over £300 million.

For Lynch, the foundations were laid for a new business, founded in 1996 – Autonomy. It would create life-changing wealth and lifelong friendships.

But it would also create a good deal of pain.

aut.on.omy (n.): Freedom of the will. Independence, freedom from external control or influence.

The definition of 'autonomy' was emblazoned on the front page of its business plan, with a picture of a cartoon dog under the heading 'Neural Autonomous Agent Software' and three globes, turned to America, Africa and Asia. Autonomy was, in effect, the commercialization of the Dynamic Reasoning Engine. The name was a masterful piece of marketing, suggesting something that was futuristic but grounded in serious capability, which could search, link and categorize content churned out electronically.

The DRE was trained by indexing a body of data, such as a company's intranet. For example, 'Apollo' would throw up the space programme and the Greek god, in a circle around the central key word. A click would take the user in the particular direction they were interested in, rather than them having to sit down and work out exactly what their query was. One developer said 'analysis engine' would have been a more appropriate name.

The internet was an emerging giant, slowly changing everything. Lynch and Gaunt thought the obvious next step was to take the reasoning engine, spin it out as a separate company, and apply it to the world wide web, which they laid out to their investors. Lynch had a way of painting a compelling vision and the others were really there to act as sounding boards. McMonigall and the rest of the Apax crowd were impressed.

The product they came up with was called Agentware: '*your complete solution to finding exactly what you want on the internet*'. It was sold in one of those plastic-wrapped chunky cardboard boxes that computer software used to come in, plastered in a sky-blue font and featuring the aforementioned, rather evil-looking, cartoon dog (there was more than a little of Hanna-Barbera's Muttley about him), one paw and one eyebrow raised, poised and ready for action. The mascot was based on Lynch's dog Gromit, himself named after the animated character, an otterhound who, Lynch said, had the air of a 'pot-smoking hippy'. Written over a star in a small roundel was: 'Includes a unique offline search feature'.

The Agentware suite featured four hunting dogs, or 'agents': the Web Agent to find information online; the Mail Agent, to filter email; the Press Agent, to customize newspapers, picking out articles you might want to read; and the Guardian Agent, to protect or restrict access to data such as pornography. These hunting dogs were the user's 'personalised intelligent agents for the internet'.

Fortune was firmly on their side. Autonomy was riding the internet wave, as the cost of sending and saving information fell and the adoption of computers grew. In February 1996, one of the first mentions of Autonomy appeared in the national press, and it soon started to make more of a splash. *The Sunday Times* reported that Cambridge Neurodynamics had produced the world's first intelligent 'Internet surfer'. 'Its AutoNomy software programme can understand what its user wants and will weed out information it considers irrelevant,' the article said.

'The dog analogy is a good one,' Gaunt told *The Sunday Times*. 'The autonomous agent could have the ability to get up in the morning and get the electronic papers, looking through them to find articles of particular interest to you. Or, if you get hundreds of e-mails, it could prepare them for you with the really important ones on top.' (There are echoes of this in the recent hype around 'autonomous agents', AI bots which can carry out lengthy computerized tasks for people).

'The idea here was could we get the computer to read something and do the work, make the decision and so it would be autonomous. It would be able to act on its own,' Lynch said. The new company raised £10 million from some top backers. It was spun out of Neurodynamics in exchange for the issue of 10 million shares each to Lynch and Apax Funds, in the same 51 to 49 per cent split in which they owned Neurodynamics. The fundraising was organized by Durlachers – stockbrokers and a big name in tech at the time.

Aside from Apax, another early investor was Lynch's Cambridge friend Daniel Levy, through the English National Investment Company (ENIC), which the businessman part owned with the billionaire Joe Lewis. (All names that became widely known outside business circles when ENIC became the owner of Tottenham Hotspur Football Club in 2001). ENIC's investment valued the business at £30 million. Already, Lynch could have cashed out and been set for life, but his ambitions for the company remained.

The product started selling quickly. In the first three months of 1996, Autonomy made £164,000 from its 'Agentware Desktop' branded consumer products. Operating expenses were £983,000 and, after paying a £2 million licence fee back to Cambridge Neurodynamics for the DRE, an overall loss of £2.7 million was recorded. But by the end of 1996, Autonomy still had £4.5 million in the bank and its business was beginning to take off.

Lynch's clashes with his staff were also just beginning. In mid-1996, Lynch had approached his old school friend and fellow Christ's man, Richard Anton, and persuaded him to leave his job at Apax Partners to become his finance director at Autonomy. It was an important job with rather unusual shoes to fill, taking over from the fictitious Frank Bridges.

John Snyder, also Anton's friend, tried to convince him not to make the move, sharing his bruising experience of negotiating with Lynch and the falling out over Muscat. In the event, Anton stayed at Autonomy for less than two years, disliking how the company was being run and fed up with the shouting. Life was too short. There was later a bitter dispute over his share options, which Anton settled.

It proved to be another bruising encounter, and yet another personal relationship which would never heal.

LYNCH WAS ALWAYS a king of spin, and he knew that for technology to fly, it had to have a good story.

There was a healthy amount of bombast in communications as the company got off the ground. Lynch described himself as 'an internationally renowned expert in the field of adaptive pattern recognition'. A press release by Autonomy in 1997 claimed that 'Autonomy's technology is based on core technology developed over the past six years by Cambridge Neurodynamics, a world leader in the commercial application of neural network and pattern recognition technologies also based in Cambridge'.

Conveniently, the release does not mention they are one and the same company.

Early reviews of the software were mixed. Independent journalist David Bowen wrote in April 1997:

> *Autonomy is a jet, or maybe a rocket. Trouble is, as with the early jets and rockets, the technology does not quite live up to its promise.*

> *To criticise Autonomy harshly now is like looking at the crash of the Comet airliner in 1954, and saying jets will never catch on. But the functionality does not yet live up to the delightful promise of those dogs; I hope it does soon.*

Lynch would tell anyone who would listen, then and forevermore, that Autonomy could have been Google. Its technology was actually far superior to Google's at that point, he said. Instead, it became one of his biggest business regrets that he abandoned the consumer search market. Autonomy pulled the plug on the hunting dogs. Lynch made the mistake, he said, of listening to tech-industry analysts Gartner, claiming they had declared that the internet ad model was dead. Had it not been for them, Lynch believed he could have ended up running one of the biggest companies in the world. More Lynch lore. Those who knew him felt that his listening to other people, let alone analysts, was an unlikely story. Google was founded in 1998, two years after Autonomy – although Larry Page and Sergey Brin had been working on the idea for a couple of years before that.

So, instead, Autonomy pivoted to corporate search, which was more obviously lucrative, and would laser in on managing all the 'unstructured' information generated by emails, presentations, even phone calls – all of the stuff that companies create in their day-to-day work. In contrast, the US tech giant Oracle, founded by Larry Ellison in 1977, helped companies to manage and use their 'structured data' set out in neat spreadsheets, like customer lists or employee records, rather like a smart digital filing cabinet. Lynch wanted Autonomy to be 'the Oracle of unstructured data'.

These comparisons with Google and Oracle were not surprising. Lynch always had an eye on Silicon Valley. Britain felt like small beer for a tech company with big ambitions. Cambridge Neurodynamics had had a small presence in America – more of a branch office, really, run by his semi-retired uncle, mainly because he happened to be there – but Autonomy needed more than that. In 1997, with twenty people in the UK and twenty in the US, it opened a headquarters in Palo Alto, California, to try to be seen as American by customers and investors. By 1999, there was an enormous Autonomy billboard on Route 101 as it passed through Silicon Valley. The company was making its presence known.

Setting up shop on the other side of the world was no mean feat. It was difficult finding the correct person to take on the role, and Richard Gaunt ended up regularly flying back and forth between continents.

While Lynch adored and romanticized the quirky academic culture of Cambridge, he had a love–hate relationship with the global home of technology. It was 'completely and utterly self-referential', he said. He claimed that everyone there did everything by proxy, and that you could turn up with a working time machine and be ignored unless you had got the right person on your board. Another favourite Lynch anecdote was that he and his team invented a game they would play at Silicon Valley parties, a tech version of Chinese whispers. One would start a rumour about an incredible but fictitious startup, then wait to see how long it took for news of this amazing opportunity to do the rounds. 'And you know what?' Lynch said. 'It always happened by the end of the evening.'

What the game also proved was that there was an abundance of deep-pocketed investors, and an abundance of money to be made.

SIX

Quacking Ducks

When the ducks are quacking, keep feeding them.

– Mike Lynch

It was the dotcom boom, the late 1990s, the era of what Yale Professor Robert Schiller called 'Irrational Exuberance'. Investors were putting vast sums into over-hyped tech businesses that might turn the internet era into gold. And Autonomy obediently gave them something to speculate on – by going public three times in two years. Winning venture-capital funding was one thing, but this was the big time.

Stellar banks worked on the floats, which made everyone involved stellar sums of money. Lynch was sometimes hailed as 'Britain's Bill Gates', as the tech magnate that the UK wanted desperately to create.

Autonomy, though, had something to it, Lynch said, unlike other overvalued basket cases. Investing in it was like the difference between buying a racehorse and being sold a pregnant carthorse. Privately, he used to describe these businesses which lacked any substance beyond a website as 'the BringToothpasteToMyDoor.coms'.

Through the three IPOs, Lynch made £80 million and became

a FTSE 100 chief executive at the age of just thirty-five. The floats also made a crew of twenty-something geeks in Cambridge a lot of money, thanks to the share options Lynch had given them in Autonomy, unusual for Brits. Envious stories did the rounds of young software developers spread-eagled on Thai beaches drinking.

Autonomy's first foray onto the stock market took place on 17 June 1998, on an obscure index known as the EASDAQ (or, to use its full name, the European Association of Securities Dealers Automated Quotation), which had been established just two years before. It was theoretically set up as a challenger to New York's NASDAQ, accepting startups – companies like Autonomy that had yet to establish a profitable track record – that would not have met the requirements of the senior stock exchanges.

Lynch said publicly that the move was meant to raise money to buy the intellectual property rights to the Dynamic Reasoning Engine, but it was also a marketing event. A chance to show the business should be taken seriously. Listing companies publicly means you have to make public quite a lot about what is going on under the bonnet, in what is known as a 'prospectus'. Autonomy's EASDAQ prospectus was published on 11 July, together with the share price of $3.70.

Some investors were put off by thirty-three-year-old Lynch's ponytail, his casual attitude and his obvious superiority complex, by his seeming unwillingness to explain what was going on within the black box of his technology, and by the way he talked down to them. For others, this easy arrogance was a huge attraction. This guy seemed to know what he was on about.

Autonomy achieved a valuation of around £100 million, which was off the charts for a relatively new and untried business with a turnover of under £2 million, facing such risks and making such losses. It gave the company a further boost of cash, and an enthusiastic shareholder base eager to launch a 'significant marketing campaign' in the

US and grow, grow, grow. Nonetheless, Lynch said 'we are still a mere fleck of dandruff on the shoulders of Silicon Valley'.

The entry into the year 2000 was unexpectedly uneventful for the tech world. The much anticipated 'millennium bug', a glitch predicted to wreak havoc on the world's digital systems, did not happen. It was the start of an action-packed year for Autonomy. In February, fresh from being named the Confederation of British Industry's Entrepreneur of the Year, Lynch became the UK's first dotcom billionaire, as the value of the company's shares soared.

Wall Street beckoned. Lynch had a phrase: 'When the ducks are quacking, keep feeding them.' Even though the dotcom bubble was deflating, the ducks had not stopped quacking, and listing in America was a prestigious, ballsy move to increase the company's profile. Plus, Lynch thought that American clients would be apprehensive to work with a technology company that wasn't listed on NASDAQ.

Lynch and Gaunt went on a roadshow around the US to drum up interest. In one particularly memorable pitch, Lynch described going to see a billionaire porn baron in New York. As Lynch tried to explain what Autonomy did, the US company's finance director stepped in, wafting around a large cigar, and suggested it worked just like the human brain. 'It doesn't at all,' Lynch said later, 'because we have no idea how the human brain works, but I said yes, and they put $25 million into the business.' *People believe what they want to believe*, Lynch thought. *If it works for me, let them.*

Beefing up Autonomy's US credentials, Lynch headhunted Richard Perle as a non-executive director. A notorious US hawk, the fifty-eight-year-old had been an advisor under Ronald Reagan and was nicknamed the 'Prince of Darkness' for his ideological zeal and aggressive policy positions. Not long after joining Autonomy, he became a key advisor to the Bush administration, which Lynch smirked would be 'useful'.

Amid the excitement, there was an early flicker of the troubled relationship that would go on to blossom between Autonomy and the world of finance. On a conference call with around fifty people in New York, there was a discussion about how to set the share price. The banking sales team said that the shares *could* fetch a certain price, but suggested they should be sold for less. Lynch wanted to know why. The bankers replied that it was 'important to keep people happy'.

Lynch balked and accused the bankers of only wanting the shares sold at the lower price as they themselves were intending to buy them and make a guaranteed profit. The bankers retorted that this was 'standard market practice'. The phrase 'standard market practice' came to be a joke inside Autonomy, a synonym for financiers' entitlement and the attitude of 'we make money by screwing you'.

Meanwhile, the company's sales were shooting up, growing from $8.3 million in 1998 to $22 million in 1999, but the business remained firmly loss-making each year. This was mainly because it was ramping up its sales and marketing costs in line with Autonomy's strategy, and this chimed with dotcom investors at the time, with a 'get large or get lost' approach to growth.

Autonomy issued its NASDAQ prospectus on 8 May 2000: over two million shares at $124 a pop, valuing the company at $5.2 billion.

The US float brought more than just money. During the process, Lynch was introduced to someone who would become important throughout his life, effectively acting as his consigliere, Andy Kanter.

The dogged US lawyer met Lynch after coming to London for a two-year transfer in the late 1990s, when he was drafted in to work on Autonomy's US IPO. The move ended up lasting a lot longer. He would go on to become Lynch's general counsel, his enforcer, his man who got shit done, someone he could always lean on and guarantee total discretion.

Aged just thirty-one at the time, but already jaded with a career in law firms, Kanter asked Lynch for a job shortly after the float. At Autonomy, Lynch started to deploy him in all sorts of capacities, to deal with problems through the businesses and beyond. Bald, with a piercing stare, Kanter was bright, resilient and determined, the qualities that Lynch loved. The diminutive New Yorker, who never lost his accent, was known for being good company and exceptionally charming, unless he needed not to be, when he could be 'fucking rude', one staffer said.

In a business growing as fast as Autonomy, it felt like there was always a fire to put out, some unexpected disaster popping up somewhere, but little phased the capable Kanter. Those around Lynch knew that if Kanter rang you out of hours, you needed to take the call; he would be phoning on Mike business and something was up. He expected people to do what they were told and did not tolerate dissent. He was popular among the Autonomy staff, but they knew where his loyalties lay and would be wary of speaking too freely with him. Everything that was said to Kanter would go straight back to Lynch.

THE DUCKS WERE just about still quacking in the autumn of 2000. Britain was calling. 'We are coming home after wandering around the world for a couple of years,' Lynch announced. Autonomy was going public in London just five months after its successful float on the NASDAQ.

Lynch always wanted to bang the drum for Cambridge and the UK tech scene. Plus, Autonomy's market value would make its shares eligible for inclusion in the FTSE 100 index – the list of the 100 most valuable UK public companies – alongside the likes of BP, Tesco and Legal & General. It was a chance that was too good to miss, since some investment funds were effectively required to buy shares included in the index.

On 31 October 2000, Halloween, an appropriately ghoulish beginning to Autonomy's ghoulish end, the company floated its shares on the London Stock Exchange. Demand was huge, and the press was congratulatory, for now, with the *Standard* among others calling it 'one of Britain's most successful technology companies', although one

Deutsche analyst, Ross Jobber, was already a bit lukewarm about the product on the day of its London debut: 'Autonomy is a binary investment phenomena: you either think it's going to be the global leader, or you think it will disappear beneath the waves.'

At almost £33 a share, the float raised £218 million and valued the company at an astonishing £4.1 billion (about $5.9 billion), netting Lynch personally almost £50 million. Its stock market ticker symbol was AU, the chemical symbol for gold. The share price jumped seven per cent on the first day. (It would never get so high again.)

To celebrate, Lynch and Gaunt were invited on a sailing trip organized by one of the underwriters, who hired two America's Cup yachts for a little race near Southampton. It was rather a damp squib. The wind was far too strong and ripped a highly strung sail, and the excursion had to be swiftly abandoned.

Unlike the celebratory sailboat, Autonomy was zipping along at a rate of knots, which put 'significant strain on our management, systems and resources', it warned. Rather like a teenage popstar, it was getting massive attention from the media (and investors), it had an influence far beyond its age or experience, and there were high expectations about its performance.

These quickly turned to disappointment. When it entered the FTSE 100 in December 2001, Autonomy had a 'lacklustre' debut, with shares dropping to £24.30. Nonetheless, a massive sum for what was still a startup.

There were other problems as the business was still growing up. This billion-dollar company was still based in the St John's Innovation Centre co-working space, running off one power outlet with a daisy chain of extension leads which felt like it could blow up the entire building at any moment, taking the Cambridge startup ecosystem with it. Then there were the staff. Critics picked up on Lynch's lack of experience running a listed business. While his nous was beyond his years, he lacked the polish, the experience, of a public company boss from central casting. Then there were the sales – tiny compared to Autonomy's massive market value.

Yet the company was growing steadily. The number of people it employed was ever-expanding. In 1997, it had 33 employees, but by mid-2000 it had 157 – of which about half were in sales and marketing – with fourteen offices in seven countries. It finally hit profitability and, when it did, it boasted an enormous profit margin, over 91 per cent, confirming the low costs associated with licence sales and delivering software products to customers.

Its new-found public status meant changes for the business. The share price provided a live indicator of how the world perceived that Autonomy was doing. That had its advantages in good times, and severe disadvantages in the bad. It also meant that there were a whole host of external people involved in the company's fortunes.

The business began to publish trading updates about how it was doing every three months, revealing key information about its financial and business performance. It did this quarterly, which put it more in line with US competitors; in the UK, half- and full-year results are the norm.

Reporting this often, Lynch found, was like being on a journey with children in the back of the car, having to tell them every five minutes where you are going, if you're nearly there yet. Autonomy would have to say what it expected its numbers to be and outline its direction of travel. In addition, those in finance who followed the company would also predict how it would do. This created a constant pressure for the company to perform as anticipated. As a result, the 'end of the quarter' was a frantic time, marked by tight deadlines, shifting targets and last-minute deal scrambles. Analysts would set expectations of where they thought the finances should be, and if Autonomy wasn't on track, its share price would fall.

One reason why investors love putting their money into software companies is because the profits can be enormous. Unlike manufacturing, which has high labour and machine costs, a piece of software can be remade and resold as many times as you want, giving you a very high margin. Yet software also comes with its downsides. Unlike selling a piece of hardware, which has a fixed manufacturing and delivery time frame, and which generates an accurately estimable monthly income, software is more unpredictable. It can be sold, pushed out and delivered to a customer right up until the very last second of a given quarter.

Ultimately, reporting with that kind of frequency distorted the way the company was run, as it drove its results towards the three-monthly deadlines – and it was this that would prove to be the source of so many of Autonomy's problems.

MEANWHILE, THERE WERE major changes happening in Lynch's personal life too.

On 16 November 2000, the *Daily Mail* called him a 'most eligible bachelor', but he wasn't to remain one for long. Out in New York attending some investor meetings at Deutsche Bank, Lynch met a bright, young, married banker called Angela Bacares, just a couple of years his junior. Originally from Colombia, Bacares' parents had emigrated to New York, where she was raised in the tough district of Queens. Speaking several languages, she attended Brown and Dartmouth, heading on to a career in finance.

Lynch had dated lots of women along the way, but Angela was different. The pair started a relationship while she was in the process of moving to work in London. As a beautiful young woman of South American heritage, she stood out: a rare beast on the almost exclusively white male trading floor of the time.

Angela had a certain quality that everyone remarked on. She softened Lynch, at least at first. People were so wowed by meeting her that they felt more warmly towards him – they felt that he must have something special for her to be with him. About a year after the

NASDAQ float, in May 2001, Lynch and Bacares announced their engagement in *The Times*.

Despite his increasing wealth, Lynch had never changed his dress sense or fixed his teeth. Friends would laugh about the ketchup stains on his shirt, or at a torn pocket he had stitched up himself. Ideas were more important to him than appearance. Since childhood, his imagination had been kept busy by technology, not by his looks. As his business got bigger, so did his waistline. This did not bother Lynch. He told one friend that if he stood with his back to the wall, moving to the side of the room, nobody could tell that he'd put on weight. Besides, he had other matters at hand – his profile and influence were growing too.

With Gaunt as best man, Mike married Angela in London, with the reception at the Lanesborough Hotel. Due to the limitations on travel still in place after the 9/11 terrorist attacks, the guest list was smaller than it was supposed to be.

For Lynch, the pay-off for several rounds of going public was a windfall, and a guarantee of lifelong financial stability. He loved good restaurants and nice cars, but he did not crave an overtly glamorous lifestyle. Money for money's sake was never the end goal, but it brought him great creature comforts, as well as immense power and status, even if he did not always like spending it on frivolities. There was a rumour that Angela bought a pair of Gucci shoes and hid them from her husband in the front garden as a joke.

Ilford was by now a distant memory. Instead, Lynch had a house near the seaside village of Aldeburgh in Suffolk, where software took a back seat. Here, he would tinker with technology and machinery from the past – 'old rubbish', he called it – which filled his shed and overflowed into the garden, where he had a miniature steam engine and railway line. 'I like old things, you can learn from them. People always seem to think that we are cleverer than our ancestors but it's just not true,' he said.

Suffolk, or 'nowhere on the road to nowhere', as he frequently described it, would from then on become his home. The rural spot was a world away from where he grew up. It had kept that old-fashioned feeling and he loved the history of the place. It is a part of England where local 'old boys' gather in pubs that never really change much, to drink beer at the bar with an open fire crackling nearby. Corduroy and flat caps abound. Lynch liked the traditions and the pubs, and the folk songs. As with old technology, he liked places with history, and with heritage.

One thing was going south, however: his hearing. It was around this time that Lynch started to grow deaf, an enormous blow for a man with such a passion for music. He'd noticed that he often failed to hear doorbells, and doctors said vaguely that a virus was to blame. He speculated to friends that his work on music tech might have caused some damage along the way. Recordings from before and after this time show clearly that his voice changed with his ear troubles, developing a flatness common in deaf people, who may not be able to hear how their own voice sounds in terms of highs and lows. It made his speech sound robotic and mechanical, sometimes devoid of emphasis and emotion, with no natural pauses or shifts in pace.

As his hearing deteriorated further, he could understand most things, as long as he was not speaking to someone with a strong accent and there was no background noise. To help, he would lip-read and use visual cues, and began wearing hearing aids.

As usual, he joked around the hardship: 'I generally hear the question. I then pause while I desperately try and work out what "my aardvark is red" could possibly mean. I look into the corner and then I answer a question that is completely different to what was asked. Luckily, people think I'm a visionary when I do that.'

SEVEN

The Bubble Bursts

This is the sort of issue that should have been dealt with as quietly as possible. Behaving like this makes you enemies. Obviously factual errors should be corrected, but there are ways and means of doing it. I think Lynch looks like a berk.

– Anonymous 'senior City figure', quoted in The Sunday Times, *11 February 2001*

Autonomy caught the tail wind of investors' frenzy to invest in technology companies, but it wasn't long before the ducks stopped quacking and the dotcom merry-go-round of money ground to a halt. A *Guardian* article from the period said presciently that for the toppy valuations of the dotcom boom to be justified, every person on earth would have to be surfing the net twenty-four hours a day with a mobile phone clamped to each ear.

That time was yet to come. Ballooning share prices had collapsed. It was a total bloodbath, even for those who survived. By January 2001, a few months after the spectacular success of Autonomy's

London float, the company's share price had more than halved and, with it, Lynch's paper fortune.

He was not alone. The tech-heavy US NASDAQ had risen 88 per cent in 1999, which continued to a peak in March 2000. Then, the crash came. Giants like Microsoft and Amazon fell dramatically in value. At least 130 internet companies folded. By October, the NASDAQ was down 77 per cent from its height seven months earlier.

Some managed to get out at the right time. Star tech investor Katie Potts, who had invested £500,000 at Autonomy's first listing, sold all her shares between January and November 2000, making a £17.4 million profit. This irritated Lynch – it seemed to him like a slight to the company. In short, it was. Potts never reinvested because she always felt uncomfortable about the numbers and Autonomy's valuation. Apax Partners, Autonomy's original investors, also sold out, divesting its final 7 per cent share in February 2001, which knocked the share price ten per cent on the day.

Yet Lynch, in his usual bullish fashion, insisted that everything was fine: 'There have been a lot of rumours in the market about Autonomy slowing down, which is completely untrue,' he said.

Not for long. In a sign of the times, in March 2001, Autonomy fell out of the FTSE 100 and was replaced by a brewer, Scottish & Newcastle. When Autonomy went on to announce plunging sales that April, it wiped more than 40 per cent off the value of the company. By this point, Lynch had changed his tune, and said the drop in the share price was due to a stalling of technology spending in Europe, a volte face after Autonomy had been telling investors it was recession-proof. Trust in the Autonomy story was beginning to fade.

As the stock continued to fall, the British press snarkily pointed out that Autonomy had joined the '90 per cent club' – an 'exclusive' club of half a dozen or so companies which had seen the value of their shares fall by more than 90 per cent in less than a year. At one point, Lynch's shares lost £55 million in value in twenty-four hours. This seeming enjoyment of someone else's misfortune made him despise the media. It was all very well for half-baked business journalists to be rude and critical, Lynch thought, but they were not doing anything remotely valuable. He claimed to not mind the ups and downs: 'You don't put to sea if you don't understand that there are going to be storms and waves,' he said.

Storms and waves there were.

Before the floats, Lynch's public profile had been quite controlled. He was portrayed in lighter feature pieces that gave a rose-coloured picture of his entrepreneurial journey. There were a few newspaper write-ups from press releases that he had authored. But now, running a public company, he was under far more scrutiny. He found it nigh-on impossible to absorb the barbs or take them on the chin. He took each one intensely personally.

Every single time he was wounded, he wanted to fight back. 'Always take a gun to a knife fight' was a classic Lynch-ism. It was a quick way to make enemies.

AT THE START of February 2001, Lynch exploded with anger and growled, red-faced, at those around him. He had long been critical of financial research coming out of the City, but this was the last straw.

Merrill Lynch's sales department was advising its clients to sell Autonomy stock, telling an untrue story that Microsoft had pinched some of its staff and was launching a competing piece of software. Karen Spärck-Jones was named by Merrill Lynch as one of the supposed errant employees. In reality, she had never worked at Autonomy.

This story was simply false. Nevertheless, the missive (which had 'the bulletin board qualities of factual inaccuracy and appalling punctuation', according to *The Times*), sent Autonomy's shares down 10 per cent. Lynch felt the unfairness keenly. He shouted at advisors to complain to everyone – to the bank, the London Stock Exchange and the financial regulators. That a house of Merrill Lynch's stature could behave like this . . . ! He wanted to know what they were trying to do to him, what was their real motive?

'Saying Autonomy had lost all of its developers is a bit like saying Manchester United has lost all its players. It is a very bad thing to say and we were under a legal obligation to get Merrill Lynch to correct that,' he said more coherently in public. The City felt he was overreacting to a really insignificant event. The investment bank did make a correction to the erroneous staffing report, but it repeated the 'sell' advice. 'We are standing by the idea but the reference to the individuals was incorrect,' a Merrill spokeswoman said.

The idea that Autonomy's software was not unique sent Lynch through the roof. He railed against the 'posh twits in suits', financiers and lawyers, the City investors who were winning and losing a fortune off the backs of entrepreneurs like him. He believed they were all idiots and he was happy to slag them off. Most venture-capital investors did not understand how to run a business, according to Lynch. Accountants were dismissed as people who just added things up. He was vitriolic about the standard of research into companies like Autonomy by the City, accusing those who worked there of 'single brain-cell analysis'. Yet it was a world that he was now closer to than ever. As the newly London-listed company became entwined with the City, he had to deal with the 'posh twits' all the time.

As much as Lynch battled with the City, he was fascinated by it in equal measure. It was an enclosed system which he felt should be understandable and predictable. There was an input of a trade and an output of the market movement. Financial markets are made up of debates and opinions. Lynch tried to apply his mathematical mind to understanding why certain things were happening and he found it frustrating that they did not always make sense to him. He was constantly asking why. Why was the share price moving? Who was selling? Why were they selling? Who was buying? He even bought a Bloomberg machine, the information terminal favoured by financiers, to get all of the data the City had.

On 11 February 2001, *The Sunday Times* published a long article about the row between Autonomy and Merrill Lynch, headlined 'Naked Lynch'. It attracted a large, high-profile readership and, as such, was a large, high-profile slap in the face for the young businessman. He was furious about it, and became increasingly obsessed by the negativity of the press towards him.

The article detailed all of the questions being asked about the business, including whether Autonomy was only really successful because of the dotcom boom. It also criticized Lynch's love of spin, and mocked the number of press releases Autonomy published about deals. Mainly, it questioned why Lynch had gone into battle so hard against Merrill Lynch in public, rather than quietly dealing with the matter. It made him look, according to one senior City figure quoted in the piece, 'like a berk'.

Not long after, he was slapped hard again. On 26 February, in the *Financial Times*, Caroline Daniels wrote a long piece entitled 'Software star's party is over'. The detailed feature raised questions about the quality of Autonomy's technology, mentioning that it was expensive and unwieldy, that it took a long time to implement and suffered from a lack of precision in its search results. Autonomy partners, Daniels reported, were not embedding the software because of high royalty fees. 'It is a total takedown,' Lynch railed, asking his team, 'Who is she sleeping with?'

As Lynch became increasingly frustrated by what he saw as ignorance, greed and even corruption in the Square Mile, a few City slickers started to get infuriated by Autonomy's startup culture and an irascible founder who seemed incapable of being polite. It was an animosity that would only build and, in some cases, last a lifetime.

The honeymoon with the media and with the City which had followed the three floats was truly over. Something had to change. Luckily, an old friend was just around the corner.

PART TWO
Goldilocks

EIGHT

The Inner Circle

Dr Lynch ran the Autonomy group informally and through small cliques of loyal lieutenants . . . I describe them later as a cabal, of which Dr Lynch, when not ostensibly involved, was nevertheless the éminence grise. The impression I have formed is that his lieutenants would not have done anything of which they thought he might disapprove: and in practice, there was no higher authority within the group to whom they could look to justify what they did.

– *Mr Justice Hildyard, civil judgement, 17 May 2022*

Sushovan Hussain started primary school in Britain at eight years old, with only two words of English: toilet and water.

His journey to get there from a war-torn Bangladesh had been traumatic. In 1971, protests over an election in Pakistan spilled over into a bloody conflict as people in East Pakistan, now known as Bangladesh, tried to win autonomy from those in the West of the country. The Pakistani army tried to crush the movement with a ruthless campaign of terror, perpetrating horrendous massacres, killing hundreds of thousands of people and making many more homeless.

It was this confusing and brutal environment that Tahmina Hussain, Sushovan's mother, found herself in. She was exhausted, frightened, and alone, caring for two young children, just as the Pakistani army was starting to attack civilians. Not knowing which way to turn, the twenty-nine-year-old fled her home city of Bogra with her little ones, Sushovan and his sister Soma, to take refuge in a remote village. Once there, they suffered through sleepless nights as they moved from place to place to avoid the fighting. Her husband Tayyeb was away doing a chemistry PhD in Sheffield in the north of England, so it was just the three of them there, facing an uncertain future, desperate to survive.

Fortunately, survive they did. After it was all over, in March 1972, the relieved family boarded the first charter flight to the UK to join Tayyeb and start a new life. But the elation of the long-awaited reunion was not to last long.

The Pakistani government cut Tayyeb's university scholarship, and the immigrant family, with little money, scraped a living, sharing one room of a terraced house until eventually they moved into two rooms, one of which was a kitchen-cum-bathroom. Sushovan slept on the sofa. Desperate to find a job, Tahmina started cleaning in a local steel factory to make ends meet. It was a huge change from her old job in Bangladesh, where she had been an English lecturer at a girls' college. She and her husband had sacrificed everything in leaving Bangladesh, including highly paid jobs, for their children's future. This new, very different life in Britain was a huge adjustment for everyone.

At Springfield Primary in Sheffield, it did not take Sushovan long to pick up the language and catch up with his classmates. Any trace of his original accent soon disappeared. He passed the exam for a prominent grammar school and in 1976 the family moved down to

London, where he continued his studies. Education was all-important to the family, and Hussain's parents worked night and day to pay for the cost of the children's private schooling. Tayyeb got a temporary job teaching chemistry in a boys' school, while Tahmina took a job in a toy car factory and sewed clothes at home in the evenings.

Like Dolores Lynch, Hussain's parents heard about Bancroft's extraordinarily beneficent funding scheme. Their academically inclined son applied and in 1980, he joined the sixth form in the year above Mike Lynch.

Hussain's family burst with pride, just as Lynch's had, when he won a place at Christ's College Cambridge to study economics. It was there that the two young men really started to become friends. He would be at gatherings in Lynch's fancy first-year college room, and later at his house parties while Lynch was doing his PhD. At this stage, there were no plans for a business or to take over the world together. But they were pals.

Hussain was a crowd-pleaser at college, a cheerful, enthusiastic individual with an infectious grin and a genuine interest in people. He would always help out his fellow students. One of the sporty crowd, he was a brilliant squash player, an outlet for his seemingly unending energy, along with running and chess. During the holidays, he would work in the restaurant his father had opened in Walthamstow. He always took pride in doing so; it was never something he concealed from his friends. In fact, he felt that working in the restaurant over the years gave him the opportunity to mix with people from all walks of life, which had helped him during his admission interview for Cambridge.

After graduating, Hussain trod a steady, predictable path, training as a chartered accountant and settling down to start a family quickly, marrying Tracie, whom he met in his mid-twenties, in 1993. She fell for his upbeat personality and sense of humour, but it was the support he gave her while she was grieving for her brother, who had died a decade before, that really made the pair very close.

Hussain started working for an oil and gas business and, when their first child, Ayesha, was two, the family got the chance to travel and live abroad as he was offered an overseas posting to Caracas in Venezuela. It was a big decision to make, especially given the economic and political turmoil in the country, but as Tracie was considering giving up work anyway, and with no schooling to consider at this stage, the family decided to embark on a new adventure.

About eighteen months later, they moved again. This time to Karachi in Pakistan, another edgy choice given the city was still in the throes of instability. Political and communal violence were commonplace. But it was in Karachi that Tracie became pregnant with their second child. People back home were surprised to hear that she was going to stay there with a new baby, but perhaps haunted by memories from Hussain's childhood, the family did not want to be separated.

Finally, when the children were five and one, the family decided to return to the UK, and they settled in the leafy commuter town of Sevenoaks in Kent. It's an affluent, best-of-both-worlds place that has the advantage of being a short train ride to London while also being in the countryside. Hussain remained in Pakistan for work for a short time, but he was constantly looking for a way to come back.

As luck would have it, at the same time, Mike Lynch was looking for yet another new chief financial officer to help him manage the next phase of Autonomy's explosive growth, and its relatively recent status as a publicly traded business. Ever a great collector of intelligent people who he'd met along the way, he turned to Hussain in the hope that he might be 'the one'.

Since its founding, the company had not managed to make a CFO stick. Lynch was a bloody-minded, difficult man to work for. Or, as executives around him put it more diplomatically, no one CFO was quite 'the right fit'. Hussain was replacing a man named Ralph Harms, who had lasted just over a year. Before that, Jonathan Spira had done the job for two and a half years, from 1997 to 2000. His predecessor had been Lynch and Hussain's former Bancroft's and Christ's college mate, Richard Anton, who had quit, and before that, it was the infamous, non-existent, Frank Bridges.

Despite the long commute to Cambridge – an hour and a half's drive on a good day – Hussain saw working with Lynch, his old friend, as a fantastic opportunity. Hussain loved Cambridge; he had extraordinarily happy memories of Christ's College and the wider university that had cemented his academic success and kickstarted his career. And Autonomy was a fast-growing listed software company. In June 2001, he enthusiastically joined, delighted to be in a *new* industry after his time in an *old* one.

Tech was a very different beast to oil and gas but, while Hussain might not have had experience in the complex world of software accounting, he was bright, hard-working and, crucially, could work with Lynch. The two men had an intense relationship, like a corporate marriage. They spoke every single day, sometimes more than once, and both poured their heart and soul into the business. It was a toss-up to know which of the two men worked more rigorously.

Hussain was popular at work, never a grandiose type, taking an attitude that 'status was for business cards' and that no job was too menial. His colleagues, in the main, described him as genuine, generous, caring and enthusiastic. It was a running joke that the conscientious man was always working, harder and longer than anybody else. Unlike a traditional CFO, he did not spend his time having lunches with investors or writing memos about strategy. He was jolly, effervescent and wore his heart on his sleeve, all while taking the job and his allegiance to Lynch incredibly seriously. 'Mike needs this, Mike is after this,' he would always say.

A far cry from the days of the work-shy Frank Bridges, he would ring colleagues out of hours, apologizing for troubling them on a Saturday night, and they would smile at the insincerity. Lynch valued him for this: for being the details man, for his ability to see the bark on the trees rather than the wood.

The strangest thing about Hussain's role was that he was utterly enmeshed in the sales operation, to an unusual degree for a CFO. Deals were monitored on 'Sush's sheets', Autonomy-speak for the Excel spreadsheets maintained by the diligent Hussain, who had a ledger for everything, including his daughter's chess tournaments. He would meticulously keep across all the detail of who was selling what, working out the prospective revenue for the company. After work, Hussain would often hop onto the treadmill, from where he would call the Autonomy sales leaders in the US for an update on their numbers and to speak about contracts and opportunities in the pipeline.

As Hussain joined the company in the UK, Christopher Egan, known colloquially as 'Stouffer', pronounced Stow-fer, started working as a salesman for Autonomy in the US, running business development and partnerships. In less than a year, he became Autonomy's US CEO, moving with his family from Boston to the headquarters in California. It was a grandiose title which meant very little in reality, as he remained a salesman.

The company needed a US frontman, and being called the 'US CEO' gave Egan a foot in the door with companies when he was landing deals. Most of his time was focused on securing the big contracts with the large banks, the likes of Morgan Stanley, JPMorgan Chase, Deutsche Bank and Bank of America.

Egan was not chief executive material. He was a strategic thinker and good at understanding how to position the technology to sell, but he (ironically) had little autonomy within the business. The real power lay in Cambridge with Lynch and Hussain. Small, thin and bald, there was a timidity about him. He was the kind of man who would not push, would not ask for his bonus if he felt he had not done something exceptional, or not done a good job. Nonetheless, he was politically astute and knew how to play the system, not least because he was far away from the Lynch apron strings in the US.

In this period of new beginnings, Lynch also stepped down as chairman. As is common in the US but less so in Britain, he had until now served in the dual role of chief executive and chairman, but shareholders were pushing for this to end. As it turned out, this meant Autonomy would not have a permanent chair until the end of the decade. He did not relinquish any power, and there was never any doubt who was in charge. Everything came through Lynch; he was the spider at the centre of the web and he controlled everybody in it.

THE ARRIVAL OF these two executives, Hussain and Egan, signalled a change at the company. They joined at a crucial juncture, just at the tail end of the dotcom boom as Autonomy came crashing out of the FTSE 100, where it had so briefly shared a table with Britain's biggest corporate beasts. In 2002, Autonomy's share price went below a pound, quite the fall from grace from the £35 it had been at the end of 2000.

Now the challenge was to build it back up.

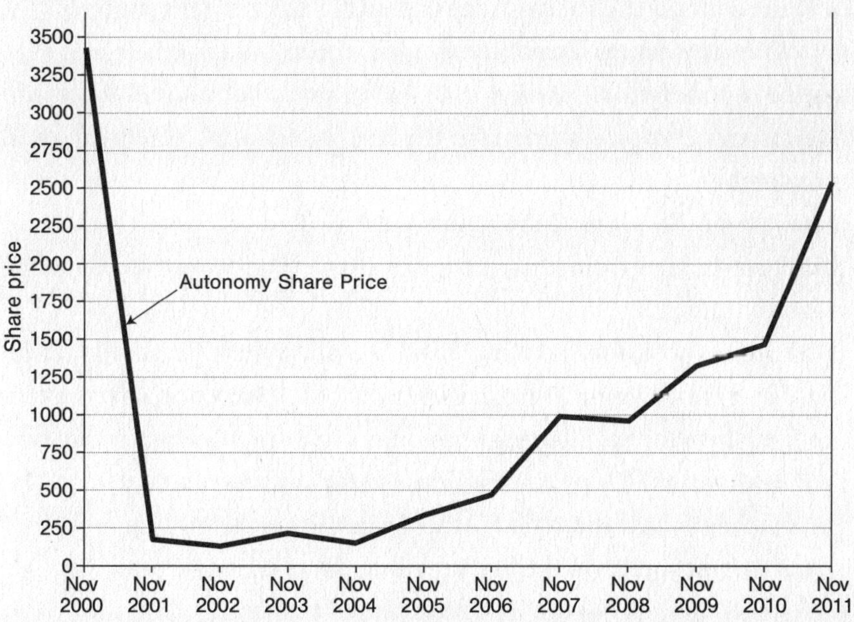

Autonomy's share price over its time listed on the London Stock Exchange.

It wasn't just the team that was changing. Autonomy was also shifting location. In February 2001, the company signed a lease to leave the St John's Innovation Centre and move into its own nearby building. Lynch and Gaunt had the opportunity to design and fit out this brand-new space exactly as they wanted.

Gaunt insisted on one thing: a circular tank of piranhas nestled in the heart of Autonomy's logo. Positioned prominently in the reception area, this predatory welcome party greeted every visitor who walked through the door. Occasionally, a half-eaten one would float along in front of the glass, sometimes still valiantly flapping a fin. Lynch liked to point out that the carnivorous fish were all exactly the same size. When one grew weaker than the others, it would be mauled by the rest. That – he said to visitors – is also the tank where the failing salespeople get dunked.

A further quirk of the new office was the meeting rooms, all named after villains from Lynch's beloved James Bond franchise: Dr No, Goldfinger and Scaramanga. It had to be villains – the list would be quite short if the rooms were named for the hero, he quipped.

While the James Bond theme was meant tongue in cheek, its sinister connotations seeped into Autonomy's culture, which reads like an archetype of workplace toxicity. Lynch's management style remained as aggressive as it had been back in the days of the small team at the St John's Innovation Centre. Few of Lynch's choleric diatribes survive from this time, but those who were there haven't forgotten them.

On one occasion, looking over a staff member's shoulder, he caught sight of an email thread that revealed a group of staff members mocking him for his Fleming obsession. He was not going to take this insubordination. 'Copy me into your reply,' he instructed her coldly. He watched while she typed 'Mike Lynch' into the cc line and then sent it to everybody on the list, including him. When he read through the emails, he lost his rag and fired one of the team.

The employee he caught was punished in other ways. Lynch later ordered her desk to be moved to just outside his office, because of her 'negativity'. He could see her computer screen through the glass and monitor her work. He would lurk over her shoulder. 'Have you done it yet?' he barked, repeating the question relentlessly again and again and again: 'Have you done it yet? Have you done it yet? Have you done it yet?'

In the mornings, he would march over to her and her breath would catch in her chest. 'What are you doing?' he'd demand. 'I need you to look at this and this and this and this,' leaving her quaking with the volume of demands. Each time she left her desk, he would ask in an accusatory tone where she was going. Her colleagues were so concerned that they kept a diary of what was going on. Eventually, she'd had enough. Driven to the edge of a breakdown, she kept a painful record of her last weeks at the business.

One day, when Lynch started to needle her, she exploded. '*Back the fuck off, Mike, don't fucking come near me. Get that fucking man away from me,*' she shouted, and left, for the last time, with no job to go to. Autonomy could have been an incredible place to work, she felt, with its amazing technology and its cohort of bright Cambridge graduates, if only Lynch had been a bit nicer, less of a bully.

Lynch felt it had to be that way. 'Nice' in the cut-throat world of tech, dominated by Silicon Valley giants, would not get you very far, he believed. Major homegrown technology companies were – and still are – as rare as small piranhas in the UK, typically gobbled up by deep-pocketed American rivals. It was kill or be killed by a rival company, and it was kill or be killed inside the business. No one would get anywhere by sitting and smiling at one another.

Many former staff talk of the trauma they experienced from working under Lynch, the fear of being belittled in public, 'covered with a bucket of shit' or fired on the spot. The joke went that if he didn't like the way they smiled at him, and he was in a bad mood, they were out. Bonded by their experiences, close friendships formed among many of the young staff. It was, they said, like being in prison.

Those who worked at Autonomy became familiar with the sick feeling in their stomach that comes from living on tenterhooks, from not knowing where the next bollocking was coming from. This feeling of being stupid and incompetent made the shy ones shyer and fumbling, but the management, inspired by their leader, did not hold back from making criticisms, because 'fear got results'. After he blasted staff, Lynch would sometimes mutter to his executives, 'I can be my own worst enemy', realizing from the quaking reactions of people around him that perhaps he had gone too far.

Things always felt like a threat. He micromanaged everything to the nth degree, down to the cover of the annual report. Some in his inner circle pondered at the time how long it would be before an angry partner of a staffer would come in and beat him up for how rude and offensive he was. One former group of employees – all men – referred to themselves as 'battered wives'.

External advisors noticed his behaviour too, and stories abound about what a nasty person he was to work with. Once, during a pitch for Autonomy's business, Lynch picked on the most junior member of a public relations team and unnecessarily ripped him to shreds. 'Do we really want to do business with this guy?' the PR team asked, stunned, as Lynch left the room. During another pitch, Lynch was so terrifying that the shirt of the man presenting went see-through with sweat.

Bits of this bubbled out into media reports at the time, and Lynch's reputation in the small world of British tech was quickly sullied by the stories. Those few who survived and rose to the top of his businesses adored him, and he had a small cohort of worshippers. 'This is not the place for you if you want to work nine to five and don't love your work,' he once blandly told the *Financial Times*.

Some, especially in Autonomy's tech teams, did love the place. The tech team really mattered to Lynch, and he put them on a pedestal, making sure they were paid and feted on a par with the sales teams. One software developer who tried to leave was summoned by Lynch himself, compared to David Beckham, and offered a foreign posting to stay.

A small group inside the company, a handful of prized engineers, was given free rein to experiment, to play around and develop new products. This cohort referred to themselves as the Skunkworks team, like the group from Lockheed Martin responsible for designing and producing advanced military aircraft during the Second World War.

By this time, the Dynamic Reasoning Engine had been renamed IDOL – the Intelligent Data Operating Layer. It was like a box of Lego which could be adapted to customer needs, either sold as separate building blocks or as a complete package. As with today's AI chatbots, which allow computers to engage with natural language, the tech teams found its ability to analyse information left in human form awe-inspiring. When it worked.

A key figure was Jack Stockdale, who joined the company's tech team in its early days and never really left the Autonomy family. An enthusiastic, talented developer, he loved working on the advanced technology. His colleagues were his own age. He had the opportunity to travel. For him, Lynch was like a father figure who would dish out advice and was almost always right.

Another who thrived there was Suranga Chandratillake, a diminutive Cambridge computing graduate with a mop of curly hair who started as an engineer and quickly moved to San Francisco as US chief technology officer. Lynch would always promote brilliance over experience. With a brain as big as his smile, Chandratillake, joined by Stockdale, then spun out Blinx, a video and audio search engine, from Autonomy in 2004.

But even for the tech guys (and they were mainly guys), dealing with Lynch could be like running into machine gun fire. He was terse and would not waste unnecessary time on people. He would answer a question, but if someone started saying something that didn't matter to him, he would just ignore them and move on. Staff who understood that did well. It was not personal; his brain had just moved on to another problem. The flipside was that praise from him was high praise indeed, and would make you feel great for the rest of the day.

Just as there were two Lynches in the office, the affable, charming, kind man and the ferocious, cruel, unforgiving one, there were also two Lynches on email. Externally, he would write fully punctuated, structured messages, including appropriate platitudes – 'I hope you are well' etc. Internally, to his closest advisors, he was the exact opposite. He would write unpunctuated, quick and sparse notes – the most indecipherable just said 'o', leaving his staff scratching their heads. 'This is wrong', was another common one, perplexing its recipients. These emails would later be thrown back at him in court, where they became part of a mountain of evidence of his autocratic management style.

One example was this unedited group message, related to a deal with the US Department of Veterans Affairs in 2010. You may need to slow down to follow it.

> **nothing is said to the customer with out it being cleared by someone senior, no meetings occur with out someone with a brain present, NO F-ing abdications of responsibility or delegation. If there is any problem I WANT TO KNOW ABOUT IT IN A F***ING MILLISECOND from all of you.**

'Just one of my standard motivational emails,' Lynch would later joke. Executives remember them all too well.

His personal email address, which he used both for his friends and as the source of many of these ransom-letter style emails to colleagues, had a handle headed 'MRLdog99'. If recipients wanted replies from him, Lynch told them they needed to be brief. Lynch's head, one friend conjectured, was far ahead of his hand, and he didn't like to dress up the important stuff with niceties. Sometimes using voice recognition to type, he would not bother correcting it. Most of the time, he avoided typing altogether and liked to ring people up, bark instructions and hang up. '*Where are you? Get here now!*' *Click-buzz.*

Wherever you stood on working for Autonomy, there were some benefits. Free food on a Friday – any leftovers could be taken home in a doggie bag. The annual Christmas party, when the company took staff and their partners abroad on a three-day, all-expenses-paid trip to destinations like Bergen, Barcelona or Paris. Autonomy would charter a jet and put everyone up in extraordinary hotels, with a black-tie dinner as the centrepiece of the event. Then, there was free time to enjoy a holiday and a lot of drinking.

Plus, Cambridge was a fantastic place for young people to hang out. Nothing beats the city in the summer months, with punting on the river, open fields and beautiful old pubs. Staff forged strong cohorts of friends. Years after they left Autonomy, they kept those tight circles going. There was respite from the boss too, at least on a face-to-face basis. It was a challenge to run a global business seamlessly, with headquarters in the UK and America, so Lynch would spend three to four weeks at a time in San Francisco overseeing the company in the US. In the summers, his family would often rent a house in the upscale Pacific Heights neighbourhood.

IN 2003, QUIETLY, with no public announcement, Richard Gaunt decided to leave the business. Staff noticed that he came in less and less, until he finally stopped altogether. He was tired and a little jaded after the intense work of the previous years and was never one to give anything less than his all. Lynch was disappointed, felt let down, and the two men subsequently saw each other only sporadically. When they did, though, it was as if nothing had changed.

Gaunt would forever be referred to as a co-founder of Autonomy, yet he always saw himself as the number two, the junior partner. Lynch could tell people: 'This has to be done by tomorrow, it has to look like this', and then when they did not do it, he would say, 'I cannot believe you did this to me!' Gaunt was never able to be quite so cold.

Inevitably, as Lynch's co-founder moved on, the power dynamic inside Autonomy shifted. Dr Pete Menell took charge of the technical side, replacing Gaunt. A gangly man with dark hair falling over his forehead and a goofy expression, Menell had a habit of obfuscating and using high-flown technical language. One of his favourite phrases was 'deniable culpability' – you could claim you weren't involved, even if you were. He could never stand up to Lynch in the way Gaunt had done and was always anxious about his standing.

Hussain and Andy Kanter became more clearly defined as Lynch's right-hand men and, on 1 June 2003, Hussain joined the board as an executive director. Yet despite its public status and refreshed board, Autonomy continued to be run chaotically, like a startup, from this core inner circle of power, without the clear infrastructure of a more

L–R: Sushovan Hussain, Ian Black, Fernando Lucini (Autonomy Head of Pre-sales and Chief Architect), Pete Menell, Mike Lynch, Andy Kanter.

established company. It had not really grown up from its teenage popstar days.

Outwardly, things looked good. The contracts continued to flow and Autonomy trumpeted them mercilessly, publishing 'Contract Win' releases at every major deal. Marketing mattered as much as ever. Lynch continued to boast that the company had a 98 per cent gross margin on its sales, because as 'a pure software business', there was little cost on a sale. It continued to win prizes, such as 'Product of the Year' at the 2003 UK Information Management Awards, and it continued to open offices abroad, including one in Beijing.

In the years which followed the 9/11 attacks, the war on terror was a boon for Autonomy. During the third quarter earnings call in 2002, Lynch announced 'a particularly significant customer': the American secret services. Autonomy had been chosen as software in the fight against terrorism for a clutch of US security bodies, including the FBI. It was a coup. Plus, Bond fanatic Lynch had always loved this 'spooky stuff'. However, the win was marred by a scandal in Washington, DC.

Richard Perle, chairman of Donald Rumsfeld's Defense Policy Board and an influential architect of the Iraq War, was still one of Autonomy's non-executive directors. Autonomy was not the only company he was involved with, and he was forced to resign from the Defense Policy Board over allegations of conflicts of interest (unrelated to Autonomy), with the suspicion he was using his influence for personal gain.

Critics pointed to the stock options he held in Autonomy and raised suspicions about the validity of the company's contracts with the US army and military. Back in the UK, the National Association of Pension Funds even recommended that investors voted against Perle's re-election to Autonomy's board. But in Cambridge in April 2003, Autonomy staff voted against selecting directors based on their political beliefs. Always denying any impropriety, Perle stayed at the company until 2010.

Inwardly, things were shambolic. Managing a company growing this quickly came with many problems. A letter from 2004 flags a litany of issues at one of Autonomy's regional outposts in Australia: that staff often 'don't seem to work out', that they were resigning or becoming 'disaffected', technical support was lacking and products did not work reliably, sales staff made 'out-dated assertions about competitors'. The executive team around Lynch fought constantly to have his ear and he would play them off against one another.

With the efforts to get things back on track and bring the company back to the dizzy heights of the dotcom boom, the pressure started to intensify.

NINE

Revenue, revenue, revenue

That bald, square, CFO kid sure does a mean sales call.

– Autonomy sales video

Limbering up as if for a race around a park, dressed in running gear – sweatbands and a white sports shirt emblazoned with the number 666 – Andy Kanter puffed on a cigarette and kissed his biceps. Sushovan Hussain, sporting three dollar signs in the centre of his running top, stretched in an exaggerated fashion, jogging purposefully on the spot.

Thus caricatured as 'the devil and the money man', Lynch's two top dogs clowned around for the cameras as they were filmed in a parody of the movie *Chariots of Fire*. The production team added the film's signature music and sped up the two men's running. Hussain is shown winning, holding up his arms as he breaks through the tape.

Then a newspaper spins onto the screen. 'Sushovan stripped of title in drug bust'. Followed by another: 'Sushovan Speaks Out' and 'Kanter said it was Viagra'!

This was just one of many parody videos starring Lynch's senior leadership team which, though they have survived the intervening years, have not aged particularly well. This one was created for an Academy Awards-themed event, although it features less than Oscar-winning performances from the two executives. There was no canned laughter, but there should have been – it would have suited the style of the thing.

In another, the theme music from *The Sopranos* was the backing track as the marketing team recreated the opening credits of the New Jersey mobster series, in Cambridge.

Lynch had form for such performances. At the turn of the millennium, Autonomy had made a last-ditch attempt to crack the consumer market with a personalized search product called 'Kenjin' – Japanese for wisdom. At a fancy bar in London's Mayfair, Lynch put on a fake Asian accent and performed a surreal sketch with Bert Kwok, the actor who played Cato in the Pink Panther films. Luckily for the reputation of everyone involved, there were no cameras present, and the attendees drank so much that, apart from a few newspaper diary pieces, no one remembers much about it.

These spoofs were a staple of the company's annual sales conference, a way of keeping the sales troops amused while they were taught to sell, sell, sell. No one was spared from taking part in the skits – even when elevated to CTO, Pete Menell would often appear as a kooky scientist, and Lynch himself would occasionally star. The absurdity of the videos was in sharp contrast to the sleek, glitzy place where they were shown – the stunning venue for Autonomy's Sales Kick Off events: the Ritz Carlton Miami Beach hotel in Florida. It was the epitome of Miami glamour, with its 1950s white art deco architecture and pool overlooking the Atlantic. There was always a theme, such as James Bond, Space or the Academy Awards. In the run-up to the show, Lynch, ever the control freak, would sit in the empty auditorium watching the rehearsals, nodding curt approval or making people play their parts again and again. He was a perfectionist; everything had to be just so.

Those Miami nights at the sales shindig could be very heavy indeed. However, regardless of how much fun the night before may have been, salespeople were told to turn up on the dot in the morning, when a register would be taken to check attendance and the doors would be locked. Teams would gather in the hotel's dark ballroom, where there were demos of the latest technology. On stage, it was quite the production, just like the *Chariots of Fire* video. Hundreds of people filled the space, row upon row of chairs stacked up right to the back.

There was sometimes a culture clash between the US and UK Autonomy teams, two nations divided by a common language. The *Fawlty Towers*-esque humour of the spoof films often went over the heads of the watching American salespeople. They would catch each other's eyes during the event, more than a little baffled. At the same time, the watching Brits would smirk at the Americans on stage, talking about the big cheques they had cashed from their latest sales bonus, the watch they had bought, the car, the conservatory, finding all of it ever so slightly ridiculous too.

For the finale of the event, Lynch would stand up and give a speech. With no notes and no slides, he would deliver a pseudo-Cambridge University lecture on a random topic, such as 'Time', or 'Money'. This was as mesmerizing as it was unorthodox and played particularly well with the Americans. 'It was the best, most inspiring speech I've ever seen,' said a US attendee after one conference, 'we didn't know where he was going, but the guy was wicked-smart.'

THE SHEER EFFORT that went into organizing and producing the Miami conferences showed that sales at Autonomy meant everything. Lynch drove the company towards hitting its quarterly targets in a ruthless, utterly dogged way, which was integral to his success. One big deal could mean the difference between the company meeting the markets' and its own expectations or being way off. If the numbers were not as forecast, it would instantly affect the share price.

To keep on top of this, sales at the company were governed by the hated Sales Management System (SMS), which clocked every salesperson's numbers and was meticulously overseen by Sushovan Hussain himself. The SMS inspired fear and awe. Salespeople had to note down their pipeline of customer leads, contacts they made with potential clients and the sales they closed. It was a rigorous but highly logical system, with a culture of 'no excuses': a product of Lynch's mathematical brain. Rather than cross his fingers and let the salespeople loose on the golf course with potential clients, in the hope that one relationship might come good, his probabilistic way of viewing the world told him that sales were more likely the more meetings a salesperson did each week.

'Salespeople are like dogs,' Lynch would say. 'If you shoot one, they all get in line.' And lo, they would swiftly get fired if they did not perform. They were coin machines motivated by money, Lynch said, far down the pecking order from the technologists at the company. The weekly sales calls made for a cruel end to employees' weekends. On Sunday nights, an email would be sent round to all the salespeople with their latest statistics. On Monday mornings, they then joined a conference call to go through their updates in front of everyone. Hussain and Egan would lead the call, but some salespeople suspected Lynch listened in.

Performance on the SMS was measured with a colour-coded system: red, amber and green. If you were in the red for two quarters – in other words, if you did not land a deal in six months – you got fired. If you closed a sale, there were huge financial rewards. Terror from the various sales agents speaking on recordings of these calls is palpable. Someone was even once fired on the call itself. The calls were like interrogations, with no trust and no transparency. It was not always clear who was listening in.

There were those at the company who mocked Hussain royally

Sushovan Hussain in the *Tommy* spoof video.

for his obsession with the numbers. He was so absolutely enmeshed in the SMS that the marketing team once made a parody of 'Pinball Wizard' from the 1975 film *Tommy*, with Hussain's smiling corporate photo superimposed onto Elton John's rocking body, tapping his gold boots and bobbing to the beat.

The reworked lyrics?

> *Ever since I was a young sales, I've done the SMS call.*
> *From Cambridge down to San Fran, I've listened to 'em all.*
> *But I ain't heard nothing like him, never heard him stall.*
> *That bald square CFO kid, sure does a mean sales call!*

He even '*does Excel in bed with his wife!*', amateur singers warbled out, to a picture of Hussain lying under the sheets.

Bald and square Hussain may have been, but the Monday morning calls inspired fear, and in the eyes of the Autonomy leadership team, fear got results. Autonomy was the best sales organization that many people had ever seen. You could do very well financially, as long as you didn't drop dead from anxiety. Bonuses could be massive. One salesperson got $1 million from a $9 million deal signed in 2010.

Yet successes in getting deals done sometimes masked a chaotic strategy behind the scenes. For instance, in contrast to the slick sales management system, pricing was haphazard. Hussain appeared to pluck numbers out of the air for contracts, based on what he believed the client could pay. And a problematic drawback of the quarterly reporting system was that, to hit the targets, close deals and collect their bonuses, salespeople would sometimes promise whatever the client wanted, often with alarming consequences for the tech teams who had to then subsequently deliver the product. When the software would come to be installed, clients would get angry because the promised features were not there, and then irate software developers would have to work overtime to implement them.

When this happened in the early days, one underhand tactic was to dispatch boxes of blank CDs out to the customer, printed with the requisite design. The fake shipment would buy the developers a couple of extra weeks to do whatever the salesperson had promised they could do once the 'error' was discovered by the customer. *Oh, we sent you blank CDs? Sorry, our mistake.* There is a story among Autonomy folk that once a box of old telephones was even shipped, although that might be apocryphal.

AUTONOMY DIDN'T JUST grow by selling software directly to customers. It also sold to other big companies like Oracle, Symantec and Adobe, which then included Autonomy's software in their own products. These companies were called OEMs, short for Original Equipment Manufacturers. By 2010, OEM deals made up a significant part of Autonomy's revenue. This was, Lynch liked to say, the piña colada sales model: his sales guys could sit on the beach drinking piña coladas and the rest of the industry was selling on their behalf.

But the most significant way that the company expanded was by buying other businesses and combining them with Autonomy's own technology Each time a company was bought, Autonomy's powerful IDOL software was apparently added to its products, like upgrading the engine on an older machine. Lynch once memorably put it as like 'bolting a jet engine onto a propeller aeroplane.' These acquisitions were central to the strategy, and could happen very quickly.

One new recruit found this out the moment he arrived. In the summer of 2005, at the age of thirty-three, Stephen Chamberlain (always known as Steve) joined the company as its Vice-President of Finance, running the day-to-day operations of Autonomy's accounts department in Cambridge. He knew the company well, having worked for its auditors Deloitte, a blue-chip business known as one of the Big Four accounting and professional services firms in the world. Yet, despite this, he couldn't have been prepared for the onslaught. On just his second day, he was forced to take a last-minute flight to Texas with zero notice, to negotiate the acquisition of a company called eTalk. It was a fittingly dramatic start to what would become a turbulent two decades for the Chamberlain family.

Indeed, Deloitte would be a recurring source of talent for the Autonomy accounts department over the years. Others who would move across included Poppy Gustafsson, the UK's former Minister of State for Investment, then known under her maiden name of Prentis. Cambridge was a satellite hub of Deloitte, a far smaller office than its mainstay in London. There, in Silicon Fen, Autonomy was its most important client and, later, its only one in the FTSE 100. It gave its staff a good grounding in the details of audit work, but once they had grasped it, many wanted to fly the nest into more lucrative jobs.

Another acquisition swiftly followed eTalk, and this one would capture global attention. In the early days, Autonomy's main rival at pitches for deals was a US search-and-retrieval company called Verity, an older firm founded back in 1988 that had hit on the niche of searching and filtering information. Anthony Bettencourt was its chief executive. Like Lynch, he had a rags-to-riches story. He was a bright man who worked hard and got lucky, and found himself in the right place at the right time during Silicon Valley's technology gold rush.

When Lynch and Bettencourt met for the first time, the two circled one another, sizing each other up, each man weighed down with mutual suspicion. At first, Bettencourt was rather jealous of Lynch's hyper-intelligence, and Lynch was not quite sure about this brash American CEO.

Yet there was a spark of camaraderie between them, and the men began meeting regularly – but always in secret, as their companies were sworn enemies. One clandestine meeting led to another and, over time, a kind of friendship formed. It gave the peers a chance to talk freely, swap war stories and connect on a more personal level. Bettencourt saw a softer side of Lynch. 'There were people on his team who were mean, and they thought they were being like Mike,' Bettencourt said. 'But Mike wasn't that way. Mike was blunt for a reason, because his brain was so goddamn big and he was so smart.'

In 2005, Lynch made a move. He decided to make a leap for the '600-pound gorilla', his name for Verity. It was a 'bear hug' – an offer so generous that receiving it feels like being squeezed tightly – which came totally out of the blue for Bettencourt. The deal got off to an inauspicious start when the Autonomy team flew to San Francisco to meet Bettencourt. Lynch, Hussain, US CEO Christopher Egan and Scott Shute – the cowboy-hatted Texan who ran eTalk – gathered outside their hotel, lingering on the pavement as they waited for their ride, Andy Kanter. The Inner Circle had added Shute to the gang for the day because they felt they needed more Americans on board.

Then, in the plush streets of the Bay Area, where bigger usually means better, Kanter rolled up in a Toyota Prius compact. It looked like something out of *Wacky Races* as the five men squeezed in, hat and all. As they turned onto Bettencourt's immaculate street, lined with rows of grand houses, Bettencourt politely suggested they park the tiny car elsewhere. He then gave them a tour of his impressive collection, which included a full-sized Batmobile.

The deal went ahead – Autonomy agreed to acquire the NASDAQ-listed company for $500 million. The Autonomy share price bounced: Verity had US federal security clearance, which meant that Autonomy was now in a more solid position to conduct business with the US Federal Government. It was a 'Silicon Fen coup', *The Guardian* said, for a Cambridge-based British tech business to buy such a well-established American one.

Lynch had eaten the competition.

Autonomy welcomed the Verity team to London with all the traditional British bells and whistles, including putting them up at the Ritz. In return, Bettencourt, a bit of a firecracker, took them all out and got them steaming drunk in celebration. But the real party was still to come, when Lynch took them all on the *Orient Express* from London to Paris. A classy, expensive treat.

After the acquisition, Lynch was scathing about Verity's technology, but he could not get enough of its marketing. He always felt the Brits were best at engineering but the Americans could not be beaten at sales. Verity's marketing was overseen by a woman named Nicole Eagan. Silicon Valley through and through, she was an all-American girl with pristinely coiffed blonde hair and a Hollywood smile. She had previously worked at Oracle, the US tech giant, under its founder Larry Ellison. She was initially irate about Autonomy's takeover, but Bettencourt convinced her it would be a good thing for her career to stick around.

Despite her experience working with the flamboyant, fiercely competitive Ellison, Eagan found Lynch to be one of a kind. He was the antithesis of Silicon Valley. Lynch joked that he had a job to 'de-programme' her, to fit into the very British Autonomy. De-programme her he did. Eagan would become one of his most trusted team members, taking over as chief marketing officer of the entire business. While others found him tricky to deal with, Eagan had no such problems. The pair would clash heads, but they always managed to find common ground.

After a while, Bettencourt decided to go back to university; he had dropped out of his studies early on and always wanted a degree. Lynch treated his former rival well – he was a fellow CEO, after all – keeping him on a $100,000 annual retainer. There was no show of ruthlessness in this relationship. Later, Bettencourt returned to the company to smooth the transition periods after other Autonomy acquisitions.

For more followed. In 2007, Autonomy bought Zantaz, which owned a product used by heavily regulated companies, like banks and insurers, to archive their emails, in compliance with growing legal requirements. Here, a man named Mike Sullivan entered the fray. Zantaz's Senior VP of Operations looked a bit like a marine, with a square head and a crop of short, spiky hair, and he would prove to be a tremendously effective foot soldier.

Sullivan was a survivor. Someone who always falls on their feet, he was one of the few people who kept his job throughout the Autonomy acquisition culls. He had already clung on when Zantaz bought his own business, SteelPoint Technologies, and he went on to take a senior role at Autonomy's cloud business, reporting directly to Lynch. He was important. If a big deal was in play, Lynch and Sullivan would speak a couple of times a day.

With all of these acquisitions, Autonomy's critics said it became very hard to know whether the company was growing 'organically', because it was selling more of its IDOL software, or whether it was just buying other people's business to make itself look bigger than it really was.

One thing was certain – each new company in its stable made Autonomy's accounts that much harder to decipher.

TEN

Meanwhile, in Suffolk

The only thing I'm dying to do is have a hot bath. It's the only luxury I want.

– *Mike Lynch,* Financial Times, *29 January 2000*

Concurrent to Autonomy's ascent, Lynch's own stature rose ever higher. Along with actress Imelda Staunton, chefs Gordon Ramsay and Heston Blumenthal, fashion designer Ozwald Boateng and tech entrepreneur Ian Livingstone, Lynch received an OBE in the 2006 New Year's Honours, for services to enterprise. From then on, he would always proudly list the three letters after his name. His real ambition was to become a Lord one day, but it was a start.

He was almost prouder of his appointment as a Fellow of the Royal Society of Engineering, which came in 2008, bringing another new title and even more letters. It was a recognition of his scientific achievements, and it meant he had the opportunity to spend time with people who understood technology and could speak on his level, as he saw it.

With his burgeoning reputation as a technology genius, Lynch was catapulted right into the heart of the British establishment. In

2006, he was invited to join the top-tier executive board at the BBC. The fusty broadcaster, undergoing one of its cyclical identity crises, had started a brand-new governing body aimed at including more commercially minded people. Lynch might not always have agreed with its way of doing things, but he was proud of being part of the BBC, appreciating its significance to the cultural and political fabric of the UK. He always loved rubbing shoulders with the great and the good – for the intrigue, status and drama alone, even if he didn't always love them as people.

The BBC wasn't a natural habitat for someone used to running their own show and making quick decisions. Under Mark Thompson, the new BBC Director General who also chaired the latest governing body, Lynch sat alongside a heavyweight group that included City stalwart Marcus Agius, the patrician former chairman of Barclays; Robert Webb KC, the former top lawyer for British Airways; and Samir Shah, the current BBC Chair. Lynch and his peers would roll their eyes at the grandstanding which went on at the large meetings, bewildered by long pointless speeches.

The old executives were somewhat suspicious of having this new bunch of people, who knew very little about television and radio, on their board, and they were not always particularly welcoming or helpful. Nonetheless, Lynch's contributions were always well-received and he was a respected member of the body, speaking concisely and pithily when consulted. Perhaps because it was not his own organization, he showed a certain respect and tolerance to the group, something that was often lacking within Autonomy.

At the time, the BBC's streaming service, iPlayer, was being developed. There were worries about what would happen to all the mountains of tape the BBC had made over the decades, as the priceless archive was also being digitized. Lynch, with his technological and business expertise, was in a good place to advise amid the chaos of trying to work out how to organize the mammoth task, and would show amused confusion as to why they were being so uncommercial and tech-unsavvy about it. (It's worth noting that the BBC was also a repeat Autonomy customer, and had been so since at least 1999. But it would later have problems with the technology within its monitoring service, responsible for tracking and analysing global media, and switch to another supplier.)

AWAY FROM THE world of business, Lynch's status also changed significantly – he had become a father. Mike and Angela had two daughters, Esme in 2003 and Hannah in 2006. Both parents were fiercely protective of the girls and worked hard to shield them from the limelight throughout their childhood.

The girls' arrival changed Lynch. The man who had always thought everyone else was an idiot started to chill out. He still believed that everyone else was an idiot, but he started to explain the world on their level, as he saw it, and became more reasonable. His children transformed him, friends said, from being scary into more of a human being.

As the family expanded, Mike and Angela started to look for a family home to create the environment they wanted for the children and that Mike had always wanted for himself. Eventually, they came across Loudham Hall, a substantial country house set amid the quiet majesty of a traditional estate. It offered not just space, but sanctuary – a retreat that would come to hold deep and lasting significance for the rest of his days. The family, including their beloved dogs, would continue to spend a lot of time in their townhouse in London's Chelsea, but the Suffolk house was perhaps closer to his heart, constant and grounding, no matter where life pulled him.

Its beauty was an instant draw. The colour of the solid, red-brick house was offset by the green climbers which rambled over its frontage and around the edges of the white-framed sash windows. Originally built as a hunting lodge in the late sixteenth century, the building underwent extensive changes in the eighteenth century. It had more than ten bedrooms, five reception rooms, a swimming pool, and plenty of space for Lynch's classic cars, including his Aston Martin DB5, iconically featured in the James Bond film *Goldfinger*. An assortment of cottages dotted the estate, where friends and staff could stay.

When the Lynch family bought the seventy-acre estate in 2009, it needed some renovation, and they spent years on the project. Lynch was never one to fully switch off. The renovation brought real enjoyment – a welcome change of pace and perspective – but it was no idle pursuit. It came with long hours, constant decisions, and no shortage of hard work. They inherited a farmyard of animals from the eccentric previous owners, including llamas and peacocks. They would add to this menagerie over the years, and Lynch took on his new role as lord of the manor with gusto. Always joking about his Irish heritage, he would wave his hand over the forty acres in front of his grand manor that he'd planted with potatoes, saying, 'This Irishman won't be getting caught out like that again.'

When the family was in Suffolk, which was not all the time, Lynch could disappear into a part of England that time had forgotten. Loudham Hall constantly needed maintenance, and there Lynch was a country squire in tweed, living in a world like *Downton Abbey*, complete with a full quota of staff who kept the place immaculately. Anything out of place stuck out like a sore thumb, and the rule was to repair, not replace. It often struck new guests how low-tech the house and its contents were, and Lynch would talk about the pleasure of returning to a home where 'the clocks still tick'. His adored train sets fitted right in.

Metal gates marked the entrance to the drive, flanked by a pair of stone lions standing guard. Discreet signs along the perimeter paths reminded passing walkers that the land beyond was private, but friends were to be welcomed with open arms. In their new surroundings, the Lynches had the glorious space to really entertain properly in their own self-contained world.

Loudham opened the door to a new circle of friends, which consolidated around the Lynch family in Suffolk – businesspeople, landowners, writers and just those with children the same age as Esme and Hannah, all of whom would gather around dinner tables and firesides, forming a warm and varied community. While life beyond the county could be uncertain, especially as Autonomy grew and grew, Suffolk remained steady – a haven of friendship and familiar faces. Lynch family gatherings would feature a mix of people from all different walks of life, not just those imported from Cambridge or London, which was remarked upon by Suffolk's more staid and snobbish figures.

Just like in the office, Lynch had little patience for those he deemed fools and made no effort to conceal it. He liked who he liked – and if a dinner companion failed to hold his interest, he would simply get up and leave, unapologetically. He had a knack of charmingly deflating the egos of Suffolk's more pompous inhabitants with a well-aimed remark and a twinkle in his eye that would make those around him burst out laughing.

Some locals were initially wary of what the tech entrepreneur would be like in person. Others had never heard of him, and others still were slightly baffled at the rather unkempt version of Lynch which presented itself at parties. He did not like spending money on food and drink at home. A lunch served at Loudham would never be very exotic or imaginative, and would be reliably based around the staples: meat and veg. Barbecues would serve burgers from the local supermarket; wine was a bottle of cheap plonk.

Wine wasn't ever something Lynch took much of an interest in at all. This was not a puritanical decision, nor one taken for health reasons; he simply had no desire to top up his glass, in the same way as he had no desire to try new things when he was quite happy with meat and two veg. He liked a curry, and enjoyed some of Mayfair's finest South Asian restaurants, but at home it was meat and potatoes.

When she was a young girl, Hannah announced to her parents that she wanted to be a vegetarian. This did not go down well at all. Lynch would challenge her on her arguments about carbon emissions from farming, even bring up the debate at the dinner table in front of guests. Emotional and ethical arguments were dismissed. He would not budge on his views.

Among his closest friends in Suffolk was Patrick Jacob – an affable former investment banker and Suffolk native. He often teased Lynch about his hopeless dress sense, which Lynch bore with good humour and total indifference. His disregard for appearances became something of a running joke between them, endearing rather than embarrassing. They'd met shortly after the Loudham purchase at a local supper party, bonding over their mutual love of restoration, forestry, history, and support for the local arts scene. Jacob kept Lynch enthralled with stories of folk songs, about the musical oral history passed through generations at the Suffolk pubs he'd grown up in.

Unlike those who bore the brunt of it, Jacob always felt that Lynch's business reputation, 'corporate Mike', was a caricature. While Lynch was thin-skinned, short-tempered and rude to journalists, much of the time Jacob thought it was with very good reason. At home in Suffolk, Lynch was a man like any other, only more insightful, interesting and entertaining. His charm came from his quick wit and comic timing, although Jacob and Lynch would invariably start arguing over politics at the dinner table.

Lynch was also unfailingly welcoming to the children and grandchildren of his friends, and when Jacob's daughter and her young family would visit, her maths-obsessed young girl would set Lynch puzzles to do before he was allowed to sit down for lunch. He always humoured her, and enjoyed the levity of it, while genuinely encouraging her curiosity in mathematics.

Another longstanding friend was John Gummer – Lord Deben – a Conservative peer who had been the MP for Suffolk Coastal for years, before Lynch had even arrived in the county. His political career is perhaps best remembered for the moment he gave his young daughter a burger to eat on camera to prove the safety of British beef during the BSE crisis. Such was the Suffolk bubble, however, that Lynch and Deben were more likely to speak about hedgerows and cattle when they were together rather than business or politics. They found a mutual interest in the rare breed Red Poll, a glossy deep red chestnut cow native to East Anglia that Lynch was cultivating at Loudham. There were a couple of other significant friends of the Lynch family in Suffolk. David Robbie, a co-conspirator from Lynch's time on the BBC board, also became close, and Tim Davie, the director general of the BBC from 2020, was a visitor.

Then there were household staff members who became part of family life. Restoring the grand, flat-fronted house was a multi-year project, much of which required around-the-clock attention. Working on everything from the staircases to the window frames was local carpenter and joiner Jeff Parish. When he and Mike first met, there was a classic Lynch test as he poked Parish about how he would deal with an old door lock. He was surprised to get a call the next week asking if he had time to take on some work at the Hall. Parish's first project was the tearoom, a lovely wooden building which was virtually in ruins. Lynch, who loved bringing old things back to life, asked him to restore it to the highest standard possible. Parish stayed on full-time.

A few years later Lynch bought Ashe Abbey, with land backing onto Loudham, next to the River Deben. One of the interesting features of the abbey was an old water wheel, which in the past had been used to grind grain. Lynch was over the moon when Parish rebuilt it and got it turning. A little later, Parish got a call from Angela: the Lynches were so delighted with the mill they wanted to invite him and his wife to Mallorca for a mini-break, on a private jet. Parish soon became Loudham Hall's estate manager.

Lynch and his family also grew closer to Anthony Bettencourt over in California, who needed friends more than ever. The former

Verity chief executive had made a major life decision – to transition to being a woman. Her voice and body changed hugely as she became Michele. Some things stayed the same – she stayed married and remained 'Dad' to her kids. Yet there were friends and family who did not know how to treat her after her transition.

The Lynches did not blink. When others ran away, they stayed close. Lynch would send her supportive messages on Facebook, sometimes just a simple 'you look great'. Angela invited her shopping in Milan. When Bettencourt's daughter was struggling to work out what she wanted to do next with her education, Lynch stepped in to offer guidance during a visit to the family. She was a talented mathematician but lacked any confidence. Lynch took her aside for half an hour and spoke to her, sweetly and gently, about her next steps – he is one of the people she today credits with shaping her career.

It is a recurring theme that despite Lynch's cruel and cantankerous business persona, he was often kind and supportive to children and young people, always taking lots of time with even the shyest. He would concoct elaborate stories that would keep them enthralled, organize inventive treasure hunts, and listen to them. This was a side of him that only his family and select friends were privy to.

AWAY FROM THE tranquillity of Suffolk, Lynch would later find himself in a more raucous environment he was not naturally au fait with: White Hart Lane, the home of Tottenham Hotspur Football Club.

On 14 August 2010, Spurs kicked off their season at home against Manchester City. The Tottenham players, including Welsh superstar Gareth Bale and England strikers Peter Crouch and Jermain Defoe, ran out onto the pitch with 'Autonomy' emblazoned on their chests. It was a 0-0 draw.

Perversely, it was not a particularly proud moment for Lynch. A relationship with the team could make Autonomy look grubby, he worried, and the partnership was not a good fit for a company which sold to businesses rather than the general public – whom he thought cared more about beer, betting or the latest trainers.

The sponsorship came about through Lynch's relationship with Daniel Levy, chairman of the club. Levy knew Lynch from his university days and he was one of the original Autonomy investors. The two old friends did a shirt-sponsorship deal worth £63 million over five seasons.

Like Tottenham's first match sponsored by Autonomy, there was something of a draw about this transaction too. Levy had been hunting for a sponsor for the football club and Autonomy fit the bill nicely. In turn, Spurs would help Autonomy find more clients, as well as become a client itself. Autonomy sold the club some £3.9 million worth of software, as well as inking an undefined and rather woolly agreement for Autonomy to update the club's systems and website.

The deal also meant that Autonomy executives could enjoy the White Hart Lane VIP experience. There's a picture of Sushovan Hussain – a passionate Arsenal supporter – turning round to ask David Beckham for his autograph at a game against Manchester United in January 2011. The midfielder was training with Spurs for a month. The image of the two men smiling at one another was splashed across the papers the next day and made the Autonomy team laugh.

Lynch was an infrequent visitor, though. Autonomy would get requests from celebrities in the TV and business world to join its corporate box at the stadium. Advisors were surprised when Lynch often did not want to join them at a game, even to meet some really famous and influential people, including investors from Silicon Valley and celebrated TV newscasters. His deafness was a problem in very loud environments, which may have been a factor, but he also disliked the atmosphere in the stands around the box, which he sneered at and thought was loutish. He was never going to be one of those chanting from the stands – he didn't even really follow the game.

Lynch wasn't a sports fan generally, and being unable to engage on the topic with other men, he said, was where he often fell down socially. Nevertheless, the association with the club and rubbing elbows with world-famous celebrities when he did use the box only furthered his growing reputation as a VIP.

Yet even while Lynch was on the rise in his personal life, trouble was quietly brewing in the economic landscape – trouble that threatened to shake the very foundations of both his success and his company's stability.

ELEVEN

2008

I would tend to accept that 'gilding the lily' in justifying large commission payments is a commonplace of commercial life, but in the context, and all the circumstances here, it is a further illustration of a disturbing culture within the management of Autonomy and an unsettling and unsatisfactory approach to disclosure on the part of Dr Lynch himself.

– Mr Justice Hildyard, civil judgement, 17 May 2022

The City of London is compact, crowded, and constantly in motion. Its narrow streets teem with people in sharp suits, weaving between towering glass skyscrapers that cast shadows over centuries-old churches and cosy pubs. The financial district which powers the UK economy is like a beehive, where bankers, lawyers and consultants make honey off the success or failure of companies, currencies and commodities. It is the heart of money and power and what happens there affects everybody around the world; a singular ecosystem; a dense, self-sustaining world where finance, law, politics, and tradition intertwine.

It boomed in the aftermath of the modernizing Big Bang, just as some of Lynch's Cambridge peers were graduating, netting those who went to work there a fortune. Two decades later, it was once again rocked to the core as the global financial crisis started to rumble in 2007. Soon, the world would be facing the most severe economic downturn since the Great Depression of the 1930s.

American banks had been giving high-risk home loans to people with poor credit histories during the massive housing boom of the early 2000s. These loans were bundled into packages and sold to investors around the world as if they were safe. But then interest rates rose and borrowers could not pay off their debts, and the bubble burst. Market deregulation had enabled many financial organizations to wildly over-speculate, and they were now horribly overexposed.

Infamously, in September 2008, Lehman Brothers, a venerable American investment bank, collapsed. Panic spread, and global financial markets began to freeze, triggering further bank failures and government bailouts around the world. After years of easy money, spending spluttered to a standstill. That same month, Merrill Lynch, the old Autonomy nemesis, was sold to Bank of America; short-selling of financial stocks was banned in London and New York; and the giant insurer American International Group suffered a liquidity crisis.

Autonomy suffered during the financial crash, like all other businesses at the time, as its clients sat on their hands to ride out the storm. It threw the company's daily sales operations into disarray. Nobody wanted to spend money until they knew what the outcome was going to be. Yet it had a better September 2008 than most. It was back in the FTSE 100 for the first time in seven years and would go on to win the London Stock Exchange's techMARK Company of the Year award. Ever since it went public, Autonomy's fortunes had been bound to the City. With its new high-profile position in Britain's top one hundred businesses, that was truer than ever.

Even without the pain of this turbulent economic period, the City was very different to the place where Lynch first floated Autonomy at the turn of the century, and his business was feeling the effects of it. After the dotcom bust, a new group of investors emerged: hedge funds. Their interest was piqued by the amount of money that could be made in falling markets – as well as rising ones. In other words, this new group of players made money by betting that a company would fail.

Lynch was deeply distrustful of hedge funds; they triggered his suspicion of analysts in the City, who he believed might be in cahoots with them. Lynch thought that hedge funds were manipulating Autonomy's share price up and down as they pleased by spreading untrue rumours about his company, all in order to make a quick buck. He even alleged, with no obvious proof, that the short-sellers (who bet on the share price going down) were launching attacks on the company's infrastructure to prevent software being delivered at the end of the month, all in order to make Autonomy miss financial targets. Lynch's supporters said he was running a company which was being used as a gambling chip by the 'twits in suits'.

Lynch had always felt that people in the Square Mile were parasitic, making money off the backs of others rather than doing anything for the advancement of society, and the concept of making money by betting on failure just fanned the flames and served to convince him further of a belief he'd long held and that became ever-more entrenched as the crisis took hold: the City only exists to benefit the City.

There was a silver lining amid the financial turbulence for Autonomy. In a bid to rein in the banks' greedy behaviour and make sure a similar crisis did not happen again, regulators squeezed their grip on financial practices. They soon introduced new requirements which meant companies in the financial services industry had to modernize how they collected, stored and managed their data. Conveniently, one of the Lego kits on Autonomy's shelf was an archiving product which helped companies to keep tabs on their records.

It made for a strong sales pitch: 'If you don't buy the software, you go to jail,' Lynch told Autonomy salespeople on stage at one Sales Kick Off event. The clever marketing campaign Lynch devised for this was 'get your ducks in a row'. Banks, fearing being sued, felt compelled to buy such software to comply with the new rules. It became a major selling point for the company. Yet despite this new avenue for sales, numbers for Autonomy's key IDOL product started to nosedive in the aftermath of the crash, and Autonomy executives started to panic. Hussain set it out in an email in September 2009:

> **U.S. IDOL is weak. Will probably only close about 35 deals, half the number of 3 years ago with more reps, managers, no competition and more products to sell.**

Against this tricky economic backdrop, competition for Autonomy did start to rise, and from some powerful quarters. In 2006, Google had released a far cheaper rival product which cost in the region of $21,000 for a two-year subscription, in stark contrast to Autonomy's six-figure price tag, and continued to hone it. In 2008, Microsoft bought Fast Search and Transfer (FAST), a Norwegian competitor to Autonomy, and later integrated the tech into its widely used software packages, which spread its tentacles wide. Lynch always said these players did not hold a torch to Autonomy, but most companies found their functionality was perfectly adequate.

On top of all of this, more sharks were circling, this time in the seemingly benign form of industry analysts. This group included Gartner, a consultancy that looks at trends in the tech sector, that Lynch had fallen out with years before. He derided such consultancies as prostitutes: because companies could pay for their advice, he would say they 'put out' for the highest bidder. He was still furious over the idea that Autonomy could have been Google, had he only ignored Gartner's advice all those years before (as explored in Chapter 5).

The relationship only worsened, particularly when some at Gartner started raising questions about Autonomy's products. There was, analysts said, a chasm between Autonomy's marketing spin and the reality of using the software. It was not the sophistication of the product, but rather its application and integration, which emerged as the issue. One analyst in particular drew Lynch's ire: Whit Andrews. The whippet-smart man had started his career as a beat reporter for a local US paper and later worked as a tech journalist. He knew Lynch from his early days. Coming from the journalistic school that teaches 'if your mother says she loves you, check it out', he spoke directly to customers about their experiences of technology products. At the coalface, he found that Autonomy's expensive and complex software was often being left on the shelf, as companies simply didn't know what to do with it. One senior technician from Autonomy described its software as 'spaghetti code' – it had been added to so much over the years that it had become a bewildering tangle.

Furthermore, procurement departments were finding the process of dealing with Autonomy frustrating; there was no set price list, and its salespeople were excessively aggressive.

Lynch reacted in the way he always did when met with dissent. He was furious and categorically denied that there were any issues with Autonomy's products. He indirectly accused Andrews of being in the pocket of Autonomy's rivals, reportedly asking, 'Has he been given cash, drugs or women?' Industry analysts were yet another part of the status quo that he detested.

DESPITE LYNCH'S DENIALS, there were some undeniable examples of problems with Autonomy's tech offering. The most high-profile of them emerging during the BP Deepwater Horizon disaster.

On 20 April 2010, an explosion tore through an oil rig forty-nine miles off the coast of Louisiana, killing eleven men working on it and seriously injuring several others. Four million barrels' worth of oil from the well began gushing uncontrollably into the Gulf of Mexico – damaging the precious surrounding environment and threatening livelihoods in tourism and fishing. BP had been drilling for oil from beneath 5,000 feet of water, and then across 13,000 feet of sea floor beyond that. It was a technologically challenging and risky operation, and the rescue and clean-up would prove equally difficult.

The inevitable resulting litigation was complex too. Autonomy won the contract to manage the vast amounts of information related to it – the process of identifying, collecting and producing electronically stored information during legal proceedings, which at the time was one of the largest e-Discovery projects to date.

The system simply could not cope. There were technical problems and the software did not always work as it should. Lynch called it a crisis. Autonomy executives were called into BP's headquarters and told that they might lose the client. BP was considering switching to a competitor, evidently because Autonomy kept making careless quality control mistakes, such as not providing some of the documents for a deposition until after the deposition. Lynch was furious and told his team to do whatever it took to fix it. There was a lot of firefighting, and money was spent hand over fist as Autonomy grappled to salvage the contract.

More problems would follow as the company failed to win a contract with the US Department of Veterans Affairs in August 2010. Lynch made his feelings about losing out to another company very clear. His email – typos and bizarre formatting included – read as below:

I swear if I could squeeze down a telephone line to
California you would get to know directly how the f***
I feel about this

YOUR HIGHLY PAID SALES MANAGEMENT COLLEAGUES WERE SITTING IN THE BACK AS THEY SAY ABOUT DIM PILOTS IN AVIATION CIRCUMSTANCES 'FAT DUMB AND HAPPY' AS THE PLANE FLEW INTO THE MOUNTAIN . . .

FOLKS I AM NOT PUTTING UP WITH THIS SHIT, KNOW THE DEALS, MONITOR THE TECH, CHECK THE PROPOSALS, BEING ASLEEP AND THEN AFTER THE FACT THROWING SOMEONE ELSE UNDER BUS IS TOTALLY UNACCEPTABLE. AN EMAIL TO ME ABOUT WHATS GOING WRONG BEFORE IS GREAT AND GETS YOU OFF THE HOOK, SEND IT AFTER AND YOU ARE TOAST.

And all the time, with these fires raging, the company had to report its numbers to the City every three months, trying to hit its financial targets. Autonomy had become known as a 'beat and raise' stock, which meant it would often beat the market's expectations and raise its forecasts for the next quarter. Hopes for it were always high, but the quarterly period looped around relentlessly and it made the company increasingly short-termist in its approach.

The market's forecast is called 'consensus', and is the average of all the analysts that cover the stock. Hitting this bullseye, with the slow-down in spending and the stiff competition, was incredibly tough. When Autonomy missed it, the share price would fall. Sometimes, even hitting the targets was not enough to satisfy the financiers.

In the second quarter of 2009, Autonomy reported an impressive set of sales numbers almost $200 million, a 55 per cent increase on the previous year. Yet despite the massive rise in sales and a slew of new deals with organizations including Barclays, eBay and global intelligence agencies, its share price fell 8 per cent. The market expected upgrades. Analysts murmured about where it was showing 'organic' growth.

'*Revenue, revenue, revenue*', Lynch thumped out on emails to his hardworking chief financial officer. This merry-go-round took its toll on Hussain. Deeply conscientious, he got anxious about things which didn't overtly worry Lynch. Everyone was only focused on the current quarter. When it was over, it was on to the next. Recordings of the Monday sales calls reveal the cut-throat pressure this put on the entire company. For Autonomy, a big deal could mean the difference between a hit or miss in the numbers, with the resulting impact on its share price and confidence in the company and its products.

It was clear that a new strategy was needed. What followed appeared to be sparked by a feeling that the company was untouchable and that nobody would find out.

TWELVE

Hardware Is Hard

Companies sell printers at a loss to sell ink. Companies sell razors to sell blades. We were a software company. We gave away professional services for free to get software deals. We gave away training for free to get software deals. In the end what matters is you make more than you don't make when you add it all up and group it together. That's the way I looked at it.

– Mike Sullivan, testimony at Sushovan Hussain's trial, 27 February 2018

It was 20 October 2009, and Autonomy had just published what looked like a blinding set of third quarter results. Its year-on-year sales had leapt by over 50 per cent to $192 million, this off the back of the 55 per cent increase posted in quarter two. As usual, the numbers were pored over. As usual, the company's volatile share price reacted. And this time, badly.

It was the biggest faller on the FTSE 100 on the day. Why? Well, although its sales were better than expected, its gross profit margin was worse. It was 86 per cent, down from 92 per cent the year before. The watching analysts wanted to know what was going on. Autonomy's management was determined not to tell them. 'Why should we show them the colour of our underwear?' Lynch mused.

A quick accounting lesson: Gross Profit = Sales – Cost of Sales. It shows how much money a company makes *after* covering the direct costs of producing its goods or services – but *before* other expenses like marketing. Autonomy set great store by the size of its gross profit margin, which is gross profit expressed as a percentage of sales. It was, the accounts said, 'an indicator of the success of its business model'. The gross profit margin is usually big for a software business, because software costs very little to manufacture. The bigger the gross profit margin, the better. As Lynch once put it:

> *The thing about software is, it's an amazing business in that you can sell a product for a million dollars and the actual production cost is one dollar, so it's not like trying to make a tiny margin on selling biscuits.*

It had been another stressful quarter for Hussain. In the run-up to the deadline, he had sent out a series of worried emails to Lynch detailing the struggle to bring in software sales. '*Yesterday was v bad*,' he wrote in one. '*From Thursday collapse is heavy*' and '*IDOL is weak . . . Europe is also weak*'.

The pressure was building on him, as it did at the end of every quarter. Only this time something had changed – something which went some way towards easing the pain.

IN THE WARM summer of 2009, not long after the Lynch family had moved into their new home, some twenty Autonomy employees, including Hussain, US CEO Christopher Egan, the company's US general counsel Joel Scott, and Mike Sullivan (CEO of Autonomy

Protect, the archiving and litigation discovery division of Autonomy) gathered for a couple of days at Loudham Hall to talk shop. Surrounded by the model trains, ticking clocks and the gentle lowing of Red Poll cattle – their mahogany-coloured coats gleaming in the sunlight – Suffolk felt like a nice reprieve from reality. Aside from the odd picture of Lynch at events scattered in corners of the manor house, you would never know it belonged to a tech entrepreneur.

The conversation at hand pulled their minds away from the relaxed setting. During a coffee break, Sullivan overheard Lynch, Egan and Hussain talking about the idea of reselling some products to a customer, and considering offering them a steep discount to get the deal over the line. This was not a typical Autonomy deal. Rather than the software that Autonomy was famous for, this was a deal to sell mice, keyboards and monitors. In other words: hardware. 'I bet I can do that,' Sullivan piped up. He had the contacts book after all – the archiving and storage part of the business he ran dealt with hardware.

Lynch laughed at him. 'If you can sell up to ten million dollars of hardware, you can have a Porsche.' It became a running joke. Sullivan loved a challenge. He did not care about a car, but he did care about the massive commission.

The deal was struck. Shortly afterwards, Sullivan sent a buoyant message from the US to Lynch and the team back in the UK:

> **I have verbal commitments for up to $20 million and could probably get twice that if you want. My biggest concern is that 4 or 5 Porsches are not practical for me. Perhaps we need to discuss a small plane or yacht?**

Cash, though, was enough. Instead of a fancy vehicle, Hussain told him, Sullivan's prize would be a special $200,000 bonus if he delivered $30 million of recognizable revenue by 30 September. If he managed to make $50 million in sales, the bonus would rise to

$300,000. 'Recognizable revenue' was vital – that is the term for revenue that a company can consider as already earnt, which means it can be recorded in that quarter's financial statements.

One of Sullivan's main sources of computer equipment was EMC, a multinational technology company founded in 1979 that specialized in data storage. Autonomy, with one of the largest storage businesses in the world, was a top customer. It had thousands of servers and bought all its storage equipment from EMC.

Autonomy soon negotiated a deal with EMC to buy hardware. Hardware which it would then sell onwards, in separate deals it negotiated with its own separate customers, at a loss. Despite the obvious problems with spending more on your product than you can sell it for, this worked, because Autonomy wasn't interested in the paltry profits (by software standards) EMC was making on the hardware, it was only interested in registering those loss-making deals as sales in the accounts.

For example, on 22 September 2009 Autonomy paid EMC $10 million for a job lot of hardware, which it then sold on to Bloomberg for $8.7 million at a clear loss of $1.3 million. This represented a win-win-win scenario for everyone involved. Bloomberg got a discount of almost 15 per cent on their order, EMC pocketed the actual profit from the hardware, and Autonomy heaped more 'sales' onto its books.

Internally, this hardware business began to be referred to (rather euphemistically) as 'low-margin sales'. While Autonomy had sold a little of this stuff before, selling large quantities of hardware was a big change for the company.

Ultimately, Autonomy was selling these bog-standard computer products at a loss: buying high from a manufacturer and selling low to customers. It had to be explained. Lynch's argument for the new strategy was always that the hardware sales gave Autonomy a foot in the door to sell companies the more valuable software – that it was a sales and marketing tool. Lynch also claimed that the strategy gave

Hussain a degree of flexibility, another ingredient when making what Lynch called the 'cake' of the quarterly accounts.

Companies were slimming down their supplier lists, and Lynch wanted to make sure Autonomy could be a one-stop shop for his customers. The strategy would, Lynch claimed, help Autonomy to build relationships with both hardware suppliers and buyers, who might then use its software in their products.

It's not always easy to verify the effectiveness of sales and marketing, yet Bloomberg did not buy any software licences from Autonomy in 2009 or 2010, so all that hardware was simply sold at a loss, with no resulting high-margin software sale.

On the face of it, nothing about these hardware sales was wrong... except for two key issues: first, Autonomy did everything it could to *not* publicly reveal it was booking revenue by selling other people's IT equipment and bundling the hardware in with its software sales; and second, it accounted for this revenue in a very fishy way.

In its annual reports, Autonomy repeatedly stated that the company was: 'one of the very rare examples of a pure software model'. As a result, having not been told that Autonomy was selling mice and keyboards – in fact, being explicitly told the opposite – investors were actively misled about how the company was generating revenues. Hardware sales were viewed as low margin and low quality by investors and the wider financial markets. Later in court, Lynch fudged it:

> *Selling hardware for a software company is a bit like a peach company selling jars with the peaches in. It's not the bit that's interesting most of the time, because it's the jar, it's not the peaches.*

While it kept the new strategy to itself, Autonomy did, however, have to reveal information about the peach jar to Deloitte, its Cambridge-based auditor. What follows is a salutary tale about how professional advisors can be misled. Autonomy did it with aplomb.

The lead Deloitte partner on the Autonomy account was named Richard Knights. A tall, kindly man with a Roman nose and a thoughtful manner, he had been at Deloitte for ever and had worked with Autonomy since 2006. He knew the company well, not least because a roster of his former staff ended up working within the business.

His job, along with a team of around fifteen auditors who would spend three months a year on site in the Cambridge offices of Autonomy, was to sign off Autonomy's accounts, to check that the sales they were making were really sales and that the numbers were accurate.

It was a relentless task with a tight turnaround, involving a limited sign-off for the quarterly figures and a more gold-plated fuller audit of the annual accounts. Deloitte wouldn't review every individual sale or line item on the balance sheet; instead, it would select a strong sample and check the supporting evidence to verify their accuracy.

The scale of the hardware sales started to cause a stir within Deloitte, who raised eyebrows at how Autonomy wanted to account for the losses on them: as 'sales and marketing expenses', rather than as a cost of sales. This was significant. By classifying some of the hardware losses as a marketing cost, it did not cut into the company's gross margin as much as it should have done. Once again, a company's gross profit equals its sales minus its cost of sales, *before* expenses such as marketing.

Autonomy tried to spin the planned accounting treatment to Deloitte through an elegantly titled 'Strategic Deals Memorandum', referring to the $45 million it was spending on hardware as 'partnership costs', and claimed that selling at a loss was an 'incentive to deepen and widen the relationship' with EMC.

It was not enough. Deloitte wanted to see some paperwork about the nature of the transactions, proof they were for relationship-building and marketing, proof of attendance at trade shows – anything – and the two sides went back and forth on how the hardware sales should be recorded on the company's books. It was odd, the auditors remarked, that Autonomy was selling all this gear at such a loss.

'Sullivan, you can get an extra $50,000 if you obtain the paperwork needed by the auditor from EMC,' Hussain emailed him, copying in Kanter and Lynch. The bonus would be payable once Deloitte signed off the 2009 third quarter numbers. Deloitte was unaware of these internal Autonomy emails.

Sullivan replied to say he was not optimistic, because EMC was 'extremely sensitive to these kinds of letters', and the company refused to say that what Autonomy had paid for was anything other than the product it bought, or to say that the money it had received was a marketing expense. On 12 October 2009, a Deloitte executive asked Hussain and VP of Finance Stephen Chamberlain whether there was 'a set marketing programme or any further information available which can help us to quantify the marketing element – e.g. a joint marketing plan or similar'. Nothing of substance was forthcoming.

Tempers were fraying on both sides. Knights went home from the office on the evening of 13 October 2009 and wondered what to do. He decided to pour oil on troubled waters by striking a jovial, light-hearted tone and pulling together all of the documents that had been pinging back and forth, to try to reach some conclusion.

He sent the note from his wife's email account, sitting down after dinner and a couple of drinks because, he later said, he was not allowed to take his computer out of the office. This is the typo-ridden missive that would later come back to haunt him:

> **After a glass or two of red wine and a plate ful of Mrs K medieval pasta i've had a stab at writing the Autonomy paper on EMC . . . This needs to come form [sic] you to us. I need it to sqaure [sic] the position on cost of goods allocation – i've still not seen anything from EMC.**

Here, he said, was what Autonomy needed to do to get its

accounting plans over the line. Knights went so far as to write out a plan, with convenient gaps left where the company should fill in the blanks. He concluded his note with a sycophantic, conciliatory flourish:

> **As mentioned above this was rattled out pretty quickly and fortified with a few liveners so as a modest bookkeeper it would benefit from the cutting edge of you software gurus . . . !!**

The Autonomy software gurus eventually got their way. To classify the hardware sales as organic growth for the IDOL software in the 2009 quarterly sales report required some 'word smithing', as Knights put it – but they managed it. This despite the 'biggest concern' being 'that hardware sales were neither IDOL based or organic!!' as Knights wrote to Hussain on 16 October.

The noise didn't entirely go away, at least within Deloitte. Even after the report was released, another partner was worried 'by the total lack of reference to the fact that nearly 20 per cent of Autonomy's third quarter revenues represented a major strategic change in the nature of its business, but that there had been no comment on that'.

Autonomy's audit committee – made up of Barry Ariko, Richard Perle and John McMonigall – was concerned too. All three members wrote to Lynch, worried about the lack of discussion about and disclosure of the hardware reselling strategy in the draft press release regarding the results. They were ignored. Knights, too, warned Autonomy that the third quarter results for 2009 should not set a precedent for the future. But, of course, they did.

The final press release was a masterstroke in public relations obfuscation, proclaiming 'RECORD Q3 RESULTS WITH STRONG ORGANIC GROWTH' and explaining, misleadingly, that 'the unexpected demand for our new product programs had a small depressing effect on gross margins. We do not expect this to be a trend'. It made no reference to hardware.

Remarkably, in that 2009 report, almost a fifth of Autonomy's standout sales numbers came from selling computer equipment made by other companies at a loss. You would not know it from the accounts. The hardware sales were bundled into 'revenue' alongside licence sales, with only $17 million of a total of $45 million in hardware costs being allocated to the 'cost of sales' – what it costs to develop a product, keep it running and deliver it to users. The remaining $28 million were reported as sales and marketing expenses.

This reporting kept Autonomy's gross margin at a respectable 86 per cent, the sort of level that outwardly confirmed Autonomy's claim to be a 'pure software company'. It was still smaller than the market was used to, but it was a better result than using the more accurate number, which would have been 71 per cent.

But changing numbers in the accounts is a bit like squeezing a balloon – it creates a bulge somewhere else. Calling the loss-making hardware sales 'marketing expenses' may have wiped them from the gross margin, but it meant that Autonomy's sales and marketing costs shot up exponentially, by $24 million.

Lynch knew the market was going to react to this and he needed a strategy to deal with it: so he embellished the launch of a whizzy new product: the Structured Probabilistic Engine, or SPE. 'This is a very exciting time for us,' he told investors on the conference call, who were wondering about the unusual rise in marketing spend. Autonomy was launching something, Lynch said, that was 'years in the making', aimed at structured data, representing an '$18 billion opportunity, a radical technology, which can clip on to pretty much any relational database.

'It's exciting, it's different, and it will take a little while for people to understand it, this is not a normal run-of-the-mill product announcement from us'. He was right. It was fiction: a tactic to cover up the marketing spend. He claimed that Autonomy had spent almost $24 million on the launch of this shiny piece of software, including flying key customers from around the world to special selective seminars.

'Now it has to be said, this is geek stuff at the moment,' he bluffed:

> *You can't really explain something as complicated as this in an ad. What you can do is just let people know that the game has changed.*

He told the market there was a QuickStart and a Beta programme in place, that some especially chosen customers were using it.

He concluded that the tech was so advanced that the whole thing might be slow to show much of an impact. 'Rather like Autonomy's first big piece of technology, we think it will take time for people to understand it . . . What we'd like to do is get to the end of the BETA programme and get evidence before we actually start to quantify that effect'. In fact, it was so radical, Lynch told a Goldman Sachs representative on the call, that putting a number on it was difficult because the 'variability' was so large.

Like many of Lynch's stories, the SPE was not a total fabrication. The SPE existed, it was just not a standalone product, marketed with millions of dollars. Autonomy had only spent around $100,000 on marketing the product. Creating it was not expensive either – all it took was a few small tweaks from the technology team to software that Autonomy already owned. What's more, as it was 'bundled' into deals, it is unclear whether anyone really used it or if they knew or cared if they were buying it. There was no evidence of a Beta programme. Customers who requested to trial it were told that it was closed due to over-demand.

Sean Blanchflower, Head of Research and Development for IDOL at Autonomy, later said SPE was just a label used for certain structured data features *within* IDOL. A quick Google search by another senior staff member revealed that the press release trumpeting the

SPE was a rip-off of a very old one describing one of Lynch's other businesses, NCorp, which was spun out of Cambridge Neurodynamics and then bought back by Autonomy in 2005.

OVER THE COMING years, the hardware sales, characterized internally as 'Strategic Deals' and 'low-margin sales', or less prosaically as 'selling knock-off computer equipment', would continue in the same vein. Lynch and Hussain would give Mike Sullivan goals every quarter, setting out the revenue they needed from hardware, and structure his bonus around that. Hardware was referred to by one employee in the accounts department as the 'bouncing number at the bottom' of the company's sales forecasts, an elastic figure adjusted as needed to close gaps in quarterly targets.

After its relationship with EMC ended, Autonomy would form partnerships with companies including Dell and Hitachi. Overall, the

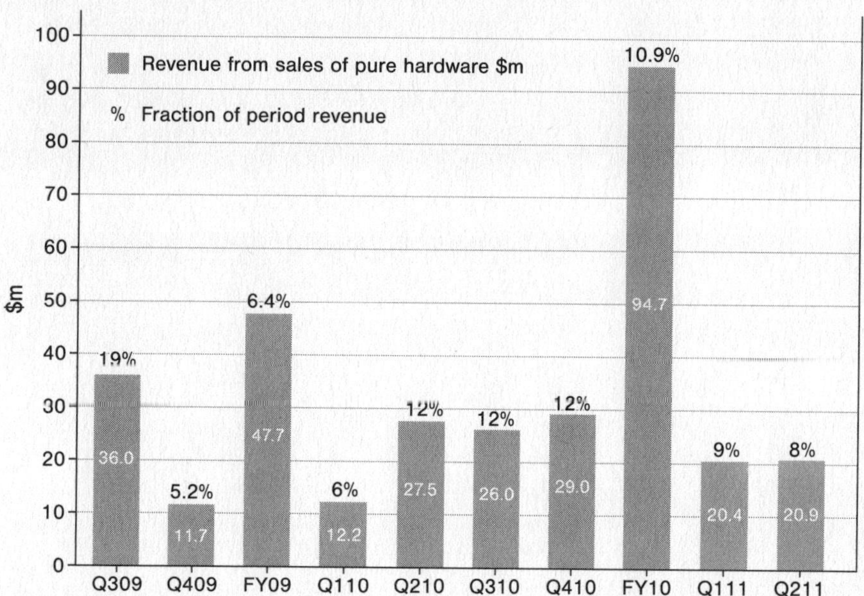

Percentage of Autonomy's revenue made up of hardware (Source: Financial Reporting Council)

revenue generated by the ruse was huge. From 2009 to 2011, hardware sales made up about 11 per cent of total reported sales, $200 million, including $105 million in 2010 alone. The handy graph on the previous page shows the impact on the company's revenues.

Had Autonomy revealed it was selling computer kit, as it should have done, it would have led to a fall in the share price and to a lot of ribbing from the razor-toothed City and media. Lynch was far too proud to allow it. It would be an admission of business failure, only serving to prove the Autonomy naysayers right. 'The truth is,' Mr Justice Hildyard would later say, 'that [Lynch and Hussain] were prepared to mislead to keep analysts and the market away from the nature and extent of the hardware sales.'

In the months after the 2009 report, Autonomy appeared to have got away with its scheme, but some people were getting increasingly suspicious.

THIRTEEN

The Three Bears

I take pleasure in winding up Lynch. Thorn in his side. Then a dagger. Then an AK-47.

– Daud Khan, 28 March 2009

The people sitting in the room were not sure why they had been called in to see Autonomy executives that Friday morning in May 2009.They chatted among themselves as they waited for the meeting to begin, the low buzz of conversation filling the room.

In the company's Mayfair office, the wood-panelled boardroom had been specially staged for the occasion, with a wing-backed chair, a standing lamp and a screen to show slides. The visitors sat in rows of chairs facing the set, slightly bemused. Then there was a lull. Ian Black, one of Lynch's executives, strode to the front of the room, carrying a large leatherbound book which looked like it could be a fancy old copy of *Grimms' Fairy Tales*. He sat down in the large chair. There was a click as he turned on the lamp above his head. The room stopped, stunned into silence. This wasn't your standard-issue financial presentation – it felt more like *Jackanory*.

'Fucking ham this up!' Lynch had shouted at Black a few moments earlier. Black, who had barely any time to rehearse these theatrics, duly followed instructions. 'Well, hello boys and girls,' he started. 'Are you sitting comfortably?' He paused for effect. 'Then I'll begin.'

The first slide didn't feature bar graphs or bullet points like most presentations, but instead displayed an open book titled *The Autonomy Book of Short Stories*, written in the kind of curly, whimsical font usually reserved for fairy tales. Underneath, hunched over a scroll and holding a dramatically oversized quill, was none other than Winnie-the-Pooh. On the adjacent page, Christopher Robin and Tigger were shown in a bucolic Hundred Acre Wood.

Sushovan Hussain came to the front to join Black, as the next slide revealed 'Chapter One: The House at Bear Corner' in the same swirly writing and yet more pictures of the bear with very little brain. Black read from the pseudo storybook, while a visibly shaking Hussain went through the slides. Lynch stood at the back, quietly watching the drama unfold.

Those watching this charade were taken aback. A serious breed of City of London investors and fund managers, they were more accustomed to being read balance sheets than bedtime stories. This was *not* their usual Friday-morning fare.

Peppered throughout the storybook presentation were quotes from bearish financial analysts who had bad-mouthed the company: 'We continue to believe that Autonomy is not immune to a slowing economy'; 'Growth is being driven by acquisitions'. The aim of the presentation was to rip them apart. Next to these comments were graphs showing Autonomy outperforming other companies in the stock market and 'errors in analyst revenue estimates'. The thrust of the remarkable show was simple: these guys are idiots, do not listen to them.

Financial analysts play a crucial role in the investment world. They dig deep into a company's financials, assess how the business is performing and share their insights through detailed reports. Based on their analysis, they issue one of three straightforward recommendations – buy, sell or hold – guiding investors, such as pension funds, in making informed decisions about whether to invest in a company's shares.

Analysts need to build strong relationships with the executives of the companies they cover, but simultaneously maintain enough distance to ask them the tough questions and hold them to account – much like a journalist reporting on a specific industry. They are expected to dig into every corner of a company's operations, piecing together an honest picture of how it's really performing – whether thriving or struggling. To do that, they rely not only on what companies tell them, but also on their own investigative research and market insight. Their bonuses are based on the quality of their research, the views of their clients – investors – and their bosses' discretion as to the quality of their work.

Some go above and beyond. One City analyst famously went undercover as a takeaway driver just to get a first-hand look at the inner workings of the gig economy. CEOs either like or loathe the analysts who follow them and, as with journalists, tend to like the ones who are sympathetic to them and are riled by the rest.

Publicly listed companies like Autonomy hold regular analyst meetings, like press conferences, which are a chance to ask companies questions in a public forum, often in response to the results that public businesses publish. Attending the same events and company briefings, the analysts inevitably get to know each other – always rivals, but all doing the same job. In London, where tech companies are relatively scarce, the circle of analysts covering the sector is naturally a small one.

There were about twenty-two analysts covering Autonomy. A handful had been taking a rather dim view of the business, raising questions about its accounting and its future prospects. Lynch had decided to call investors in on that Friday morning to prove them wrong. The elaborate Winnie-the-Pooh slideshow had taken a while to prepare. In advance, he emailed Hussain with a warning: 'This is your one chance to get it perfect, pls work on it.' The investors watching this presentation relied on these analysts, the very people that Lynch was ripping apart.

When the presentation was over, the watching audience was stunned. 'They were all really insulted by that,' Black relayed to his boss. It was tone-deaf investor messaging at a critical moment. 'Fuck them,' said Lynch. He was at war.

ONE OF THE City's key arteries is Moorgate, taking its name from a medieval gate in London's old city wall, a busy road running north from the grandiose Bank of England towards trendy Shoreditch. A year or so before Autonomy's Friday-morning fiasco, Daud Khan was sitting at his desk at Number 20, the home of Cazenove – the blue-blooded investment banking firm later absorbed into the big US bank JP Morgan. Khan was an established tech analyst responsible for covering Autonomy at Cazenove, and he was about to sow the seeds of Lynch's war.

A measured, softly spoken South Londoner with a steely core, like Lynch, Khan had studied at Cambridge, graduating in 1994. A strict Muslim who would lay his prayer mat out in the office, he trained as a chartered accountant and started his City career at Merrill Lynch in 1999. In fact, he had been working there at the time of the bank's massive bust-up with Lynch in the early noughties.

Over the previous year, Khan believed he had spotted something strange in Autonomy's numbers – some of his comments would even make their way into the Pooh Bear slideshow, and his critical publications about the company sparked a series of explosive confrontations with Lynch.

It hadn't always been that way – the two men once shared a good relationship. They first met in 2001, when Khan was given the job of covering Autonomy at Merrill Lynch. After the row with the bank, Lynch expressed delight that someone who really understood technology was going to be following his business; someone with an accounting background; someone with a proper, solid, scientific Cambridge University degree. At this stage, Lynch was the most amenable company leader that Khan had ever dealt with.

Lynch took time to make the younger man feel comfortable, always available for a phone call and responding directly to emails with questions about Autonomy or requests to join in with roadshows. It was the best relationship Khan had with any chief executive. Lynch was kind, warm and charming. When Khan was having a crisis about the future direction of his career, he even approached Lynch for advice and the two men met for a warm lunch in Mayfair.

The relationship could not get too cosy, however. Khan's job was to keep an independent, impartial eye on Autonomy. Fast-forward to the ballooning financial crisis which was taking hold in 2007, and Khan (correctly) had a hunch that an economic downturn would mean that companies' budgets for tech software would be squeezed, which would hit Autonomy's sales hard. In January 2008, he published a report saying so. There was no response from the company, but Lynch was on high alert to suppress information that he did not like.

Khan went one further. He had a theory that organic growth at Autonomy was overstated, that it was getting bigger through buying other businesses rather than by selling more of its own software. After a forensic review of Autonomy's numbers, he drafted another note in April 2008, setting out his arguments and giving the business a negative rating. When it was written, he sent the preliminary copy to Lynch to read and review. It was a polite gesture, a heads-up to Autonomy that this was about to land on the market and a chance for the company to point out any glaring errors in Khan's work.

Most chief executives reading such a note take it on the chin and agree to disagree. Khan had no idea that his draft would provoke the storm it did, smashing his previously cordial relationship with the Autonomy CEO to bits.

As usual, Lynch took his gun to this particular knife fight. He replied:

> **Daud, I'm rather surprised as this note contains a significant number of factual inaccuracies and misquotes the company. While we, in no way, have any issue with the opinions and conclusions you may draw, the fact that your note knowingly contains inaccurate information is deeply disturbing.**

All we ask, Lynch said, is that Khan be accurate on the facts. He could then draw his own conclusions. A confrontational response, but perhaps understandable. The pile-on continued, though. Andy Kanter emailed Khan's boss, David Knox, the head of research at Cazenove, to say again that the report was full of inaccuracies.

They all decided to meet face to face and thrash it out in person. It was never going to be a comfortable meeting. Khan felt confident in his numbers, but Lynch was a ferocious negotiator and never backed down.

Lynch arrived at the office with Hussain. It was the first time Khan had met 'angry Mike', and it wouldn't be the last. Lynch and Hussain continued to argue against the publication of Khan's report and said that if Cazenove published without consultation, it would be seen as a criticism of their professional advisors and the company would have to respond.

Knox wanted to know if Lynch was trying to threaten Khan, or threaten the bank itself, and asked him so directly. Lynch retorted that Autonomy was a public company and needed to ensure that it defended itself. The atmosphere was tense, and didn't lighten as the meeting was wrapped up. When Khan reached out and touched Lynch's shoulder in what he thought was a friendly gesture, Lynch flinched away and his face went red. Lynch followed up with an email to Knox: 'Thanks for your time today. I think it was very useful. In the words of Vinnie

Jones, "that was emotional"." The phrasing could be read as conciliatory, but the tone felt sarcastic. The saga was not over yet.

The threats continued. Kanter emailed Knox with a warning to say that Autonomy had tapes of Khan which they felt proved that he had breached the UK financial regulator's guidelines. It was a thinly veiled jab at Cazenove – an implicit message to back off, or their analyst would face serious consequences. Khan was slightly terrified. He believed he hadn't done anything wrong, but the threat of involving the regulator was extreme – and it heightened an already tense situation. Cazenove's compliance department reviewed all of the recordings of Khan's calls and concluded that there was nothing wrong with them.

In May 2008, they published the note. Khan's report began:

> *Standing as the minority negative voice in a torrent of positive opinion warrants some clarification. Autonomy remains the darling of European technology. However, we have raised a number of issues which we believe need to be thoroughly addressed. More detailed disclosure would help to alleviate our concerns.*

The report argued that Autonomy was more exposed to the shock in the global economy than it let on to the public, and called for greater transparency, for the company to break out revenue by brand or business unit. In other words: spell out more clearly how it was making its money.

Everything suddenly became very personal. Khan was banned from attending the company's presentations, with a colleague invited instead. He was left out in the cold to listen in remotely, and he did not have his questions answered.

He is not the only one who remembers this feeling of being frozen out because of their negative views. On Autonomy conference calls, a sing-song voice would say: 'If you would like to ask a question, please press star followed by the hash key.' One frustrated naysayer recalls that pressing the requisite keys would result in . . . nothing. 'No other questions?' Star-hash. Silence. Star-hash. Silence. 'OK. Thanks very much, that's it for today. Have a great morning everyone.' Star-hash star-hash star-hash.

Autonomy always stated this was not the case; that the company struck a fair balance between questions from those who were positive and the critics. Nonetheless, the stories about how these meetings were handled showed Lynch's war with the City was intensifying. It was reminiscent of Alex Ferguson, the hugely successful but fiercely cut-throat Manchester United football manager, who did not speak to the BBC for seven years after it raised questions about his son's dealings as an agent, and refused press conference access to certain sports reporters.

AFTER LYNCH'S EXTRAORDINARILY sensitive reaction to his report, Khan's antennae were on high alert, and he started to dig into the numbers still further. He believed that Autonomy was overstating its success because, while the company showed strong profits on paper, those profits weren't generating the corresponding cash flow ('cash conversion') they should.

Software companies sell licences for an upfront fee, along with maintenance and support contracts. These contracts are typically paid a year in advance, but the revenue is recognized gradually over that year. As a result, cash conversion – how much cash is generated from profit – is usually close to 100 per cent for software companies, because the incoming monthly cash is all already collected before the incoming monthly revenue is fully recognized in the accounts. With Autonomy, this was not happening.

Analysts noticed that the collection period for Autonomy was unusually long – it was not collecting cash from customers as quickly as it should have been, suggesting that it was signing deals and recognizing revenue, but the cash was not coming in. It was, they felt, a total smoking gun.

At the offices of Peel Hunt, a respected second-tier stockbroker in the midst of the gossipy hive that is the Square Mile, Paul Morland was also having doubts about Autonomy's numbers. A tall, slim, energetic and quite eccentric man, Morland questions everything, talks nineteen to the dozen, ferreting out the details of whatever topic is brought up and constantly asking 'why?' He tends to lean towards unconventional theories, sceptical of mainstream or more straightforward views.

The father of four started working in the City of London in 1985, training as a chartered accountant with PricewaterhouseCoopers (PwC – like Deloitte, a Big Four accountancy firm). His job at Peel Hunt was to burrow into companies and advise fund managers whether they should buy into them, and he was curious about Khan's stance on Autonomy. (It is no coincidence that those in this story with an accounting background were the ones who were most curious about what was going on.)

In June 2008 he got in touch with him, keen to hear more about his theories. This interaction was completely unorthodox. It was like a journalist sharing confidences with someone on a rival newspaper. Khan *umm*ed and *ahhh*ed about getting together but, at odds with others in the market in his views on Autonomy, he felt rather lonely, and was pleased that someone wanted to understand his take. The two men met in a Starbucks near Moorgate tube station, and Khan decided to share his research. Morland agreed with his findings.

However, these two analysts were swimming against the tide. Their negative notes did not have an impact. Even as they argued that it shouldn't, the Autonomy share price continued to rise. On 1 September 2008, Khan published another note:

Despite the relentless revenue and profit growth that Autonomy publishes in its quarterly results, we remain concerned by the lack of cash conversion relative to its software peers.

The two analysts started to speak more regularly. Along with Roger Phillips at Evolution Securities, a small and scrappy firm, the men called themselves the Three Bears – in finance, a bear is someone who thinks the market – or a particular stock – is going to tumble. They even started a group chat about it all – 'The Autonomy Discussion Forum' – and it became a bit of a game. Before one reporting round, Morland messaged Khan: 'Looking forward to getting back to some Autonomy bashing on Monday. Working on a pre-results note that I will run past you.'

Another of those questioning Autonomy was David Toms, one of London's most respected tech analysts, who had covered the stock for a firm called Numis since 2005. Everyone wanted to know what Toms was writing about, what he thought about the companies he covered. In his mid-thirties by this time, like Lynch he had studied natural sciences at Cambridge, graduating in 1996. The men always had a bit of an affinity for one another, thanks to their shared degree. Enthusiastic, bright and dogged, Toms was struggling to make Autonomy's numbers add up. He had spotted the shrunken gross margin in the third quarter of 2009 – the one hit by the hardware sales – despite Autonomy's best efforts to cover it up, and wanted to understand more.

The company had changed the way it reported between 2008 and 2009 on multiple occasions, which was odd, he felt, and like Khan he wanted to see more detailed information about the impact of the companies Autonomy was buying each quarter. All in all, he got less information and less data from Autonomy than from the other companies he followed. This was not going to change, even when he asked direct questions in Autonomy's regular forum: its results meeting.

*

COMPANY RESULTS MEETINGS are normally plodding, rather mundane affairs, but Autonomy's executive team would approach them like they were preparing for the D-Day invasion. They set out answers for every potential question, making sure everyone knew exactly what they could or couldn't say. Still, the whole rigmarole really terrified Hussain, and analysts witnessed him shaking during the meetings. Hussain emailed Lynch at one point in October 2009, right in the middle of the hardware era:

> **I am burnt out given my 'anal' nature. I am spending all my time (awake and asleep) worrying about the 10 minutes on Tuesday where I have to answer the analyst questions and I'm not doing anything else. I need you to take the questions this time round unless they are really easy. I don't want to deal with the analysts anymore.**

Hussain hated public speaking, Lynch claimed, and this fear was getting worse from being continually baited by the analysts. So, to keep control and make things easier for Hussain and the team, Autonomy included a set of cue words at the top of their meeting prep notes, to guide everyone on how to handle tough questions from analysts and investors.

Lynch could point to these words – unnoticed by the analysts – to signal to his team how they should respond, depending on whether the question was 'straightforward', which was acceptable and could be answered immediately; a 'trick', something that should be redirected to him; answered briefly; or referred to the company's website. Lynch would also sometimes cut across Hussain in the middle of an answer – he was just as across the financials as his CFO.

On the day, in a typical analyst meeting, hands go up and a microphone is passed around so attendees can ask their questions one by one. With Autonomy, these meetings got increasingly fractious. At the end of a meeting, there's a scrum when analysts gather informally around company bosses, while they are packing their things away and preparing to leave. The scrum was always bigger and more protracted at an Autonomy meeting.

Autonomy's website was also becoming an increasingly important deflection strategy. Rather than respond to individual questions or criticism, Autonomy executives would often post answers online. This was all part of the playbook that Autonomy built to tackle negative commentary, once again taken from the Lynch school of 'Always Take a Gun to a Knife Fight'.

Any negative analyst notes that were released to the public would immediately be seized upon by Lynch's team and pored over with a fine-tooth comb. Then Autonomy would go into attack mode, picking up the most minor errors and throwing them back at the analyst concerned in order to discredit them. Lynch called it 'looking for the silver bullet', ripping apart the research by revealing any mistakes.

A company document from December 2010 actually went so far as to allocate the analysts who covered Autonomy to one of four different classifications, depending on how they treated the company in public: 'Corrupt', 'Feeble-minded', 'Drifters' or – the highest accolade attainable – 'Sound'. The 'Corrupt' category, coloured in an angry bright-red shade, included Khan, Morland, Phillips and Toms. Helpfully, all the analysts were displayed up on a pie chart. Just under half were 'Sound', coloured in a reassuringly calm pale blue.

There was about to be another twist in the tale. For while the Three Bears and others were starting to suspect someone had messed with the porridge, Autonomy had figured out a new way to stir the pot – bringing in someone else to pick up the tab.

FOURTEEN

The Vatican Deal and 2010

Radical action is required, really radical, we can't wait any more.

– Email from Sushovan Hussain to Mike Lynch, 10 December 2010

Footsteps clacked smartly across the chessboard marble floor and echoed around the vaulted ceilings. Then they stopped and all around was silence. It was broken by a collective gasp.

Mike Lynch looked upwards at the brightly coloured frescos which decorated the walls and ceilings above him, the glimmering white stone surrounding them. It was December 2010. He was standing inside the hallowed space of the Vatican Library; the home of ancient maps, illuminated manuscripts and one of the oldest surviving fragments of the New Testament.

Lynch had always loved history, and these buildings, commissioned in the sixteenth century by Pope Sixtus V, are totally unique. 'An absolutely incredible archive of Western thought in the last 2,000 years,' Lynch later said; 'there's nothing like it anywhere in the world.'

Proudly showing Lynch, Angela, Sushovan Hussain and his wife Tracie around was Cesare Pasini, Prefect Emeritus of the Vatican Library. La Biblioteca Apostolica Vaticana, to give its official name, is not open to the public, making this private tour within its secretive walls all the more special. But the tour was for business, not pleasure. Autonomy was bidding to be part of a project to bring the treasure trove into the twenty-first century, and to open it up to the world. The guests were bowled over by the long underground tunnels which seemed to stretch on forever, stuffed with ancient treasures.

Since January 2009, Autonomy had been vying for the contract to digitize the library's contents: some 80,000 manuscripts and over 40 million pages of documents, a contract worth around €70 million. It would have been up there with the biggest deals that Autonomy had ever done – and would be an extremely prestigious one, at that.

At first, things looked positive. In February 2010, Autonomy started and funded a testbed project which involved taking high-definition photographs of many manuscripts with an expensive camera that the company had shipped to Rome. Technology teams went back and forth to supervise proceedings. It was frustrating and intense, but also a very interesting programme to be involved with.

Time ticked on and there was no white smoke from the Vatican to confirm that the deal could go ahead. Hussain started to worry that the utterly critical contract would not come through. If it didn't, Autonomy would not meet its target sales numbers for the first quarter of 2010. The day before the results were due, the Autonomy salesman on the ground in Italy eagerly reported that the deal would be signed in half an hour. It was not to be. The deal was still some way off, but the need to fill the financial gaps, in order to hit the company's sales forecast, remained.

Lynch and Hussain had a solution, one which they would come to use again and again. Right in the dying hour of the quarter, 11.30 p.m. on 31 March, Lynch told Hussain that Autonomy somehow needed to register $10 million from the Vatican deal.

They roped in Christopher 'Stouffer' Egan, the US CEO. On the West Coast of the US, it was early afternoon. Egan picked up the phone to a contact, Dave Truitt, who was lounging in a chair on West Palm Beach, Florida, enjoying a well-deserved holiday with his family. Truitt was the chief executive and founder of a confusing clutch of three technology resellers: MicroLink, MicroTech and DiscoverTech, companies which were all related to one another in some capacity.

Egan wanted to know if MicroTech would be interested in coming on board with the Vatican deal – if it would buy the software instead, then sell it on to the Vatican in Autonomy's stead after the close of the quarter. The bosses loved it, and everyone was very excited about it, Egan said breathlessly. Truitt called his brother Steve, who was running operations at MicroTech and who gave it the nod. In a flash, a deal was on.

And so, Autonomy sold $11.5 million worth of software – intended to be used to digitize the Vatican Library's files – to MicroTech, rather than to the Vatican Library itself, with further deals with the Vatican expected to follow as the work progressed. Autonomy had not signed a deal with the Vatican, but if you sell to a middleman (a reseller), and they take on the risk of the deal, that counts as a sale. Everyone breathed a sigh of relief. This deal was crucial to the company reporting, which was claiming $194.2 million worth of sales that quarter, up about 50 per cent from the year before. Analysts' consensus forecast was for $193 million.

The problem was that, apart from clocking the revenue, there was no obvious reason as to why MicroTech should have been involved. If it had been a legitimate arrangement, MicroTech would have taken on the negotiations with the Vatican in the deal's immediate aftermath, which did not happen. In technical terms, the deal 'lacked commercial substance'. MicroTech had not really taken on the risk.

*

LIKE OTHER SOFTWARE companies, Autonomy had a long history of using Value Added Resellers (VARs), who acted like middlemen, with a twist. These companies buy software, such as a licence for a business tool, and then 'add value' by customizing it, bundling it with hardware or providing support services. They then resell the final solution to end users at a higher price.

Logical enough, if more complex than a direct sale. But things were a little more complicated here, not only because MicroTech didn't seem to be adding any value, but because in 2009 Autonomy had bought MicroLink – one of the two other VARs Truitt had founded – for $55 million. So, by this point, Truitt was the CEO of a subsidiary of Autonomy, as well as being heavily involved with two of Autonomy's reselling partners.

MicroTech was a long-standing partner. It had become an Autonomy reseller in 2006, mainly because it specialized in US federal contracts. When it took on a deal from the government, MicroTech would pay for the Autonomy software. When the deal closed and the software was delivered, MicroTech would get back what it had paid Autonomy, plus a 10 per cent profit.

MicroLink had operated in a similar way, but Autonomy's acquisition of that company had been a controversial one. Lynch argued it was done in order to give Autonomy federal clearance in the USA; critics argued it was to wipe the slate clean of all the money MicroLink owed Autonomy for software it did not manage to resell. In effect, the acquisition avoided a bad debt.

There was surprise inside Autonomy about the involvement of the US reseller in the Vatican Library deal. As far as anyone could tell, MicroTech had had nothing to do with preparations in the run-up to the deal. MicroTech did not have international experience or anyone who spoke the appropriate languages – Latin or Italian – and was completely unfamiliar with the library. In a crucial omission, no one appeared to have told the Vatican Library itself, the potential client, about MicroTech's involvement.

Furthermore, the deal was at odds with what Lynch had once told David Toms, the City analyst: that sales at Autonomy were not booked until they were sold to the end user, which in this case would have been the library.

Back in Cambridge, members of the accounts team were incredulous, claiming that the Vatican Library deal, and others in the quarter, were garbage, and that they had only refrained from speaking out because they didn't want to snitch to the auditors – Deloitte – whom many of them had, of course, worked for before joining Autonomy. Their boss, Steve Chamberlain – who ran the accounting department day-to-day – agreed that the reporting had been strange, but insisted that their jobs were to do what they were told.

The Vatican Library deal formed part of a pattern of behaviour at Autonomy which would increasingly emerge during certain major transactions. If a deal looked uncertain, a Value Added Reseller would be used at the last minute to allow Autonomy to log the sale in its books. The VARs always signed the standard Autonomy contract, stating that they were on the hook for the deals they were buying – i.e. that they had to deliver the software to the end client – and always confirmed this to the auditors.

But the tacit understanding between the two parties was sometimes quite different to the contractual one. There was no expectation that a VAR would do anything other than take on a debt it knew it wouldn't have to pay. Autonomy would try to recompense the VARs for taking on the risk, paying them for their troubles – and for software they bought that then didn't sell on to the end client after deals fell apart – through other deals. All the while, the paper trails became increasingly complex.

In the instance of the Vatican Library deal, Autonomy started paying MicroTech back by signing a $9.6 million, three-year contract with the reseller on New Year's Eve 2010, for the use of a brand-new mobile demonstration facility called ATIC. Demonstrating exactly how seriously Autonomy was taking the deal, the only paperwork for this elaborate-sounding tech facility was a one-page purchase order which featured scant details and none of the terms and conditions you would expect for such a big expense. Remarkably conveniently, the cost of ATIC exactly matched the amount that MicroTech owed Autonomy for the Vatican software. Steve Truitt later said as much in court, implying that the figure was reverse-engineered. No mention was made of Autonomy in ATIC promotional videos, and other customers paid MicroTech considerably less for the facility.

By July 2011, due to various deals similar to the Vatican one, MicroTech owed Autonomy more than $25 million – of which $10.3 million had already become overdue on 30 June. As for the Vatican Library, despite the Italian sales reps' optimism back in 2009, Autonomy had never won the deal. And because the transactions never closed, MicroTech was never paid by the Vatican, and was 'left holding the bag'. It would later go to court and sue Autonomy – then owned by HP – over the matter.

As for Deloitte, neither they nor Autonomy's audit committee had a clue what was really going on.

BETWEEN MARCH AND June 2010, the (unpronounceable) Eyjafjallajökull volcano in Iceland repeatedly erupted, wreaking havoc on global air travel. The phenomenon happens every five years, but this time its impact was unprecedented. The soaring height of the dense ash cloud stopped planes flying and caused enormous disruption across Western Europe. The Lynches, with their two young children, were stuck over in California.

It meant that on 21 April Lynch had to do the Autonomy earnings call for the first quarter of the year remotely via his mobile phone. Given his deafness, he would later claim in court it was not always easy to hear what was being said.

The buying and selling of hardware, and using those sales to plug revenue gaps, had left Autonomy with more strange bulges in its accounting balloon. Buying bulky equipment was not a quick process – far removed from the click of a button by which software which could be instantly dispensed. If it was bought and not sold, it sat on the company's books and was not an easy thing to cover up.

Lynch had the job of explaining why the company owned $10 million worth of hardware, twenty times more than it usually did. This was so unusual that it piqued analysts' interest. It jumped off the page. What was going on? Daud Khan, allowed back into the meeting for the first time since he had been excommunicated, was among those who wanted to know.

Lynch, always so confident in the superiority of his intelligence over that of everyone around him, spun a tale. He said that Autonomy was taking advantage of 'discounted offers' and said that it was increasing the sales of a product called Arcpliance – hardware which came pre-loaded with the company's valuable software, known as an 'appliance' in tech jargon.

David Toms, confused, asked for clarification. He wanted to know how the sales of the product would be reported in the accounts. Would Autonomy break with tradition and start spelling out where sales were coming from, line by line? Lynch's reply dodged the question:

> *David, I think you may have misunderstood what that revenue is. It's not hardware revenue. We have very little interest in just selling hardware, and consequently the revenue that that goes for is not related to the hardware cost. It's solely a component of that sale. So, what we are not doing here is acting as a generic company that resells hardware . . . obviously those people do that business and we have no interest in it.*

It was vague, repetitive and ultimately incorrect – Autonomy *was* generically reselling hardware, at a loss, and misrepresenting its accounting. In 2012, Lynch told a journalist: 'One of the very interesting periods in a child's development is when it first becomes deceitful. Deceit's a fascinating thing, because to be deceitful you have to realize that not everyone has the same information you have.'

It seems this is exactly the theory he was applying here.

Auditors at Deloitte, on the phone, were listening to this startling untruth, but did not say anything. Over the coming months, correspondence flew to and from the auditor over the issue. In July 2010, Nigel Mercer, who had taken over as the lead partner for the company, wrote to his predecessor Richard Knights: 'Sparks likely to fly. May need your help.'

After the summer, Autonomy failed to 'beat or raise' in its quarterly figures. It's a marker of the feeling of distrust around the company that, when it forecast that its sales would be a mere three per cent down year-on-year, its share price plummeted by a full fifth. This was another sharp example of how volatile the Autonomy stock was, and of how reactive investors were to the company's sales figures. Autonomy had announced sales of $210 million, of which $26 million – over 10 per cent – was made up of hardware, something still unbeknown to the market. On 10 December 2010, Hussain wrote Lynch a panicked email:

> **Really don't know what to do mike. As I guessed revenue fell away completely . . . There are swathes of reps with nothing to do maybe chase imaginary deals. So radical action is required, really radical, we can't wait any more.**
>
> **Everywhere I look . . . it's bad.**

FIFTEEN

The Fightback

Doesn't he fucking realize? I've got £100 million pounds in the bank. Surely we can fix this with a big bag of drugs and a bag of money and a prostitute?

– *Mike Lynch*

And still the Bears would not go away.

With good reason. City analysts were on particularly high alert when it came to technology companies and their accounts because of a series of accounting scandals over the years, such as at iSOFT, an NHS software supplier, in 2006, and Informix in the late 1990s. In software, where delivery is often intangible, the timing of recognizing when a sale happens can be murky and open to manipulation.

In 2007, three executives were sent to prison for falsifying documents after revelations of accounting irregularities at Torex Retail, a British public software business which sold card machine terminals to shops. Like a scene from *The Sopranos*, during the unfolding drama the executive who revealed the fraud went into hiding, fearing for his life. Then there was FAST, Autonomy's rival, which was bought by Microsoft in a deal that was swiftly followed by revelations of an accounting scandal. The company's offices were raided and its chief executive, John Lervik, stepped down. Microsoft mainly shrugged off the misdemeanour.

Khan was continuing to dig. He had heard noises about issues with Autonomy's technology and what it was like dealing with the business. In 2010, he went straight to a primary source and asked the tech procurement team at JP Morgan – now his ultimate employer after its acquisition of Cazenove.

He heard a strange tale. The bank had a rolling contract with Autonomy; a regular subscription payment. In June 2010, Stouffer Egan rang and asked to convert it to a one-off, upfront payment for substantially less money; a lump sum. When JP Morgan demurred, Egan almost broke down in tears, desperate to get the deal done. Shortly afterwards, Lynch himself came on the phone and demanded to know what price the bank wanted. At a minute to midnight on 30 June, the end of that quarter, the revised deal was signed.

The reason for this strange decision, to bring in less money overall but more in the short term, was so that more *revenue, revenue, revenue,* that favourite Lynchism, would be recognized in the quarter in order to hit targets, even though this meant less money for the business in the future.

This internal conversation with his own tech people cemented Khan's view that Autonomy was speeding up its recording of sales. Khan developed a theory about why keeping the share price high was so important. He believed that as Autonomy's share price kept climbing, so did the value of its equity – giving the company a powerful currency for acquisitions. But the model depended on that upward momentum. If the share price stopped rising, they'd hit a wall – limiting their ability to buy bigger companies. And without those deals, it would become harder to mask the lack of real growth in the core business.

He became convinced that the answers that were coming from

the company were a deflection from the truth, and could well be outright lies. Khan approached John Calonico, the former chief financial officer of Interwoven, an Autonomy company, for information. This overtly direct step sparked an internal furore at Autonomy. The company was fed up of Khan's troublemaking and suspected he was only doing it to feed information to his hedge-fund clients.

Andy Kanter emailed a warning to Calonico:

> **We have been told that his [Khan's] work is a front for hedge funds and those seeking to concoct stories in order to damage the company and get negative momentum in the stock. He has also come awfully close to soliciting inside information. He should be treated very carefully.**

It became increasingly clear to Lynch that he had to do something to stem Khan's momentum, to fight back and display that Autonomy was as strong and profitable as ever.

ONE STRATEGY LYNCH came up with to hit at the naysayers in the City was to get some solid names and reputations on board. Specifically, onto *the* board of the company. Despite its growth, Autonomy's board was unusually weak and small for a FTSE 100 company. A strong board, packed with experience, implies a company with good governance that is capable of intelligent decision-making – in short, a sound investment.

In 2009, the company had appointed its first permanent chairman: Robert Webb KC. Always known as Rob, he had served on the BBC board alongside Lynch. It had taken the pair a few years to speak to each other in depth at the broadcaster's meetings, but eventually they became quite friendly. Webb had a keen sense of humour and quick way with words, qualities which ultimately took him into the upper echelons of a career as a barrister.

What Webb lacked in technical expertise he made up for with his ferocious intelligence and boardroom experience. Lynch wanted someone who would add value to the company, he said, not someone he would have to teach. A former general counsel at British Airways, Webb had spent a lot of his life in businesses which looked safe and turned out to be less so – for instance, he moved to Rolls-Royce when it was investigated by the Serious Fraud Office over a global corruption scandal.

Before accepting the role, Webb therefore did his due diligence, spending a lot of time speaking to everyone on the board, as well as Deloitte, to see what they thought of Autonomy. He heard that it was a high-growth and high-risk company, but that did not put him off.

That quarter, the sales of hardware made up six per cent of the total, a smaller number than it had been. The new chairman set out his stall for change during the third quarter results call of his first year, right in the midst of the hardware era. He spotted that the board was 'few in number and long in service', and that a shake-up was overdue. Webb wanted to add more external figures around the table. Around the same time, Barry Ariko and Richard Perle, two men who had been non-executive directors of Autonomy since 2000, stepped down. Under the UK corporate governance code, non-executive directors serving more than nine years were no longer regarded as independent. Non-executives play an important role in questioning their executive directors, to check everything is as it should be. They should act as strategic sounding boards. Autonomy's non-executive directors still numbered co-founder Richard Gaunt and early investor John McMonigall, long-standing Lynch associates who had both served more than nine years. It did not feel like a particularly challenging group.

It was time for some new faces.

In August 2010, Jonathan Bloomer took the role of overseeing the numbers as the audit committee chair. He was meant to be a hefty name to complement Deloitte, as the primary auditor, and to work alongside Sushovan Hussain, who had been named the FTSE 100's CFO of the Year that May. Bloomer had been chief executive of Prudential before he was pushed out as the board lost faith in his strategy for the company, but he bounced back and dusted himself off, starting Lucida, a pensions insurance company which was eventually acquired by Legal & General for over £150 million. Bombastic and spiky in the business world, more introverted at home, Bloomer was intelligent, clear-thinking and a good orator. He mixed his knowledge and experience with a rare humility. He would later become the chair of Hiscox, the insurer, and Morgan Stanley International.

The second appointment Lynch made was Dr Frank Kelly, then the Master of Lynch's beloved Christ's College Cambridge. He was also Emeritus Professor of the Mathematics of Systems at the university, a maths don. Kelly's titles may have been grandiose, but he was not – he is a slight, grey-haired, casually dressed man lacking airs and graces, well-liked by his college community. Like Lynch, Kelly's parents were Irish immigrants. His father was a builder who came to the UK in the late 1940s, while his mother was a maid in a London hotel. There was an affinity and an understanding between the two men; they knew other worlds beyond Cambridge and commerce.

Far from the pompous figureheads of some Oxbridge colleges, Kelly is a professor first and foremost. Warm and modest, he took the role as Master after his predecessor sadly died, but insisted that he continue his academic pursuits at the same time, feeling that it was important to keep his hand dipped into all facets of university life. When it came to Autonomy, he was not a businessman, but he did understand Bayes' formula. It seemed like a convincing enough reason for him to sign on.

It was quite a coup to get Webb, Bloomer and Kelly, and the men were surprised, but pleased, to be approached. They soon had the desired effect: the diplomatic Kelly, for one, was dispatched to speak to some of the groups that Lynch had a fraught relationship with, which helped to heal some of the fractures with scarred stakeholders. But Lynch's next strategy for soothing relations with the City would come back to bite him.

WALKING DOWN PICCADILLY one day, Lynch was fuming. He had a tendency to get into long funks where he wouldn't speak out loud, but would mutter and move his face bizarrely. He would be having an entire argument with someone in his head, the back and forth written all over his countenance. Suddenly, he burst out, 'Doesn't he fucking realize? I've got £100 million pounds in the bank? Surely we can fix this with a big bag of drugs and a bag of money and a prostitute?'

The target of his ire? Marc Geall. Autonomy's former Investor Relations Director. Geall had been very much a part of the team at one time, even appearing in one of the comic sales films, an *Alien*-style skit that ended with the head of Mike Mooney – Autonomy's US head of sales at the time – bursting through his chest. '*In sales, no one can hear you scream, except Mike Mooney*', appeared on the screen. Perhaps it summed up the horror of working in the Autonomy sales department.

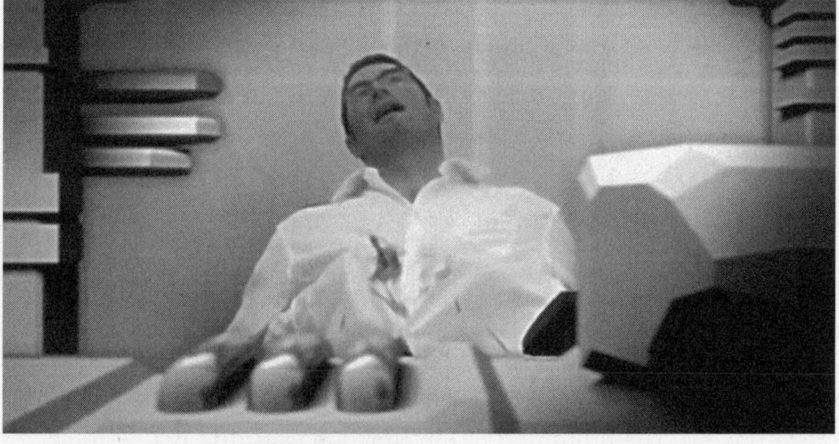

Mark Geall taking part in an Autonomy spoof video.

Lynch may have thought very little of some analysts, but he took others on as employees. Geall was another Cambridge engineering graduate, and had covered Autonomy since 1999 as an analyst at Citigroup. He got to know Lynch and Hussain as part of building relationships with management teams, which was standard practice for an analyst. In 2008, he jumped ship and was hired by Autonomy to run a company it had acquired called Virage.

Geall took a pay cut to take the Autonomy job. He had been making £400,000 a year in the City and Autonomy paid him £125,000, matching his base salary with the promise of a bonus that never materialized – although Hussain gave him some stock options, which made up some of the difference. There was surprise about his move in the City. His former colleagues whispered that he had sold his soul to Mike Lynch. The outcome was not quite as he had expected. His initially positive view of the business turned sour as he found it was a brutal place to work, even for someone used to the cut-throat world of the City.

After his stint at Virage, he moved into Autonomy's Investor Relations team. This job meant dealing with the City, explaining to his former analyst peers what was going on inside the company. Lynch hoped that by presenting analysts with one of their own he could improve their general perception of the company. The appointment was a bit like the hunter becoming the hunted. Geall's analyst friends would take him aside in the pub and say things like: 'Mate, you've moved to the dark side. It's dangerous, they're cooking the books – and you're now their mouthpiece!' They did not think he was listening, but he realized everything was not as it should be.

On one occasion, Geall had just returned from holiday in Barbados, during a 'closed period' for the company – normally two to three weeks before the end of the quarter where a management team is not allowed to talk to analysts to prevent any insider trading – when Lynch called him into a meeting. New notes had been published by analysts in Geall's absence, which caused the consensus – the average forecast for the forthcoming financial results – to move.

'This is your fucking fault,' Lynch swore at Geall across the boardroom table. Fuming, he railed that Geall had let the consensus get ahead of itself. All the good work they had done to deliver revenues was now lost because market expectations were too high, he said. Geall argued back that there was nothing he could do, as it was a closed period and speaking to anyone would have been against the rules. It was futile. Lynch was furious with him and would not listen to reason. 'People just didn't question him,' Geall said. 'I don't know of anyone who really questioned him, including other board members.'

Geall didn't like being treated like crap, but that wasn't the strangest thing about his time at the business. He started to get suspicious about how it was being run. At the end of September 2009, Peter Goodman, Geall's deputy, spotted a piece of paper left on a printer. A $45 million contract for hardware between Autonomy and EMC. He wondered what it was about.

Geall told Goodman to check if Andy Kanter was in the office. When he couldn't find Kanter, Geall then instructed Goodman to either shred the contract or lock it up. Three weeks later, the quarterly results were issued with that unusually high marketing expenditure on the SPE, designed to cover up the hardware sales (see Chapter 12). Geall kept quiet, but it bothered him that the results were potentially inaccurate.

Geall was becoming increasingly concerned by some of these 'red flags' and believed that Autonomy was misleading analysts, people he used to work with and had known for many years. It made him feel extremely uncomfortable. There was a string of things that bothered him – how acquisitions were being presented to accelerate growth for the business, the real size of the core business selling software to OEMs, the hardware sales and the real value of the SPE – was it even really a product at all? He also did not like the banning of some people from company gatherings; he was the one who invited Khan back into the analyst meetings.

Lynch, in turn, was scathing about Geall, saying he had failed at Virage and that's why he found himself 'demoted' to the investor relations role. Years later, in court, Lynch would go on to accuse Geall of lying about his reasons for wanting to join Autonomy, and claim that Geall had been pushed out of his previous job at Citigroup but hadn't disclosed this to Autonomy. As always, Lynch was searching for the silver bullet to discredit perceived critics.

Geall needed to tell someone. In May 2010, he met Rob Webb, Autonomy's chairman, to raise his concerns. Webb was busy at an event, so Geall went to find him in a courtyard behind the central London venue, and explained what he believed was going on. Nothing is recorded of the outcome, but that June, Geall left Autonomy. He departed on seemingly cordial terms, promising to catch up for a drink with Andy Kanter. He soon started work at Deutsche Bank, back doing his old job as an analyst – and once again writing about Autonomy.

Geall's return to the analyst fold was a major moment for the business. Autonomy had welcomed him inside its inner sanctum, revealed some of its innermost workings. Now, Geall was back outside the tent and he was throwing rocks. The hunted had returned to being the hunter.

Everything Geall said about Autonomy was taken more seriously by the City because he'd been on the Autonomy payroll. He did not disclose his suspicions about what he had really found within the company, but he came as close as he could to warning the market to stay well clear. He downgraded the company from a 'hold' to a 'sell' rating, and published a twenty-six-page critical note.

The tight chain of command reporting into Lynch was more representative of a startup than a major global player, he wrote. It was a business run by a small group at the top who were stretched far too thin. Salespeople were hunters, not farmers, he said, who were no good at account management. Autonomy was spending too much time hunting for deals and too little time actually making sure customers were happy and the tech worked for them, he claimed. This meant deals were not being renewed and subscriptions cancelled.

The note's release in October 2010 sent Autonomy's share price tumbling and raised Lynch's ire even further. But there was little he could do except try again. In June 2010, to replace Geall, Lynch turned once more to the analyst community, choosing Derek Brown, an unassuming, mild-mannered man. He did not know what to expect from the new job, but he felt like a change and he had long had a good relationship with Lynch, who had been supportive of him over the years. Whatever he thought would happen, it was not that he would be treated like a child.

Brown, who would prove to be Autonomy's last Investor Relations Director, now looks back on his tenure with an air of bewilderment. Whenever he left the office, even just to get a coffee, his phone would ring. Lynch would want to know where he was, paranoid that Brown was meeting analysts and saying things that Autonomy didn't want him to say. Brown encountered a poisonous atmosphere of secrecy inside the business, a strange bunker mentality of 'us against the world'. Like Geall, he endured his fair share of angry tellings-off from Lynch, who would call and instruct him to 'get down here', before administering a tongue-lashing. It would all have been deeply upsetting, if it hadn't been so patently ridiculous.

Yet, after a while, incredibly, relations with the City seemed to improve. Lynch wisely brought in the calm, poised Vanessa Colomar as a public relations advisor to act as a peacemaker. She, too, was to prove another loyal lieutenant during subsequent years.

Then things improved further still. On 1 February 2011, Autonomy unveiled record-breaking annual results – sending its share price soaring and fuelling a wave of exuberance around the company's future.

'Good morning, ladies and gentlemen!' Lynch began the upbeat earnings call with analysts, announcing sales of $870 million, up 18 per cent. Pre-tax profits were also up on the year before. He boasted that Autonomy had signed almost 100 seven-figure deals in 2010, up 42 per cent from 2009, and that the company had a staggering average selling price of $800,000. On top of that, he said, Autonomy had plenty of money in the bank and big plans to spend it. It registered nearly a billion dollars in cash at the end of 2010, including $500 million raised through a convertible bond – a type of loan that can later be converted into shares – intended for buying yet another company. New deals were on the horizon. Lynch said that customers were feeling more confident and Autonomy was signing an ever-increasing number of cloud-computing deals – Lynch was again very early to this tech revolution, where Autonomy had a major business.

The company's share price rose over six per cent that day. It had defied its critics and beaten the market's expectations. On the analysts call, Geall, Daud Khan and David Toms all asked questions and had them answered. It felt like a turning point. Analysts described the numbers as a 'relief', while Lynch optimistically called 2010 a 'year of transition'. He advised the market that there would be almost $1 billion of sales in 2011.

What wasn't disclosed was that in 2010, Autonomy had sold approximately $100 million of hardware, which constituted 11 per cent of its sales. Nor was there any mention of the various outstanding VAR deals, which cut into the true revenue figure.

And one man was determined not to accept that everything was as joyful as it appeared to be.

LIKE LYNCH, TIM Steer had got stuck into the music tech scene in the 1980s. He had previously worked as a sound engineer for acts like Meatloaf, the Jam and Diana Ross. The height of his cool came when he managed the light and sound systems used for Pink Floyd's 'The Wall Tour'. As if he wasn't already enough of a rockstar, he then decided to take his street cred to new heights by . . . training as a chartered accountant.

After qualifying in 1988, while Lynch was still an undergraduate in Cambridge, he worked at Merrill Lynch as a research analyst, specializing in writing 'sell' notes about companies that had dodgy accounting. He rather made a name for himself out of it; he was never squeamish about sticking the boot in. Steer's senses were particularly attuned to software companies, which had quite a lot of freedom in the early days, as the sector was developing.

He then became a successful fund manager at Artemis, running its £300 million UK growth fund. In 2010, he was a few years away from retirement and had assumed near-legendary status in the City. With his dishevelled grey hair, he was comedically world-weary, always wearing a slightly bemused expression, as if to say, 'Oh, here we go again.'

Steer was looking for companies that he thought were going to do badly; he was betting money on certain share prices going down. By 2011, he had placed a large bet against Autonomy's share price, which meant he would make money if it dropped. He might have been short on stocks, but he was not short of self-confidence.

He thought there was 'aggressive accounting' going on, something funny in the company's numbers. It was so bad that, in March 2011, after reading Autonomy's record-breaking annual report, he took the unusual step of writing to Nigel Mercer, the audit partner at Deloitte in Cambridge, to let him know about his concerns. He didn't expect much to come of it, but thought it might just spark an investigation, especially if others were raising similar concerns.

In his letter, he listed out the issues he spotted, concluding:

> *Some people might think that there is much effort in these accounts to ensure, where possible, costs avoid the profit & loss account whilst revenues are maximised, with the happy consequence that the key Earnings Per Share figure keeps moving ahead.*

He received no response. Steer thought that wasn't good enough, and wrote to Mercer again, this time copying in Deloitte's senior partner and chief executive, John Connolly. Even though they were marked private and confidential, Deloitte passed his letters to Sushovan Hussain, who replied in April 2011, politely, pointing out that Steer didn't really understand the business.

> *We can understand how some of these questions may arise, given the lack of comparable companies in the FTSE100. Autonomy is a rare example of a pure software company in the industry. As a pure software company almost the entire revenue stream for the company comes from the licensing of the company's standard software.*
>
> *The company's revenue recognition criteria are simple, strict and straightforward. Because of Autonomy's pure software model, the policies are actually stricter than many other UK technology companies which may recognise revenue based on estimates of work completed; Autonomy does not do this.*

Autonomy knew Steer held a short position, and that he had a financial interest in their share price going down. But the use of the phrase 'pure software' in the letter was problematic. As David Toms later said, 'I took it to mean that they sold purely software.'

And that wasn't the case at all.

SIXTEEN

The Whistleblower

The 'Hogenson Episode' provides further support for the conclusion I have reached that both [Lynch and Hussain] knew that the VAR sales were illusory and improper, and were determined to avoid investigation that would reveal this.

– Mr Justice Hildyard, civil judgement, 17 May 2022

In Autonomy's San Francisco offices, the team scrambled around early one morning to try to find batteries for a remote control to make the conference call system work.

It was an important day. It was the summer of 2010, and Brent Hogenson, the man running the company's US finances, had a remote meeting with John McMonigall, one of its directors and original backers. Rob Webb, the company's chairman, was listening in.

Hogenson wanted to raise concerns about what he alleged were some weird things going on in the company accounts – to *blow the whistle* on Autonomy's books. After listening to his rambling description of what he believed was going on, McMonigall and Webb came to the quiet conclusion that he was looking for a pay-off. Shortly afterwards, he disappeared, and no one was told where he had gone. Staff were confused.

Any questions about him were met with a stony silence from the management team.

BRENT HOGENSON HAD started his career auditing tech companies at Arthur Anderson, a major accountancy firm that was complicit in the Enron scandal and was dissolved in 2002. He had come to Autonomy quite by chance. He had joined a document management company named Interwoven in 2003, which Autonomy bought in 2009. Hogenson was absorbed as the head of finance for the US arm of the company.

He first raised questions about Autonomy's accounting practices during his first year at the company, when he wrote a note to Sushovan Hussain and Stephen Chamberlain asking whether he should continue ensuring that salespeople were not engaging in so-called 'side letters' – informal promises about deals that were not recorded in proper contracts. It was always a danger with salespeople, that they might do something on a handshake and a nod, which was a little bit naughty. He was told that it was not necessary. Early on, after the Interwoven acquisition, he recalled that Hussain told him, 'Don't worry about Deloitte, they work for me.' It struck him as odd.

Hogenson got a bee in his bonnet then, and began actively scratching around for details. As he combed through how the company was run, executives were pumped for information even about minor things such as holiday pay. The level of detail he went into quickly became a source of frustration for those around him – his concerns were persistent and hard to ignore. His bee would not stop buzzing, and everyone knew it.

A series of conversations led him to uncover the dodgy VAR deals. He found that a system was in place whereby an Autonomy reseller would buy software as if it were for an end user, but without having a customer to sell it on to. Autonomy would register this as a sale in their books and, at a later date, buy something without real value from the reseller to compensate them. It was either that, he thought, or deals were being registered in the accounts before they were signed. In other words, he felt Autonomy was making itself look like it was selling more software than it really was.

Hogenson then came to believe that Autonomy made the $55 million acquisition of MicroLink, one of the Truitt resellers, in order to write off $20 million worth of unpaid invoices and avoid a bad debt, and therefore avoid a hit to its own profits. He noted that three businesses – MicroLink, MicroTech and DiscoverTech – were more than four months overdue with their payments to Autonomy. Yet on the accounts, the company claimed that extra revenue from them was 'probable'. He did not understand the claim. How can accounts state that a payment was likely to come in from a customer when that customer still hadn't coughed up $14 million that was over four months late?

Hogenson felt he needed to tell those in charge. He sent a series of dynamite emails to Lynch and the board from June 2010 onwards, alleging that the company may have materially mis-stated bits of its accounts from 2008 to 2010. He said he had gathered evidence to suggest that some in the senior management team may have been engaging in multimillion-dollar fictitious transactions with resellers where there was no customer and where the reseller could not pay Autonomy. Furthermore, he was curious about the close ties of the resellers involved in the sales to Autonomy, which raised questions about whether those deals were truly independent. And then another detonation. There appeared, he thought, to be barter deals – where both sides swapped goods or services – but the value of what each side got seems to have been exaggerated. He presented these bombshells to the board 'in good faith', a carefully chosen phrase intended to give him legal whistleblowing protection and protect him from retaliation.

The phrase 'in good faith' is important, because it shows someone is raising concerns honestly and with the belief that something is genuinely wrong. It helps protect whistleblowers under the law, since many protections only apply if the person wasn't acting out of revenge or an intent to cause harm. It also strengthens their credibility, showing they were motivated by a sense of responsibility, not personal gain.

In another company, executives may have taken such a discovery in their stride. At Autonomy, Lynch's baby, still young, still nurtured by him and those who had been there from the early days, such allegations were intensely personal and his team was determined to quash them. Outwardly calm, Lynch suggested that Hogenson get into the specifics of his concerns and blustered that he may be confusing the different requirements of Generally Accepted Accounting Principles (GAAP) – the regulations used in the US – and of International Financial Reporting Standard (IFRS) – the UK rules. Lynch then got on the phone to Andy Kanter, who emailed Hogenson:

> **We know of a couple of rather dishonest characters who are fronting hedge funds, and by coincidence a couple of phrases you used were reminiscent of them. Please can I ask that if you are getting outside IFRS advice please be very mindful of the need for discretion and please be careful who you consult with.**

Hogenson, after a bit of back and forth, felt as if he was being fobbed off. He then went over Lynch's head and went straight to Deloitte at the end of July 2010.

Deloitte reviewed his concerns – as did Jonathan Bloomer's audit committee – but with rather less information than the management team had at their disposal. Hogenson, cautioned by Lynch about his behaviour, had watered down his emails and phrased them as a series of questions, rather than as an official whistleblowing complaint. They decided there was nothing to address, and that Hogenson simply did not have the full accounting picture – 'an incomplete understanding' was the phrase used. He was a US GAAP accountant with limited knowledge of international accounting standards, so Deloitte felt some of his questions were wide of the mark.

AUTONOMY, HOGENSON FELT, needed to find an excuse to get rid of him. Happily, one presented itself. Another curious accounting case had bubbled up in another corner of the business in June that same year. Two employees had been stealing quite a lot of money from the company.

Lourdes Dionisio, a payroll manager, and Hannah Yao, a financial analyst at Autonomy's US office, had embezzled $2.6 million over four years. They were each later sentenced to five years in prison, in a case which was led by a young prosecutor named Kamala Harris. Suspicions had been raised about the payroll fraud when, while filing for unemployment benefits, Dionisio listed her annual salary as a massive $450,000 – it was actually $63,000.

The man tasked with clearing up this mess was Joel Scott, a Canadian Stanford law graduate and Autonomy's associate general counsel in the United States. He got the job by pure chance; he saw it advertised on the listings website Craigslist, back in 2005, and leapt at it. A bit like Kanter, he was an everyman, thrown all sorts of projects which did not relate to his legal work. He latterly became Autonomy's Chief Operating Officer for the Americas, one of the most senior executives working in Autonomy's US operations. Like Stouffer Egan, his titles were grander than his positions. He had no real decision-making authority – that, he found, always lay in Kanter's hands.

Scott was given the task of 'independently' investigating the payroll fraud and, specifically, Hogenson's role in it. This murky episode was cast as an example of Hogenson's incompetence. There were other things thrown up too, such as his lapsed accounting qualification, and an altercation over a dinner expense. He also wiped his laptop – significant, those inside Autonomy felt. Hogenson himself described the payroll fraud as a lucky tool that Autonomy could use, that just happened to occur at that same time as he raised concerns about Autonomy's accounting.

Scott did not feel that there was anything independent about his investigation; he was being given strong directions. Autonomy set the forensic investigation company Kroll onto the matter, and then a second private investigator to try to dig up some dirt. No evidence was uncovered of any wrongdoing by Hogenson or anyone else other than Dionisio and Yao. Kanter, Hussain and other executives told Scott about things Hogenson was supposed to have done which violated Autonomy's policies and asked him to look at them, saying he was a troublemaker out to destroy the company. Truth be told, Scott had always found Hogenson rather irritating – the two had never got along, but Scott felt like the verdict had already been given.

On 28 July, five weeks after Hogenson's first allegation, Scott called Mike Lynch to talk to him about the prospect of firing Hogenson. Lynch told Scott that it was his decision to make, but that *if* it were him and there was somebody that was really trying to destroy the company, he wouldn't want them around. The boss had spoken. And so Scott fired Hogenson over the phone and recorded the call:

> *Well, Brent, I got to tell you what I see is a pattern of financial irregularities and mismanagement. Um, I see unauthorized partner payments where you're committing company dollars well in excess of what you're authorized to. . .*

Hogenson wanted to know who was authorizing Scott to make the decision:

> *I'd like to ask if there was any part of this decision that was related to the questions that I've raised to the audit committee, Deloitte or the FSA [the UK Financial Services Authority]?*

Scott demurred, insisting that his investigation and decision were his, and his alone. He also fired two of Hogenson's juniors – Percy Tejada and Reema Prasad, who coincidentally also had concerns about Autonomy's accounting.

It was only then that Scott found out more about the whistleblowing allegations. It made him feel extremely uncomfortable. For that matter, so did working at Autonomy. It was a really hard environment to exist in, with a fair amount of yelling. People being fired over things that didn't always make sense to him. It was, he felt, a very reactive place to work – high-intensity with contradictory instructions and no humanity.

Hogenson, meanwhile, threatened to sue Autonomy for wrongful dismissal. The company paid him three quarters of a million dollars to settle the case and to keep quiet. It was more than any other settlement Scott had ever seen Autonomy enter into, but it made Hogenson go away.

For the moment.

In the years that followed, Hogenson twice applied for money from America's whistleblower programme, which pays out up to 30 per cent of any imposed fines which come about from information a whistleblower provides.

Before he left, Hogenson had thrown one more spanner into Lynch's works. As he mentioned in the call with Scott quoted above, right before he was dismissed he had emailed the Financial Services Authority's whistleblowing email address (the FSA, at that time, regulated financial services firms in the UK), as well as the Financial Reporting Review Panel. The latter is a UK regulatory body responsible for monitoring and enforcing compliance with accounting standards. He had copied in Rob Webb, the Autonomy chairman.

Suddenly, more people outside Autonomy began to ask questions. The cracks were beginning to show, and Hogenson would not be the last to speak out.

*

THE EMAILS SPURRED the regulators into action, but the process that followed was deeply compromised by responses from Autonomy's leadership. In February 2011, the Financial Reporting Review Panel (FRRP), part of the auditor's watchdog, flagged one particular deal: a $4 million transaction between Autonomy and food manufacturing giant Kraft.

It was the usual story. Unable to get the deal over the line before the end of the quarter, Autonomy had done a deal with one of its friendly resellers – a VAR called Capax Discovery – who issued a purchase order for the software so Autonomy could clock the Kraft sale onto its books anyway. Later, when an agreement was directly signed with Kraft, money was moved around and Capax Discovery got $400,000 as a fee for the service. Capax's CEO knew when he signed the deal, he later said, that his firm was always going to get the cash back from Autonomy. The FRRP wanted to understand why Autonomy appeared to have contracted with both Capax and Kraft for the same licenses. In response to the FRRP investigation, Autonomy sent a series of responses to the regulator describing the deal as unique, which were later found to be 'materially misleading'.

And yet the company did not stop. In mid-March of the same year, Autonomy tried and failed to do a deal with Prisa, the owner of Spain's *El País* newspaper. The media business was already an Autonomy client, and was hoping to outsource its content hosting. The deal started to look precarious but Autonomy needed it to go through in order to hit its numbers.

The end of the quarter came and went and no deal was secured. Stouffer Egan once again called Dave Truitt and asked DiscoverTech to take on the contract. It was a little late this time – it was already April – so Egan organized for the paperwork to be backdated to March. Truitt sent the contract with the erroneous date back to Egan's personal email address. Nothing with an April date on it could be faxed, lest it left official fingerprints. Both men knew it was something they should not be doing, and Egan had to reassure an uncomfortable

Truitt that it would be a one-time thing. Prisa's interactions were all with Autonomy, after all, not with DiscoverTech.

In the end, it didn't matter. Months later, Prisa could not get the software and the technology to work, and so they killed the project.

Major deals were continually being done in the same chaotic manner involving resellers. It created a horrible merry-go-round each quarter. Egan was stressed out about it. He noticed that, as time went on, the number and size of each of the reseller deals increased, even as the probability that the end-user deal would actually be completed decreased. The result, he found, was that the hole in which Autonomy was starting each new quarter kept getting larger and larger – it meant constantly having to scrounge to complete old customer deals from previous quarters, or come up with another way to fix things. That burden mushroomed over time.

Pressure was intensifying within the business to the extent that there were even signs of tension between Lynch and Hussain. The diligent CFO wanted to take some of his large amount of accrued holiday: 74.5 days.

> **Btw I worked every day for 4 hours at least and had 5 meetings on top during my Boston/New York holiday and haven't claimed any of it.**
>
> **Same problem as for Pete [Menell], anyways happy to take 25 days = 5 weeks between now and q4 if you want. The problem (which is not solvable) is basically that we as a management team work all the time because we live and breathe it.**

It was met with this reply on 15 September 2010:

> **Thank you for your threat to take five weeks off between now and the [year end]. Please do that and you will see the**

consequences . . . Sushovan I am sick of dealing with this shit from people . . . do what the fuck you like.

Key people were thinking about jumping ship, including Egan. His team was underperforming. He was exhausted and desperate to leave Autonomy. The high stakes and travel away from his family were taking their toll. After a decade working there, he was done. The company had got bigger, with both the pressure on him and the numbers at stake growing with it. And there was the hangover that was being created every quarter by the reseller deals. It was all getting to be too much.

Autonomy and Lynch had also made Egan a fortune by this point. But in later years he would choke up, thinking about the pressure that was put on him and other members of the management team. They were often forced to travel at the last minute and stay away from their homes and families, in case a client needed them. Lynch would push his employees, Egan felt, until the point that they were on the edge of quitting, which was exactly what he was about to do.

He wrote a long email to Lynch in June 2011, where he set out his state of mind.

Mike, I'll preface this by saying I will kill myself to get you all of your deals through June. I know you think it helps to pile more pressure on, and I know your thinking and models of me are informed by prior, but at a certain level what may have worked before has the opposite effect.

I'm in the back of the plane again fighting fires in the enormity of front-of-the-plane issues, reps quitting, hiring not where it needs to be, excess risk . . . I sense Nicole [Eagan] and Mike Sullivan may both go this summer. Makes it much harder to do it and think it's worth it, since the relief is so temporary.

For these reasons and more, which I can't justify the time to communicate now, I need to let you know I want to exercise whatever notification is expected of me to leave. Let's get together in July and I can lie on the couch and give you the whole story.

I'm communicating this despite considering yourself, Sushovan and even Pete [Menell], whom I don't talk to much anymore, to be my best friends in the world. It's been family and that fact has probably caused me to go on too long.

Lynch responded briefly.

Let's park it till July and sort it out then. I have more information than you do.

Mike.

And then the music stopped.

PART THREE

The House Is on Fire (2011–12)

SEVENTEEN

The Birthplace of Silicon Valley

Software is eating the world.

– Marc Andreesen, 20 August 2011

In hindsight, it's perhaps embarrassingly obvious that Hewlett-Packard and Autonomy were a match made in hell.

HP was a grandee of Silicon Valley: a slow-moving, heavy beast of a business; a giant, mature company with an annual turnover of $130 billion and 330,000 staff members around the world.

Back in 2010, it had just celebrated its seventieth anniversary. The US firm had by this point become a household name from the sale of its hardware, such as PCs, printers and ink, but the world was rapidly changing. The sexy new opportunities in the tech world were in the highly profitable software industry and cloud computing, and HP was suffering from Big Company Syndrome.

It was so large and slow and unwieldy it was sometimes compared to a civil service, except that might be harsh on civil services. HP was loaded with a long and distinguished history which proved both a blessing and a curse. It lacked the energy of some of the wildly successful tech companies making waves in the Valley at the time, such as Google, Facebook, Netflix and even Apple, which was significantly older than the rest. Steve Jobs' business may have almost died in the 1990s, but it had stormed back and redefined the tech landscape with the iPhone, launched in 2007, cementing its status as the leading producer of beautifully designed, intuitive and advanced tech hardware. People loved the Cupertino company's products. Apple, in particular, felt untouchable.

But HP had been the future once. Its romantic founding story had become baked into Silicon Valley legend. The company is the embodiment of the American Dream, a shining example of success that every tech entrepreneur to pass through the Valley has tried to replicate ever since it opened its doors almost a century ago.

It all started in the 1930s with two talented and enterprising engineering students at Stanford University, Bill Hewlett and Dave Packard, who tossed a coin to decide the order of their names. The garage where HP was founded – a little wooden shed tucked down the side of a large house in Palo Alto – would later become a famous historical landmark. The State of California formally enshrined it as 'the birthplace of Silicon Valley'.

The pair's erstwhile professor at Stanford, Fred Terman, nurtured and inspired the two students through the early days of the company. Terman, often referred to as the father of Silicon Valley, had a vision for a stronger relationship between the academic and commercial worlds. Well before the founding of the St John's Innovation Centre in Cambridge, Terman wanted to foster the ideas coming out of universities and turn them into businesses. He encouraged his students to start their own ventures, rather than to join electronics firms in the area. It was a path many students would follow during Terman's tenure, one which carved out California as the home of technological innovation.

Hewlett and Packard were the first to follow his advice. The two young engineers made electronic testing and measuring equipment in their small workshop (early clients included Walt Disney's chief sound engineer) before working on a range of defence products through the Second World War. HP went public in 1957, and quickly became one of the world's most famous companies, responsible for some breakthrough technological moments. In 1964, to much media fanfare, HP engineers flew around the world synchronizing the globe's atomic clocks to one millionth of a second.

In 1966, the year after Mike Lynch was born, the company created its first computer, and went on to become one of the leaders in the consumer digital revolution – particularly famous for the shrinking size of its calculators. Its first proper personal computer was the HP 85, released in 1980, a cream and grey box with a small screen and big chunky keys more like those of a typewriter.

From then on, HP increasingly brought technology to the masses, introducing a full range of computers and equipment. Its iconic laser jet printer may be the butt of office jokes now, but on release it was nothing short of revolutionary. The company's contribution to the modern world cannot be understated: it democratized access to new technology in a way that made it a runaway success. And its success attracted talent: Steve Wozniak worked on the first Apple computer while working for HP (he even offered the company first refusal on his design but was turned down – perhaps a sign of the decline that would come).

For a while, HP was everywhere. In a bizarre parallel with Autonomy, it even sponsored Tottenham Hotspur Football Club for four years, its logo splashed across the centre of the players' crisp white shirts at the end of the 1990s, (and again for the 2012/13 season – but that was only to fulfil Autonomy's contract).

But, by the early 2000s, HP was a very different brand to what it had been in the post-war and early technology eras. As the millennium dawned, the dotcom bubble burst, which wiped out inflated company valuations; HP's shares fell by over 50 per cent. The world of technology was changing, and newer companies were now doing hardware too. HP seemed old fashioned. The market preferred Apple.

There were more competitors, there were global economic factors at play, and the US entered a recession in 2001 as the world faced geopolitical uncertainty after the 9/11 terrorist attacks.

In response to this decline, HP decided to go on a disastrous spending spree.

IN THE TEN years following the millennium, HP would announce acquisition after acquisition, starting with Compaq, which it bought for a whopping $25 billion in 2001. It was, at the time, the largest merger in the history of the computer industry, done with the aim of creating a new tech giant which could compete with IBM and Dell by combining Compaq's computing nous with HP's printing expertise, or so the theory went. The move was led by Carly Fiorina, who had been HP's chief executive since 1999 and the first female CEO of a top US business.

The deal was met with opposition. Many HP investors hated it, as did Walter Hewlett, the son of the legendary co-founder. Undeterred, Fiorina pushed it over the line by a whisker. The outcome was messy, perhaps inevitably given the scale of ill-feeling and resentment inside the business. Far from creating a new challenger to IBM, the integration process between the two companies was chaotic, and the longed-for revolution from the merger did not happen. There was an intense culture clash – a hallmark of HP's coming acquisitions haul – which created a toxic working environment. The Compaq brand was phased out while HP plodded along as it was, still focused on printers and business services. The saga has since become a Harvard Business School case study of one of the worst tech mergers ever.

After Compaq, HP's management churned. Fiorina had to go. She moved into politics, becoming an advisor to Republican senator John McCain. She later ran for US President in 2016 (exiting early in the primaries) and became the official Republican nominee for the California Senate race in 2010 but lost to the incumbent Democrat.

Fiorina's calamitous tenure was followed swiftly by a spying scandal in 2006, when Patty Dunn, HP's then chairwoman, commissioned private investigators to probe corporate leaks. Highly controversially, the investigators impersonated board members and journalists to obtain information. Dunn swerved criminal charges for fraud, but she too had to go. HP continued to struggle – that same year, 14,500 jobs were slashed.

After Fiorina, the next into the CEO's chair was Mark Hurd. Paid almost $40 million a year, he was touted by *Fortune* as one of the world's best leaders. And for a time, things seemed like they were going well. Taking charge in 2005, Hurd ruthlessly cut costs and doubled the company's share price.

But Compaq did not prove a salutary lesson. In a bid to keep growing, the company continued its rapacious strategy of buying other businesses. In 2008, Hurd oversaw HP's acquisition of Electronic Data Systems Corporation for $14 billion, which helped HP gain ground in the IT services industry. It also acquired 3Com, a networking company, for $2.7 billion. Later, as it tried to get into mobile devices in mid-2010, it bought the handheld computer business Palm for $1.2bn.

This hotchpotch of bolt-ons might have all worked out regardless, but Hurd's tenure as joint HP chairman and CEO ended earlier than expected when Jodie Fisher entered the frame. Fifty years old, Fisher was a blonde former Playboy model and reality TV personality. She worked as a hostess at some HP events, and Hurd was taken with her. Offers of sex, money and holidays allegedly followed, as it was claimed that the married chief executive tried to love-bomb Fisher into accepting his advances.

An internal HP investigation ruled that nothing untoward happened, although it concluded that Hurd had used the company dime to take Fisher out for dinner on non-work occasions. To some, this sort of offence seemed like minor shenanigans, but he was forced to resign. It was not a totally unhappy ending – with around a

$22 million severance package, Hurd jumped ship and became the co-president of Oracle alongside Larry Ellison, its founder. He oversaw sales and marketing for the tech giant until he died from cancer in 2019, aged sixty-two.

As Hurd's leadership went awry, so too did HP's sense of direction, and at the time that Hewlett-Packard joins our story in earnest – around the time of Hurd's departure – its executive leadership team was in tatters. Cathie Lesjak, its chief financial officer, had been parachuted in as interim CEO. Lesjak was an HP lifer, whose approach to the CFO role was forged in the furnace of the financial crisis, when she had first taken the job. With a straight dark bob cut just above her shoulders, the fifty-one-year-old was renowned for being direct and sharp-elbowed. But she wouldn't last – her bosses had always intended on appointing a new captain from outside, a fresh face with new ideas.

When they finally found one, it wasn't exactly who everyone was expecting.

THE GERMAN-BORN SON of Jewish-Polish refugees, fifty-seven-year-old Leo Apotheker was not the name most would have chosen to lead Hewlett-Packard into a glorious new dawn. Apotheker did not fit the California tech stereotype, and he certainly didn't come with a background selling HP's bread and butter: hardware. A graduate of the Hebrew University of Jerusalem (with a degree in International Relations and Economics), he speaks an alarmingly impressive array of languages: Dutch, English, French, German, and Hebrew. He's the first child of holocaust survivors to run a major German firm – software giant SAP, where he worked his way up the ladder to become CEO.

He's a soft-spoken man, which belies his hard interior. He dislikes chaos or lateness, going so far as to refuse to admit tardy people into his meetings. He had been at SAP – hardly a consumer-facing business – for a long time and had abruptly resigned as CEO after less than a year in charge, when its board decided not to renew his contract. He had implemented large-scale job cuts in the wake of the financial crisis, which upset the employees.

Yet, in an era where data was being touted as the new oil, HP executives believed, once again, that change was needed, that the company needed to move in a new direction, so they approached Apotheker. They didn't seem bothered by his lack of hardware or consumer experience. They liked his pitch for the job. Apotheker wanted to turn HP into a one-stop shop, offering businesses the technology they needed in one place: hardware, software and networks. A focus of his strategy would be growing HP's software business.

Software was having quite a moment. In 2011, the famous venture capitalist and HP board member Marc Andreesen declared that it was 'eating the world', in one of the most influential tech comment pieces from the period. Software companies were, he said, poised to take over large swathes of the economy.

On the other hand, as the old saying goes, 'hardware is hard'. It is costly, slow, dependent on supply chains and bound by physical constraints. And so it was to Apotheker, with his background in B2B corporate software, that HP turned for its unlikely next chief executive. They wanted 'a software guy' who would hopefully cause less tumult than his predecessors, and Apotheker fit the bill. Publicly, he lauded the potential at HP, simultaneously touting the company's willingness to embrace change and its intention to get back to its roots as he announced his revolutionary new plans. Robert Ryan, an HP board member at the time, said that he was 'exactly what we were looking for in a CEO'. Not everyone agreed. HP's share price continued to fall.

The decision to appoint Apotheker left one person in particular stunned – Larry Ellison, the founder of Oracle. Never shy about taking a sharp public swipe, he claimed that HP had several good internal candidates, but instead 'picked a guy who was recently fired because he did such a bad job of running SAP'. There was more than a little bad blood and tangled politics between HP and Oracle at this stage, including a turgid legal fight over an Intel chip, and over the coming years, Ellison would sit back with a proverbial bucket of popcorn to watch the drama at HP unfold, seemingly enjoying the demise of the company. He continued to fire the odd pot-shot in public, to liven things up still further.

Yet despite all the challenges and the grumbling around his arrival, Apotheker was determined to put HP on the map. To bring it back to its roots. To make it innovate. To make HP cool again.

So, true to the company's history, he started to hunt around for some deals.

EIGHTEEN

Not So Autonomous Any More

It would be like someone turning up and offering a native American chief 3 rifles and some firewater in return for Dakota.

– Mike Lynch, email to Frank Quattrone, 10 October 2010

At home in Loudham, the Lynch family's idyllic Suffolk estate, family life continued. Lynch's friend Patrick Jacob remembers being asked over one day to watch some trees being moved. The mechanics of the monumental process were completely fascinating to both men – the huge holes left by the excavation, the machinery lifting the tree and root and placing it elsewhere. There was something enthralling about watching these ancient anchors being revealed, these previously buried earthbound tendrils being taken from where they had always been and given new life, roots established in another deep earthen home elsewhere.

Afterwards they sat down for a cup of tea. Lynch chewed over what they had seen in a gentle way, very much in home-mode. Hannah Lynch flung herself onto her father's lap, relaxed and happy, and Lynch absent-mindedly stroked his youngest daughter's hair as he continued talking. Jacob loved these conversations – Lynch was interested in a range of things without being overbearing. The man Jacob knew was very different to the one others saw in the working world, and Loudham was a world away from the intensity of Autonomy and Lynch's other business commitments.

Aside from overseeing the transformation of Loudham Hall, one of Lynch's other new interests was farming; the estate had come with its own array of livestock which Lynch wanted to understand and to manage properly, and he was not afraid of mucking in. One night, when he came across a cow who was having a difficult birth, he turned to Google and helped to get the calf out himself, a strenuous and complex job.

But while it was a working estate, Loudham was also a home and a place to gather people together. Every summer, the Lynches held a spectacular party for friends, colleagues and neighbours from all walks of life –unusually egalitarian for Suffolk. The postman would rub shoulders with one of Lynch's banker friends or a Lord; it was a big, unsnobbish shindig for everyone in the community. At other times, groups of people would gather there for the weekend – often very clever and stimulating people. Lynch loved gathering top brains around him, even when he was supposed to be relaxing.

Sometimes, regardless of whether there was an official party going on or not, people who were passing by would drop in. On one particularly scorching August day, Matthew Porter, a friend of Lynch's from school, was driving home after a caravan holiday with his family in Norfolk, when he and his wife decided to stop in at Loudham on their way back.

After giving their surprise guests the grand tour, Lynch encouraged the children to get into Loudham's swimming pond to cool off. Porter's daughter was delighted, and happily swam across the pond. On her heels was young Hannah Lynch. Angela and Mike nudged each other's elbows in delight at this – Hannah had not taken to her swimming lessons, but here she was, happily splashing through the water.

Lynch laughed – 'Look how humans work!' – and grinned at his old school pal. Hannah wanted to follow the older girl across the pond, and so she did it. Lynch always said that you could overcome self-doubt and your own perceptions of your limits, and there was his daughter, proving it.

Outside of his role as a country gent, there were other things happening for Lynch away from Autonomy's ongoing troubles with the City. In June 2011, around the same time as Stouffer Egan was emailing him with concerns about how long he could last at the company, Lynch was drawn into an advisory role within the British government, in the hope that he could provide some support to Britain's tech sector – which was, as always, lamenting its inability to keep pace with Silicon Valley.

UK politicians have long wanted Britain to be more like America, with its capacity to seemingly spawn the next Google, Facebook or Apple at will. This desire has only surged as tech businesses have become increasingly lucrative, and successive UK governments have repeatedly looked for ways to grow the sector and create a home-grown Silicon Valley out of the country's rich scientific expertise. It never quite seems to happen. Britain works wonders at the early stages of innovation, but it rarely creates the megaliths that seem to spawn naturally in California.

Chasing the American dream, knock-offs of Silicon Valley are everywhere in Britain. Everything has been redubbed Silicon This, That or the Other, but nowhere seems to have really nailed it. Cambridge is of course Silicon Fen. Old Street in London's East End, which for a time vied with Elephant and Castle for the city's ugliest gyratory, was rebranded Silicon Roundabout in 2008. Conservative Prime Minister David Cameron called it the technology capital of Europe. In his party conference speech in 2010, he praised the digital sector: 'It will be the doers and the grafters, the inventors and the entrepreneurs who get our economy moving.' Cameron and his coalition government were once again banging the drum for UK tech. But they needed some drummers.

This is how Lynch was invited to become a Member of the Council for Science and Technology. He was one of the rare Brits who had hit the tech big-time, and he was delighted to be asked. Cameron noted his importance in a speech, claiming that companies such as Autonomy, ARM and Sage underpinned the UK's future growth. (Only one of those, Sage, remains listed in the UK.)

The job drew Lynch further into the establishment, giving him even more power, influence and connections. He was popular in government. Deeply patriotic, with a passion for Cambridge, Lynch was always willing to help and was generous with his time, whether it involved speaking at entrepreneurial events or meeting foreign dignitaries. He consistently delivered the message to anyone who would listen that the UK is a great place to build and grow a tech business and, with his brilliance at marketing and convincing even the most cynical people, he seemed to make the perfect poster child.

The vision he presented was very quickly to prove illusory. Within a matter of months, Autonomy would no longer be a British-owned.

THERE HAD BEEN long been gossip in the City that Autonomy might be sold.

Daud Khan had even mentioned it in the 2008 note that led to his furious row with Lynch, touting Oracle as a potential buyer at the time. It would make sense, financially and logistically speaking, he said, and would merely be the latest in a long line of illustrious British tech companies being sold to foreign corporations. In September 2010, the *Financial Times* called Autonomy 'the real prize in the UK technology sector'. IBM, Microsoft and Oracle were all named as potential buyers, although the *Daily Mail* said investors were 'running for the hills' over fears that Autonomy's organic growth may be slowing.

The trigger came on 6 October 2010, when Autonomy's share price fell 16 per cent following a surprise profit warning. Lynch said its customers were dithering over their spending decisions, and so Autonomy had shaved a sliver, just 3 per cent, off its annual sales forecast. Yet investors responded by cutting their holdings savagely, and the resultant fall wiped over £725 million off Autonomy's market value.

This noise had not gone unnoticed by one of the world's top tech dealmakers – who, as always, had his finger on the pulse. Frank Quattrone was watching the fracas keenly.

With his thick dark moustache, shock of curly hair and eye for a deal, Quattrone had a long-standing reputation for being *the* hotshot banker in the world of tech. Straddling the lucrative worlds of Wall Street and Silicon Valley, he was as charming as he was persuasive, dazzling everyone he met. Known as 'the prince of Silicon Valley' during the dotcom boom, his talent lay in spotting fast-growth tech businesses and introducing them to money; either through private sales or by launching them onto the public markets.

Quattrone had a Cinderella story. He came from a working-class immigrant family in Philadelphia, where his Italian father worked in clothes factories. They lived in the part of Philly where *Rocky* was set – a neighbourhood with a gritty, underdog edge. A scholarship student, bright and ambitious, Quattrone attended business school at Stanford, where he developed an obsession with the burgeoning tech industry and led the charge into the sector at several big investment banks, including Credit Suisse First Boston.

He masterminded flotation after flotation – Netscape, Cisco and Amazon were all notches on his bedpost. He had flair, once sending a donkey to a prospective client's office, with a note telling them to 'Use Credit Suisse First Boston', after the CEO mused that he was worried about looking like a donkey at IPO roadshows. It grabbed attention, and he won the client. Quattrone was, one early Facebook investor said, the Steve Jobs of tech banking.

But Quattrone's success came with some controversy. The US government investigated him over allegations that his best investment clients, dubbed 'friends of Frank', would improperly land shares in hot new IPOs. In 2004, he was tried and convicted of obstructing justice, just as his firm won the job of leading Google's float. Two years later, the Securities Exchange Commission (SEC) – in a rare and controversial move for the market regulator – overturned his lifetime ban from the industry. After that, he set up his own boutique firm, which he named Qatalyst.

Quattrone's industry connections flocked back to his fold after the legal issues ended. Between 2010 and 2011 he advised almost a dozen companies on deals, an astonishing number in such a short time, and his quoted clients saw stock market premiums of around 70 per cent when their companies were sold. *The New York Times* picked up on his momentum, writing: 'Sellers may want to make him [Quattrone] their first call. Buyers, on the other hand, should heed the approximate Latin: *Caveat Qatalyst*.' The Latin hybrid is a play on the proverb *caveat emptor*, which means 'buyer beware'. In other words, be careful when dealing with Quattrone's company.

Autonomy's lower share price meant that a bargain could be on the cards for someone, and Quattrone wanted to be a part of the action, if there was any action to be had. He had a sixth sense for these things.

Quattrone emailed Lynch, saying he believed some big players would now come crawling out of the woodwork. Many of them had been waiting for just this moment and Quattrone threw his hat in the ring, offering to help Autonomy think through and prepare for such an approach. He believed that a buyer might be prepared to pay 70 per cent more than the market value of Autonomy. Lynch was sitting on a goldmine.

Lynch replied to the opportunistic tech banker with one of his classic analogies: selling Autonomy for such a sum, even one 70 per cent higher than his company's value, would be like a Native

American chief agreeing to sell Dakota in exchange for three rifles and some firewater. In other words, someone making a disastrously unequal deal – giving up something of great value for a small, short-term or degrading pay-off. The UK does not have the same 'poison pill' protection against takeovers that US businesses do, so any offer would mean an easy win for a buyer and an immediate surrender from Autonomy's shareholders, who would not allow the deal to be stopped.

A 'poison pill' is a tactic some US companies use to stop another company from acquiring them. It's like a built-in defence system that kicks in when someone tries to buy too much of the company too quickly, making the takeover so costly or messy that the would-be buyer might back off. One common version works by giving existing shareholders the right to buy more shares at a discount. This floods the market with extra shares, making it more expensive and difficult for the buyer to take control.

Because that's impossible to do in the UK, Lynch would be at the mercy of his shareholders should any buyer come in with an offer – so he was telling Quattrone in no uncertain terms that he would do everything he could to raise the bar of 'acceptable'. To do better than firewater.

But was Autonomy even being primed for sale at this point? Did Lynch intend to sell his company? While it feels like semantics, it is a question which would be debated again and again in years to come.

Lynch was certainly tired and fed up with dealing with the pressure from critics in the City. Yet he always argued that partnering with Quattrone was just about being prepared in case a big player came knocking; Autonomy wanted others to bid and push the price up. It was about contact building and profile boosting, a subtle difference from selling.

The view was different in the world of finance; instead of Quattrone's involvement bringing Autonomy more attention and notoriety, it was interpreted as a clear signal that Autonomy had just posted a massive 'for sale' sign outside.

In any event, as Quattrone and Lynch discussed the situation still further, Qatalyst organized a series of introductory meetings between Lynch and major US companies. One of those was with Oracle, and in an April 2011 meeting with co-president Mark Hurd, the former HP CEO, Lynch walked straight into the lion's jaws. Whatever happened behind closed doors remained private until a few months later, when Lynch rubbished Oracle to the *Wall Street Journal* and denied that Autonomy had been 'shopped' to the US giant.

Ellison begged to differ, telling the same publication:

> *Either Mr. Lynch has a very poor memory or he's lying. 'Some bank' did not just happen to come to Oracle with Autonomy 'on a list.' The truth is that Mr. Lynch came to Oracle, along with his investment banker, Frank Quattrone, and met with Oracle's head of M&A, Douglas Kehring and Oracle President Mark Hurd at 11 am on April 1, 2011. The Lynch shopping visit to Oracle is easy to verify. We still have his PowerPoint slides.*

Ellison said Autonomy's price was simply too high. Lynch hit back, and said the get-together was a meeting about 'database technologies'. This response only fanned the flames: 'Another whopper from Autonomy CEO Mike Lynch', Oracle retorted in a press release. Ellison then left Lynch with a very public and a very embarrassing legacy of the meeting:

> *We have put Mike Lynch's PowerPoint slide sales-pitch up on the Oracle website – Oracle.com/PleaseBuyAutonomy – with the hope Mike Lynch will recognize his slides, his memory will be restored, and he will recall what he and Frank Quattrone discussed during their visit to Oracle last April.*

Autonomy carried on denying a sales process was underway and Quattrone took the rap, issuing a mea culpa, saying he had sent out the slides independently, pitching Autonomy as an idea to Oracle.

It was a PR dog's dinner.

Not everyone was as put off by the idea of buying Autonomy as Ellison, though. Some were undeterred by its market valuation and were interested in seeing Quattrone's slides. One such person was Leo Apotheker, still new in the HP job and looking around for targets to spruce up the ailing tech giant. It was a meeting he would live to regret.

NINETEEN

Due Diligence . . . ?

This is a highly sophisticated US corporation that employs hundreds of people to do this due diligence . . . What value would a CEO add to that? You have to trust your people.

– Leo Apotheker, in evidence given to the UK civil trial, 2 April 2019

Running HP was never going to be the easiest job, and Leo Apotheker did not have the easiest start. It was an astonishingly political organization. It was also very leaky.

Only six months after becoming HP's boss, Apotheker sent out a sensitive memo to the company's leaders, setting out that thc third quarter would be 'tough'. Two weeks later, the memo reappeared, verbatim, in a Bloomberg news report. The leak forced HP to bring forward its earnings report to officially reveal the company's lower internal sales projections, except that the whole world knew about them already. It looked amateur.

The sooner something could be done that would shake up the company, the better, Apotheker thought. His first target was TIBCO, a US software group founded in 1997 and HP's neighbour in Palo Alto. HP offered $34 a share, but executives could not agree terms and the offer was rebuffed in March 2011. Apotheker continued his hunt to see what else was out there, alighting on several businesses, including Autonomy.

Quattrone, the inveterate matchmaker, had the same idea.

He got in touch with HP about Autonomy at the start of 2011, sending over some slides with lots of detail about the British business. The two executive boards agreed to meet. Whether Lynch liked it or not, Autonomy was in play as an acquisition target, and it was his job as CEO to try to make sure that it was acquired for as much money as possible, by the most appropriate buyer. HP sounded like a good prospect.

What Apotheker and HP found so attractive about Autonomy was its core product, IDOL. The idea was that integrating the Cambridge company's clever software into HP's ubiquitous hardware, with its massive brand recognition, would result in nothing short of dynamite. Autonomy would become a software world leader, with a golden product and access to every boardroom in the world through HP.

On 4 March 2011, Hussain and Quattrone went along to HP's Palo Alto headquarters, while Lynch was beamed in via video link. Things went well. They went so well, in fact, that just a month later, Lynch and Apotheker met in person for the first time. They liked each other, and a few other get-togethers followed. Apotheker thought Lynch was knowledgeable and enthusiastic, and HP did not have the type of product which Autonomy sold. The relationship between the two men rather made sense. They were two European software bosses, a no-nonsense German and a self-made Brit, both existing in the believe-your-own-bullshit world of Silicon Valley. Many later speculated that, had Apotheker stayed the course at HP, the Autonomy and HP merger might have worked perfectly.

There was a charm offensive going on. To make the deal happen,

HP leaders knew they needed Lynch's buy-in. He was absolutely in control and it was his baby, and he still owned 8.5 per cent of the stock. On a beautiful summer's day in June 2011, Lynch met Shane Robison, HP's fifty-seven-year-old chief technology officer, at Hartwell House, a luxury country hotel in Buckinghamshire about forty miles north-west of London. In this peaceful and private setting, the two men roamed over their companies' strategies and started to explore the what-ifs of working together – an HP and Autonomy collaboration. Robison told Lynch not to think about HP's future, but to think about a future using HP's resources.

Lynch really liked him, and was taken in by Robison's vision. He was Lynch's kind of man. He was an engineer through and through, with a long and distinguished tech career which started in developing flight simulators for the military, later researching artificial intelligence, before moving to Apple when colour was introduced to the desktop computer. He had been around the technology block. At this point, he was a decade into his life at HP, having joined around the time of its Compaq deal in 2001, when Carly Fiorina was its CEO.

The flirting continued. A month later in Deauville, France – the picturesque Normandy seaside resort where Apotheker holidayed – Lynch met the HP team again. Here, he felt the odds of a deal happening started to shift. It seemed more than probable, rather than only possible, that HP would make an offer for Autonomy. But Lynch put the chance at 10 per cent.

They discussed a more serious relationship, what Lynch's role in any new company might be, the reasons for merging and the logistics of how Autonomy would be integrated into HP. In future years, Lynch always maintained that it was never his intention to sell Autonomy. At the time of HP's approach, he had already sold down a lot of his shares and was a very wealthy man. However, the HP offer did provide him with what is known as an 'exit': a way of taking money off the table after years of hard work.

And not just any exit. The proposed deal would leave all the key players wealthy and the company healthy, with a seemingly bright future under the umbrella of a big brand. In return, Autonomy and its artificial intelligence model would, Apotheker hoped, help HP move with the times. So, these were not bog-standard company meetings, Lynch felt, but 'changing-the-world' conversations.

It was not all champagne and roses, though. Lynch had a few concerns. He thought that Bill Veghte, HP's head of software, was a classic suit: a large-corporate shill, an intensely political, no-vision, no-insight creature, who might get in the way of what Autonomy was trying to do. There was also a fear that Robison, the clever chief technology officer, might leave, which could scupper a successful merger, because Lynch felt he really 'got it'.

As these meetings went on, affairs within HP started to move quite quickly. The company's financial advisors stirred up the sense of increasing urgency – Perella Weinberg Partners called buying Autonomy a 'critical offensive move', while Barclays Capital said that HP should move rapidly to formalize an offer and try to avoid a leak. The project was given a code name: Tesla. HP became 'Hawk' and Autonomy (its prey) became 'Atlantis', the mythical island.

There was wild optimism about the numbers and the future potential of Autonomy. One spreadsheet had a tab called 'waterfall', which suggested Autonomy had a standalone value of $10 billion, which rose to $27.8 billion if you included the expected benefits of merging. It was prosaically called the 'aggressive synergy case'. There was less interest in Autonomy's actual numbers – Apotheker, while he had read the 2010 annual report, had not read Autonomy's more up-to-date quarterly financial reports.

Apotheker pleaded to his board for their backing in emotive terms, telling them that Autonomy could have sales of $6 billion by 2014. 'This company [HP] is a burning platform,' he told them desperately. 'I cannot do this alone. I need your support. We're going to have to hold hands and go through this together.'

On 20 July 2011, after a meeting which dragged on from 8 a.m. to 7 p.m., the Hewlett-Packard board gave Leo Apotheker a budget of $11.7 billion and authorized him to press on.

With the board's approval in his pocket, Apotheker merrily sallied forth, sword in hand, to capture his prize. Yet, glancing back, he saw that many of his troops had already abandoned him. HP executives had started to get cold feet.

Among the first of his senior commanders to turn their back was Cathy Lesjak, HP's chief financial officer, who had run the business as interim chief executive before Apotheker stepped in. The pair grew to hate each other. Their relationship was, Lesjak said, 'a little war', while Apotheker described it as 'poisonous'. The CFO disapproved of the timing of the Autonomy deal, disliked the price and said it was not in the interests of the company. Apotheker wanted her out; he did not believe she was producing accurate financial forecasts. Lesjak openly stabbed Apotheker in the back at a board meeting on 16 August 2011 when, without warning him, she spoke out against the Autonomy deal.

Doubling down on the attack, she tapped away furiously on her phone while the meeting was still going on, and fired out some snide emails about Apotheker to Ray Lane, the chairman, who was sitting in the same room. She complained about Apotheker's lack of interest in financial details and a dearth of financial discipline about the deal. 'They're saying Leo is a dead man walking,' she told Lane, plunging in the knife still further.

AUTONOMY'S SHARE PRICE had fallen as the market took a tumble, but Lynch was always a ferocious negotiator regardless. The deal, which initially had HP offering up to 56 per cent more than Autonomy's market value, had become even more expensive as Autonomy's stock had declined. HP's advisors suggested that Apotheker try to renegotiate a lower price. However, they anticipated that Lynch would react poorly to any attempt to reduce the offer, so they tiptoed around the issue. A condition of the deal was Lynch's support. HP did not want to pursue a hostile takeover. Throughout the process, they were trying to keep him onside – the founder CEO who retained an unusual level of control for a FTSE 100 company that was still run more like a startup.

After some toing and froing over the cost – Lynch wanted £27 per share, HP offered £25 – they met in the middle. The meetings culminated on 14 August, when a deal was agreed at the last possible moment: £25.50 a share, representing an eyewatering 64 per cent premium for Autonomy's shareholders. Altogether, it meant HP would pay $11.7 billion for Autonomy, or £6.7 billion.

HP had added 'the Lynch premium', a close friend remarked, something Lynch had always managed to command since the start of his business career. The price was eleven times Autonomy's stated sales numbers for 2010, which were almost $1 billion. HP already had a $3 billion software business by sales, a small percentage of its overall $130 billion revenues, but this was a step towards making it bigger.

HP's valuation left Lynch with no choice but to sell up, even if he didn't want to. But by now he had bought into the HP vision. Apotheker and Robison told him that they liked Autonomy's culture. HP was going to create a new division which wrapped together their four or five other software businesses, including Autonomy, with the admin side of things (such as finance) still handled by HP. Lynch was to be put in charge of the whole thing, they told him. Even if it all sounded too good to be true, it was still a risk worth taking.

Once a deal was agreed, the conditions around the sale from Autonomy's side were unusually watertight. Lynch told his bankers and lawyers to make sure it got over the line – that there was absolute deal certainty.

When one company buys another, a due diligence process is typically undertaken by the acquiring firm. It should represent a rigorous look inside an organization, examining the business and the finances to give confidence and reassurance to the buyer that everything is as it seems. And when the price involved is $11 billion, a high level of due diligence is expected – a long, thorough, exploratory process.

And so, one of the most curious and most frequently raised questions about the whole acquisition – given that it would come to define much of the remainder of Lynch's life – was why HP took just eighteen days to look inside Autonomy. HP's review of Autonomy was more akin to squeezing fruit at a market stall than a full-on dissection. It was described as 'confirmatory' – simply double checking that everything was as HP thought it was.

One reason was the fear that someone else might jump into the fray. When a UK public company is going through a takeover, British rules require equal access of information to all bona fide bidders or potential bidders. Buyers are aware of this, especially of the dangers of feeding sensitive information to any other circling sharks. Internal HP memos cautioned everyone to take care with due diligence, in case it gave a potential rival bidder an advantage. The rules can drive the price up and make the acquisition take longer, which everyone wanted to avoid. The two sides agreed to keep communication and information sharing as verbal as possible, which would limit what was put out publicly. Strictly, this should not work – other parties would have to be given the same information even if it was provided verbally, but only if they asked for it specifically. They couldn't just say, 'Tell me what you told the others.'

It was felt that speed was of the essence. The checking process was done under the suspicion that another buyer was lurking somewhere in the shadows, ready to swoop in and steal Autonomy from under HP's nose. This flicker in the shadows – this phantom rival – might be IBM or Oracle, Apotheker worried. It created a sense of urgency. Of course, Ellison later made it clear what Oracle thought.

The plan was to announce the deal with HP's third quarter results report on Thursday 18 August, and that was the deadline both parties stuck to. At the last minute, Ray Lane and the HP board got cold feet.

The day before, Lane rumbled that they wanted to delay the acquisition by a few months, terrified about how the announcement was going to be received. But Apotheker was adamant that a delay might cost them the opportunity – that someone else might win. Yet, as we know, Oracle had ruled itself out by this stage – and would later mock Lynch very publicly for his approach to marketing Autonomy (the 'another whopper from Mike Lynch' statement). There was no one else coming to the table.

Apotheker was in a race against himself.

IN JULY, ANDREW Gersh, a US partner at one of the world's top accountancy firms, KPMG, was approached to run the rule over Autonomy's books. Gersh's task was to understand if the fit was right between the two businesses. An HP presentation described KPMG's role as 'validating synergies, understanding key product capabilities and retaining key executives.'

To try to make sure nothing would knock the deal off course, the two businesses signed an agreement that Autonomy wouldn't attempt to tempt anyone else to make an offer while HP was undertaking its due diligence. HP set a timetable for the review process, which began on 1 August and ran until the announcement date, 18 August. Bankers present at the time recall the process as a period of going through the motions. The CEOs on both sides wanted the deal done, so inevitably it would be done.

Lynch was astonished. He had never seen a deal done at this speed. It was certainly a very short period to review the company's books, contracts, technology and structure, especially as a chunk of that time included questions being asked of the Autonomy team that they then had to go away and ferret out the answers to. The only justification is that, as a public company, there was already a lot of audited information out there about Autonomy, signed off by Deloitte.

But there were plenty of warning signs that things within

Autonomy were not all as they seemed. There was the noisy chatter among the London analysts about its numbers, the murmurs from the tech analysts about its software. On top of that, during the due diligence period, Autonomy was actively buying hardware from HP, and Gersh knew that Autonomy was itself selling hardware too. But he simply assumed that the transactions between the two companies represented a component of software sales, that the HP products were part of appliances bundled up with software. The auditor did not ask exactly how much hardware Autonomy sold.

There was a phone call between a weary KPMG team in the US and Autonomy's auditors in Cambridge, Deloitte, where the two teams went over some of the numbers. Nigel Mercer from Deloitte brought up the Brent Hogenson event from a year earlier, but the episode did not raise alarm bells.

KPMG notes in its records that Autonomy followed the accounting standard known as IFRS, which is different from the US accounting standard, known as GAAP. It underlined that Autonomy recognized revenue for licence sales upon sell-in to its resellers (IFRS), rather than on a sale to the end customer (GAAP). While it sounds like a mundane technicality, this would later become a flashpoint of multiple civil and criminal trials.

There were other things too. Autonomy offered unusually long payment terms to its customers – sometimes over a year – something that did not meet HP's revenue recognition rules, which required payment within 90 days. KPMG also questioned how Autonomy recorded revenue for parts of contracts that hadn't yet been delivered, like training or services, noting the complexity of such packages. However, KPMG concluded that the impact of these differences would likely be short-term, since Autonomy would soon be following HP's accounting policies.

KPMG also highlighted that Autonomy was counting revenue from acquired companies as part of its own 'organic' growth. This had concerned several financial analysts, because it hid the fact that Autonomy's overall business – and especially its core product, IDOL – was seeing slowing growth. KPMG warned that Autonomy might have to keep acquiring other businesses just to keep its growth rate up. On a more positive note, it said recent acquisitions, like Iron Mountain, would help boost growth through the rest of 2011 and into 2012.

In Gersh's defence, the documents that KPMG produced for HP were heavily caveated:

> *The data and access provided to us during due diligence was very limited, but was comparable with other acquisitions involving large U.K. publicly traded companies.*

But the due diligence report was never properly finished. KPMG was supposed to investigate Autonomy's historical revenues, gross margins and operating margins. This did not happen.

HP leaders did not pay much attention anyway. Apotheker did not read the draft report and did not know that a full one was never completed. HP had a well-oiled machine for acquisitions; he later claimed that if someone had thought there was something he should read, they would have told him. You must trust your people, he said. His CFO, Lesjak, did not read the report either.

The affair has echoes of a story Lynch used to tell about a neglected pot plant in Autonomy's San Francisco office. People would walk past the sad, wilting sapling each day, presuming it was someone else's job to deal with it. Everyone, Lynch would say, needs to take responsibility for every aspect of the company – even those aspects that appear not to be part of any individual remit. It seemed as if, at HP, people were walking past the pot plant. Apotheker later told *The Telegraph*:

> *It took HP more than a year to figure out that something was potentially wrong. If it takes the owner of a business more than a year to*

figure it out, how could we have figured it out in three or four weeks of due diligence? It's impossible.

The final report to the board showed a series of green lights, claiming that KPMG had been engaged to conduct accounting due diligence, and that no material issues had been found. HP also did a limited amount of technical due diligence, all of which emerged satisfactory.

Everything was in place for the bombshell news to hit.

TWENTY

Big News

I am particularly pleased that Dr Mike Lynch, who heads a team of brilliant scientists and employees, will continue to lead Autonomy. I look forward to our collaboration as we focus on creating maximum value for the combined company, its customers and employees.

– Leo Apotheker, 18 August 2011

Autonomy's London offices were always based in Mayfair, a part of London known for hedge funds, where chauffeur-driven cars loiter by the edges of the pavements, dropping their passengers off at private members' clubs. These stuffy surroundings were a weird location for a tech company, which in those days were flooding to hipster East London and the aforementioned Silicon Roundabout. But it was an unmistakably Lynch location: solid, traditional, steeped in history.

In 2010, Autonomy moved around the corner from Piccadilly, the home of the Ritz, to the grand St James's Square, with its central garden featuring a statue of William of Orange mounted on a horse.

The Georgian square plays home to private members' clubs of the most traditional kind. Nearby, the RAC Club on Pall Mall boasts a rotating display of stunning classic cars and an extraordinary swimming pool, unique to overcrowded central London. Close by is the Institute of Directors, and around the corner is Jermyn Street, lined with gentlemen's outfitters, windows displaying bow ties, hats, smoking jackets and silk dressing gowns. Here too sits Wilton's, where it has been since 1742 – one of the few restaurants that Lynch liked to go to.

Numbers 21 and 22 St James's Square, where Autonomy was based, were two houses joined together, where the late Queen Mother lived until 1920. In homage, a portrait of her sat in one of the rooms. It was a rabbit warren decorated like a stately home, with dark wood panelling and furniture, big portraits, thick piled carpets and a long, polished lacquer dining table. It looked impressive, but there were flaws beneath the surface. The plug sockets in the heavy ornate spaces were a bit lacking, which made it tricky as a functional workspace.

At the front, there was a large, plush room with a curved front window giving onto the square, where the triumvirate – Lynch, Hussain and Kanter – had their office. Lynch's desk, the largest, naturally, was in front of the window; Hussain's and Kanter's were to either side. Behind their backs, their colleagues dubbed the room the Oval Office. It was also a cut-through, a quick route around the building.

The first indication most people had that something at Autonomy was about to change was when padlocks appeared on the Oval Office doors, with no information about why or what was going on. Suddenly it was a no-go zone. Back in Cambridge, staff suspicions were raised when a company came in to clean the carpets. Something was definitely afoot.

On Thursday, 18 August 2011, a hot summer's day in London, it became clear why – the office became the war room for the announcement of the company's sale to Hewlett-Packard.

Lynch had called a team at Brunswick, the PR advisory firm,

and asked them in for an immediate meeting. They raced around the corner to see him. Another company called Financial Dynamics had long held Autonomy's public relations contract, but now Lynch wanted extra firepower. 'Big news,' he told them. 'We're selling the company – you're hired and this is your first day.'

It was the day of HP's results. The deal was being announced immediately, chaotically and at hyper-speed. It was late in London, as the Brits waited for the close of the US markets so the announcement could be made. It all felt a bit like an election-night party, with the accompanying feeling of uncertainty about the outcome, as everyone on the London end of the sale gathered together. Unusually, Angela joined Lynch, his Inner Circle and the various PR teams in the office. They were tense and nervous, waiting for the phone call that would formally announce that the deal was approved.

The odds did not look good. On the sidelines, the bankers, lawyers and company directors involved in the deal started an unofficial sweepstake on the odds of it going through. Not a single one of them would even bet a pound that it unequivocally would. One director gave Lynch a one in ten chance of staying through the acquisition, and reasoned that it would only happen if he was named the chief executive of HP. There was no way that Lynch would report into anyone.

Another reason for their anxiety was because, while it was sunny outside, it was a thoroughly miserable day on the financial markets. More than £62 billion had been wiped off the value of shares in London that morning as traders worried that the world was sliding into a dark recession. The Eurozone debt crisis had taken hold as poorer countries could not pay their bills; it was so bad that there was even talk that the European Union could collapse. Standing around the Bloomberg terminal with Angela and Shane Robison, Lynch stared at a sea of red arrows pointing firmly downwards.

They were all wired, the adrenaline was pumping. There were billions of pounds on the line. Lynch paced around and around like a lion in a cage. He stepped outside into the garden at the heart of St James's Square and continued marching, wringing his hands, looking strangely vulnerable. It was a massive, massive story and a massive, massive moment. A British tech company on the cusp of being sold to a Silicon Valley legend for an unfathomable sum of money.

The secret, though, was already out. Before the official announcement. Someone had leaked it to Bloomberg, and the financial news giant, with its reputation for absolute accuracy, published a story at 5.35 p.m. The whole thing was played out in the press in real time. Lynch was furious. It was the worst thing that could have happened, because it meant they were now all on the back foot. He had wanted to be able to shape the news, control the message and explain on his terms, to his stakeholders, why the deal was a good idea. It was a sign he would no longer be in charge. A sign of the doom to come.

Finally, the sound they had all been waiting for. The phone rang. It was Ray Lane, HP's chairman. He exchanged some perfunctory words with Lynch. The board had unanimously approved the deal.

It held a conference call for investors at 10 p.m. to go through the news. One watching fund manager shorted HP's shares instantaneously. It was just the wrong buyer for Autonomy, he felt. Lynch asked Kanter if HP could still back out of the deal. No chance, came the reply.

LYNCH, WHO WAS wealthy before, was now unimaginably rich. He made £500 million from the sale of Autonomy, in cash. He was covered in glory and had proved those who doubted him wrong. One of the world's most venerable technology companies had chosen his business and wanted him to stay as part of it. It was a stunning comeback from the swirling suspicions about him and Autonomy.

There would be a reputational boon for everyone involved, Lynch said, to be associated with such a prestigious deal. Plus, he now had yet another new title. He was to be known as Dr Michael R. Lynch,

Executive Vice-President of Information Management at HP. He would be one of the company's top fifteen executives.

Others did very well too. Sushovan Hussain earnt £6 million. Phil Pearson at GLG Consulting, who was long on the stock and was one of its largest investors and traders, made about £20 million for his fund.

When the gathering was all over, the set-piece done, the news released, Lynch stooped over his briefcase and packed up his laptop, ready to go home. Ian Black asked him how he felt. He turned around, looked Black straight in the eye and said: 'I am never going to have to close another quarter.' Black had never seen such a sense of relief from his boss. For Lynch, quarters were the bane of the corporate world and he could not wait to be rid of that constant weight on his shoulders and on the business. He would no longer be in thrall to the whims of the City.

The sale was one in the eye for many in the Square Mile. The punch Lynch had always wanted to deliver. He laughed to everyone in the Oval Office about the number of short-sellers carried out on their backs, as he put it, by the sale – the people who had lost huge sums of money, anticipating his share price would fall. These included Tim Steer, the sceptical letter-writer, whose fund had just lost £30 million. Those twits in suits would not be able to mock him any more.

There was quite a bit of press to be done following the announcement. British newspapers wanted to spin it as yet another UK company being sold to the US. Only a year before, Kraft had bought Cadbury and shut some British factories. It was a sore point. Lynch, still wary of his role within the British government, did a lot of work to convince them he wasn't selling out of Cambridge. He emphasised that a lot of the cash would go into starting new British tech ventures. He was not the kind who was going to kick back on an island and do nothing for the rest of his days.

Lynch talked a good game about the future of Autonomy, about how it was going to become an independent division within HP. It would get to sell through their channels, get access to an enormous workforce and a huge enterprise customer base. It's going to put rocket boosters on Autonomy, he said.

Lynch, who saw his competitors as Oracle, Google, Microsoft and IBM, had always felt that it was really difficult to be a fish in that pond. He wanted the best of both worlds, which meant being both technologically independent and simultaneously part of a massive company with its resources, channels and money. And the HP deal offered him that. He had suddenly gone from fighting a war with a gun to owning a fighter jet. Autonomy now had the chance to influence the direction of one of the global technology companies, he told *The Sunday Times*, and called it a good day for UK technology.

In the event, 87 per cent of Autonomy shareholders agreed to the sale, and the process was set in motion. It is difficult to reverse a UK takeover; effectively only regulatory competition concerns or a rejection by shareholders can really change the course, neither of which was likely in this case. Once a takeover is announced, companies are marching to the beat of a drum.

Privately, Lynch was a bit apprehensive about what might happen under the new regime. But by then he had 'one billion reasons not to fret', one of his friends said, jokingly referring to his flush bank account.

The mood on either side of the Atlantic could not have been more different. While there was joy at Autonomy in Britain, there was despair at HP in the US: 18 August 2011 would forever be known as 8/18 within the company, a date laden with doom and emotion, etched into the corporate memory. The reaction to the announcement was even worse than HP's board had expected. While Autonomy's share price had taken off like a rocket, HP's had fallen sharply, down by 20 per cent in just one day. Generally, people were gobsmacked by the astonishingly high price it had paid for the British company.

It was not just because of Autonomy that HP's share price fell. The company had made a host of other major announcements at the same time, the totality of which shook up investors. One surprise might have been manageable, two perhaps careless – but the barrage was a full-on ambush.

First, HP had failed to hit its expected numbers. Second, it announced that it was considering spinning off the backbone of the company, its lucrative and world-beating personal computing business. Third, it announced that it was ceasing production of the brand-new computer tablets that it had launched just a few months prior. And then there was Autonomy.

Moody's downgraded HP's outlook from 'stable' to 'negative'.

The decision over HP's computing division in particular caused a minor uproar, catching the market unawares and making everyone nervous about what was happening to this important component of the company, which had generated over $40 billion in sales the previous year. It was what HP was known for! A large and vocal section of HP shareholders disapproved. It was a decision that would be reversed just a few months later.

Shareholders also lobbied HP's chairman, Ray Lane, and other senior directors to see whether it could get out of the Autonomy bid before it closed. Lane's nervousness about it turned to fright. HP's top brass had promised Apotheker they would hold their nerve, regardless of how the news was received by the market. They did nothing of the sort. Apotheker, though, remained completely convinced about the validity of his approach. He emailed Lynch, who used nautical analogies in response, encouraging him to weather the storm.

On Sunday, 4 September 2011, Lane emailed Apotheker, trying to backtrack, claiming to be 'haunted by Autonomy itself'. He asked Apotheker if there was a way to wriggle out of it.

I don't think it's the panacea we think it is. I read the analysis of their organic growth and I still see them as a

roll-up. I don't think the board thought (at least I don't remember that discussion) this was largely a roll-up when we contemplated the price.

Analyze for the board . . . whether there is any way to get out of the Autonomy deal.

Lane had clearly already started thinking about the future, about salvaging the most he could from the disastrous acquisition. He also asked Apotheker to work out what size of buyback HP could launch to try to recreate lost value for shareholders. Apotheker quickly shot back that he was 99 per cent sure the deal was irreversible. 'If Autonomy and more software isn't the solution,' he said to Lane, 'what is the alternative?'

A SUPERSTITIOUS PERSON might say that the chief executive job at HP was jinxed. As September rolled on, leaks had not only continued, but intensified. On 22 September 2011, Apotheker's phone rang. It was a journalist from Bloomberg, asking him if he'd lost his job. It turned out he had. He was summarily booted out of the company before the Autonomy deal was even completed, and certainly before he saw any of the longed-for collaboration that he had vaunted. In total, he had been in the HP job for less than eleven months.

While this was happening, Lynch was sitting outside the boardroom in the US, having flown out to see his new bosses. Browsing the web on his phone, he had seen the news about Apotheker on Bloomberg. Lane sent Lynch packing with a plan to convene at a later date. It was not the welcome to the new business Lynch had expected. Lynch described it as 'a very peculiar day'. Just like the announcement of the Autonomy acquisition, the HP saga was all over the press before even insiders knew what was going on.

This interaction effectively signalled the end of HP's relationship with Autonomy before it even began. Without Apotheker – the man who had so badly wanted the deal to be done – at the helm, who would take the lead on the deal? Autonomy had been acquired based on a new strategy for HP, and it looked like that new 'plan' was being thrown out of the window. It was sudden, and unexpected, and it made Lynch feel uneasy.

As it turned out, the HP board already had someone else in mind to lead the business and needed Apotheker out of the way. He had played his politics and lost and was being replaced by someone with a different approach.

TWENTY-ONE

Getting Megged

The fun is over and it's time for Autonomy to grow up.

– Meg Whitman

'No, no, no, no!'

This was Meg Whitman's first reaction to being offered the job as CEO of Hewlett-Packard.

She was inside the HP boardroom with her fellow board members, and the company was in crisis mode. It had lost faith in Apotheker and was keen to replace him as quickly as possible, so it hastily turned to one of its own members. Whitman had been on the board since January of that year, and her colleagues told her she was the woman for the role.

She was far from convinced. Life had been full-on for a long time at that stage. Whitman had spent the previous ten years first running eBay and then running unsuccessfully for Governor of California. A troubled company was not what she needed.

But the HP board was pretty persuasive. It included Marc Andreesen, the legendary Silicon Valley entrepreneur and investor best known for co-creating the first widely used web browser, Netscape, and the influential venture-capital firm Andreessen Horowitz. He was also the author of the previously mentioned piece lauding the future of software, which he published just two days after the Autonomy acquisition. Then there were some of the most influential women in tech: Ann Livermore and Pat Russo. And of course there was Ray Lane, the chairman.

Apotheker had to go after the chaotic series of announcements in August. They flattered Whitman that she was the perfect person to take on the embattled business, praising her stellar reputation, experience running large businesses and deep understanding of consumer technology. With a bit of cajoling, eventually, she agreed.

HP's reluctant new CEO, then aged fifty-five, was one of America's wealthiest women – reportedly worth almost $4 billion – with an extraordinary pedigree in Silicon Valley.

She had started at eBay in 1998, when it was a tiny auction site doing $4 million worth of yearly sales and employing just thirty people. Whitman led it through its IPO, its successful acquisition of PayPal and its less successful acquisition of Skype. By the time she resigned in 2008, the company employed over 15,000 staff and boasted annual revenues of $8 billion. Growth was slowing, the $3.4 billion purchase of Skype was written down by $900 million. It felt like time for a change.

With a fair complexion, blue eyes and shoulder-length blonde hair, the six-foot-zero Whitman has a commanding presence. She is the kind of capable person who just has to get stuff done. She was most recently the US Ambassador to Kenya, until immediately resigning following the re-election of Donald Trump in 2024.

Whitman grew up in Cold Spring Harbor, upstate New York – an exclusive East Coast enclave which includes an estate that inspired *The Great Gatsby*, the iconic story of glamour, ambition and the darker side of wealth. Her parents both came from families known as Boston Brahmins, an old-fashioned term for the Bostonian elite, lifted from the name of India's traditional ruling caste. It means old money, and not a lot of flash.

Hendricks Hallett Whitman was a financier, while his wife Margaret C. Whitman stayed at home. This belied her adventurous spirit – Meg Whitman always spoke about her mother as her inspiration. Margaret had joined the war effort during the Second World War, getting on a troop ship from Boston to the South Pacific, and learning in Papua New Guinea how to be both an aircraft and car mechanic. Whitman's mother told her three children that they could do anything they put their minds to. That mantra stuck.

Whitman was a bright, academic young person who had originally wanted to be a doctor. She went to business school only after her father advised her that it might make it easier for her to be taken seriously as a woman, going to Harvard for an MBA. When she graduated in 1977, only 10 per cent of her class were women.

Whitman's first job was at the consumer goods giant Procter & Gamble, where her first intriguing assignment was working out how big the hole in the shampoo bottle cap should be. She then moved to Bain, the management consultancy, where she worked with Mitt Romney, then to Disney and onwards to Hasbro, where she brought *Teletubbies* – the British programme beloved by babies and toddlers – to the US with huge success.

Life was not all business. She married Dr Griffith Rutherford Harsh IV, a neurosurgeon, and the couple had two sons. And after eBay, Whitman had entered politics. Her unsuccessful bid to become Governor of California drained some of her significant wealth, though not enough to cause her real concern. She may appear a cool, collected type but she had a fiery temper which had flared up along the way. In 2007, while being prepped for an interview with Reuters, Whitman swore and shoved a young communications advisor (with whom she later settled) aside.

On 22 September 2011, Whitman's appointment as HP CEO was officially announced. It was no major surprise – it had already leaked to the press along with Apotheker's unceremonious sacking. Her name received a muted reception; she may have been more of a celebrity than her predecessor, but she was seen as an odd choice. Whitman had not worked in an enterprise tech company before, and she certainly was not a software guru.

Moreover, the constant leaking and the revolving door of CEOs at HP bore all the characteristics of a corporate farce. HP was becoming a laughing stock. Was HP's board the worst in its long history? one news agency asked. Even with all her gumption and fighting spirit, the scale of the challenge Whitman faced was breathtaking.

ON HER FIRST day in the job, Whitman called everyone at HP together to address them. Staff told her confidently: 'We're live blogging you!' Sighing, she retorted: 'You all have taken leaking to a new art form.'

One of the first things Whitman did was push out Shane Robison, the chief technology officer, the man who had introduced Lynch and Apotheker. Robison turned up to her house to let her know he that he was going on holiday – he was off on an African safari for three weeks. She was surprised and asked if he really had to leave right then, suggesting that he might hold off and delay his trip, or return a little sooner. The Autonomy announcement had been a pretty rough road, she said, and she needed him. Robison would not change his mind. He was taking his trip. The challenges at HP were so great, Whitman decided, that she needed people who would step up to the plate, and she fired him. The man Lynch had so admired was gone.

In her first interview upon taking the job, Whitman said her appointment did not signal a change of strategy and that she would continue along Apotheker's path. 'We are behind the actions that were taken on 18 August. We are firmly committed to Autonomy,' she said. In private, HP had explored whether it could reverse the acquisition but, under UK takeover rules, that was not going to happen.

On 4 October 2011, the deal was finalized. Whitman was stuck with Autonomy, like an 'unwanted stepchild', as Lynch later put it.

Just a day later, one of Wall Street's most prominent activist investors quipped that investing in HP would bring him too much 'brain damage'. The main concern was with the biggest strategic decision the company had yet to make – what it was going to do about its wildly successful personal computing division, which Apotheker had announced he might spin off. It was a big, complicated mess.

And it was into this big, complicated mess that Autonomy was brought.

With Apotheker and Robison gone, there was no one left at HP who had conceived the new software strategy, with Autonomy at its heart. It was not an easy beginning to the marriage. Whitman set the tone for their future together early on. 'The fun is over and it's time for Autonomy to grow up,' she told the team. Autonomy executives characterized their interactions with her – including their unwitting acquiescence to her very charming and persuasive demeanour – as 'getting Megged'.

HP was like a cruise ship trying to dock with a speedboat. The cultural mismatch was impossible to ignore. The two firms were chalk and cheese. On the one hand was the quirky Cambridge company which ran like a startup, overstretched and frenetic, where its top executives dressed up for silly sales videos, where decisions were made quickly and where processes were few. On the other hand was an uptight, bureaucratic juggernaut where things had to be done by the (strict) rule book.

HP executives travelling around to meet the Autonomy teams soon heard worrying tales about how the company was run, which started to ring alarm bells. One HP executive was asked to stand in the doorway of a building in central Chicago, on a windy day with rubbish blowing past, just to find a private spot to speak to the Autonomy staffer. To avoid the supposed bugs. And it wasn't just the management that was the problem. HP executives also found major issues with some of Autonomy's products, such as incorrectly identifying duplicate emails and not archiving them.

On the flip side, even as HP's eyes were being opened, Autonomy staff were finding themselves baffled by their new colleagues. They couldn't understand the hundreds of people who appeared in HP meetings for no apparent reason, nor the amount of unnecessary red tape that existed within the business. They shared stories of long, time-wasting meetings where American staff members each explained how important they were, but no decisions were taken and innovation was crushed. There were more than twenty-five HP employees for each Autonomy one. Many began to feel as if the US giant was purposefully trying to overwhelm the British business. HP was, they found, the opposite of a meritocracy.

Compounding this culture clash, some of the basic steps to integrate the two businesses were simply not in place. Switching to using HP's sales process had slowed things down on the software side. Then there was the massive volume of paperwork Autonomy staff had to contend with. They struggled to do basic things, like access HP's internal systems, or expense small purchases. These problems only increased. On Valentine's Day 2012 – very far from a love-in – Lynch emailed Hussain and Kanter briefly: 'Meeting meg 2 morrow, need all craziness examples'.

They found many. Lynch already had told Whitman that HP should appoint a 'craziness czar' to stop the 'crazy processes' of HP's supposed integration of Autonomy, even alleging that Autonomy staff had been barred from HP's offices and had to go through third-party checks when working with the new parent company. Autonomy was excluded from HP's marketing activities, such as taking part in trade shows. Its sales were suffering. HP's salespeople were not working with Autonomy's and were even sometimes actively cannibalizing their deals.

It became quite clear quite quickly that Lynch and Whitman did not get along. Like their companies, they too were chalk and cheese – their humour, their way of working, their approach to life . . . even their musical tastes were different. She once played 'The Gambler' by country star Kenny Rogers to the HP executive team at a budget meeting. It was an assault on Lynch's (rather deaf) eardrums; he hated the genre, he grumbled.

They would have one or two meetings together a week, where Lynch would ask her to get things fixed and Whitman would do her best, always insisting that HP wanted to make Autonomy a success. He got more of her time and attention than anyone else, she felt. He, on the other hand, felt like he was being set up to fail.

Lynch wanted to manage the software division autonomously, but that was nigh-on impossible within the framework of HP. Whitman thought Lynch was too big for his boots. There were all sorts of cultural wars and political battles going on already at HP, and this became yet another one. It did not help that Lynch quickly started to openly belittle HP, cruelly mocking board meetings to friends and colleagues, joking about the red tape, about expenses and travel policies, about 300 people in a room trying to work on a project that six people would do better.

Overall, Whitman's relationship with Lynch was disastrous. They loathed each other; she hated his laissez-faire attitude, and he hated her interference in his business. Meanwhile, Whitman had bigger fish to fry, as problems at HP continued. Things were worse than she had thought. She compiled a report for the board on 22 March 2012 where she set out the scale of the problem:

> *[There is] a crisis of confidence among all constituents. [There are] significant business challenges across every Business Group, HP Labs and Global Sales. Suboptimal business processes, a lack of focused strategies [and an] unsustainable cost structure.*
>
> *HP culture is in tough shape, must be revitalized/realigned to be successful.*

Whitman was still dealing with the write-downs – the money HP had already lost on unsuccessful acquisitions. In 2010, HP had bought the Palm hand-held computer business for $1.2 billion, writing down almost $1.7 billion a year later. Two years before that, the company had bought Electronic Data Systems (EDS) for $13.9 billion; its value was written down by $8 billion in August 2012. Successive companies were consistently not worth nearly as much as HP had thought they were.

HP soon abandoned Apotheker's software turnaround plan and went back to focusing on its core business: the original, low-margin, hardware model.

FOR AUTONOMY, BREAKING point arrived in April 2012. Whatever Lynch had said to Ian Black, the merry-go-round pressures of three-monthly targets had not gone away under its new ownership. Panic ensued as it became clear that the company would significantly miss its quarterly revenue targets.

Hussain flagged this to Lynch in an email on Sunday 29 April, one day before the quarter closed.

> **We are faced with an unprecedented set of blockages on top of the recession (which is hitting us particularly in Europe). As we have started to close out the HP leads we are finding a set of previously unknown processes which prevent deals being signed in the quarter. Our salesforce are getting a bit demoralised because other parts of HP seem not to be interested in closing out deals. I am still working round the clock to bring as much as i can in but again i have to warn you of a sizeable miss. I am very very sorry for this news. I own all of the issues, i will not shirk from my responsibilities to you and to HP.**

Lynch forwarded the email to Whitman, with a few judicious edits.

She told him that relaying this kind of bombshell information at such short notice was 'completely unacceptable conduct for any leader'. She felt that Lynch was utterly unfit to run a company, the complete opposite of everything she held dear, such as organization, discipline, efficiency and transparency. She made her feelings plain: it was not acceptable to alert her to a problem at the last minute, underplay the scale of the issue, then sit back and watch what would happen rather than trying to sort it out. The whole affair, along with his 'authoritarian' management style, led Whitman to believe she could not trust Lynch – that he was not the right person to turn Autonomy around. It was a chaotic organization, chasing high-value deals rather than focusing on strong and steady results.

Whitman summoned Lynch onto a conference call that same Sunday night, after 10 p.m. in the UK, and gave him a piece of her mind. He tried to blame HP for Autonomy's failures. It did not wash. During the call, he dashed off one of his kidnap-style emails to Hussain: 'RING STOF ASAP AFTER CALL. Need tog et [sic] stories straight'. Which translated as, they needed to call Stouffer Egan and agree a collective reasoning as to why Autonomy would be missing its financial targets. In the end, Autonomy revealed a revenue shortfall of more than $130 million – far higher than the $30 to $50 million forecast that Lynch had optimistically set out for Whitman.

On 3 May, Hussain 'officially' tendered his resignation to Lynch – taking the fall, to outside eyes, for the quarterly results. Of course, outside the confines of a resignation email which would inevitably be leaked, the two had already discussed their next steps. Recriminations raged about the reasons for the shortfall that quarter. In public, Whitman blamed the growing pains of an entrepreneurial business and delivered a firm message of support for Autonomy. She called it a smart acquisition, and said that she felt great about the product, claiming to 'have absolutely hit one of the themes that is changing most in the technology business'.

Whatever the reasons, the business was going to continue to grow, but without its founder. Lynch was told to get out. His dismissal was formally announced at an investor meeting on 23 May 2012, around seven months after HP acquired Autonomy. The man who had fired so many others was now on the receiving end of the bullet. Though he himself had expected it, it seemed completely improbable to his teams, used to Lynch being all-powerful and all-terrifying.

The reasons given for his dismissal were damning. He had failed every which way, his letter of termination stated.

> *Your failure to adequately perform your duties and responsibilities at Autonomy . . . Including in particular a failure to meet the financial challenges with operating Autonomy in the HP environment, performance goals associated with your position, a failure to adequately manage, supervise and/or instruct the company's management team and employees, a failure to adequately communicate regarding the company's performance and operations, a failure to cooperate, communicate and work with others in a satisfactory manner and an inability to maintain the confidence of senior leadership.*

After Lynch was fired, Whitman held a conference call where she heralded loudly to staff: 'Integrity, integrity, integrity!'

It was a sorry end to a sorry relationship. By this point, Lynch was very angry, very hurt and had less than no respect for HP. He was gleeful to friends about just how many people followed him out of Autonomy. He continued to pour bile on the US giant.

Along with Hussain, others from his Inner Circle who left included Nicole Eagan, Pete Menell, Andy Kanter and Vanessa Colomar. There was a plan in place for them – a new business already afoot.

Shortly after Lynch was fired, anonymous Autonomy insiders talked to the *Financial Times* and described the tortuous experiences of having to comply with HP's bureaucratic internal controls and to sit through a long string of boring teleconferences. It was, they said, like being waterboarded.

Lynch's camp was playing a dangerous game, openly poking fun at HP. They were prodding the hornet's nest.

TWENTY-TWO

The War Begins

A senior member of Autonomy's leadership team came forward, following the departure of Autonomy founder Mike Lynch, alleging that there had been a series of questionable accounting and business practices at Autonomy prior to the acquisition by HP . . . This appears to have been a wilful effort on behalf of certain former Autonomy employees to inflate the underlying financial metrics of the company in order to mislead investors and potential buyers.

– HP statement, 20 November 2012

With Lynch gone, Autonomy and HP muddled along unhappily in their new relationship. As it became increasingly obvious that the merger was not working out, the British company's employees started to pick sides in the chaos, wary of what might happen next. Old alliances broke up and new ones were forged. Which way should they jump? Was it worth being loyal to Lynch if he was no longer in charge?

Executives from both companies were caught up in the turbulence, working out how they were going to navigate the unpleasant union with their jobs, careers and reputations intact. Suspicions grew between colleagues. Who was saying what to whom? Then, news spread that there was a new 'Autonomy whistleblower'. Amid this kerfuffle in May 2012, Joel Scott disappeared. He was Autonomy's chief operating officer and chief lawyer in the US. He was the man who had been responsible for firing Brent Hogeson, the 2010 whistleblower. It didn't take much to put two and two together.

In the run-up to what was perceived by some as his defection to HP, Scott's former colleagues noticed that something was up. He just seemed a little different, maybe a bit less warm and open in meetings. More combative. There was something in his eyes, something in his manner.

Two days after Lynch had been placed on gardening leave, Scott had gone to see John Schultz, the chief legal officer at HP, with some concerns. He wanted to talk about what he called the 'curious' hardware sales. When Scott had asked Autonomy about them, he was told that by combining hardware and software sales, the company was growing its sales but squeezing its profit margins. The conversation left him puzzled. 'I didn't go home and think, "Wow, that's really smart." I went home and thought, "I'm not sure I understand."'

Scott told Schultz a tale of Autonomy as a challenging and ruthless environment, saying that a lot of what it did made him feel uncomfortable. Later, Lynch's lawyers would try to undermine this portrayal of his Autonomy experience, pointing to his emails thanking Lynch for the opportunities he had given him, and asking for more prominence within the company. Schultz, however, believed him.

Scott's side-switching was a bazooka pointed directly at Autonomy. The meeting sparked an investigation. Stouffer Egan, Autonomy's burnt-out US chief executive, had also remained at HP and he told some of his former colleagues at the time that evidence was being compiled about Autonomy. He too had a meeting with a senior figure at HP.

Chris Yelland, the HP employee assigned to oversee Autonomy's financial operations in April 2012, started to dig into the company's numbers, assisted by consultancy company PwC, but a July report revealed no red flags. In August, HP concluded that no reduction in value of Autonomy was required, and that its value should be kept at the $11 billion that had been paid the previous year. But over time, detailed forensic work uncovered substantial issues, and by November, things had changed dramatically.

AT 4 P.M. ON 19 November 2012, Simon Case, private secretary to British Prime Minister David Cameron, received a phone call. Hewlett-Packard wanted to give him a heads up on an announcement due the next day, regarding its purchase of Autonomy. Deloitte, Autonomy's auditors, had also been informed a few weeks in advance, but for everyone else, including Lynch, it came as a complete surprise.

The first he knew about Hewlett-Packard's plans to go nuclear was through an explosive press release, which dropped while he was in a board meeting for a new venture. His phone started to light up in a way that never meant good news. Frantic messages from all sides urged him to check his emails.

Then he got a call from Vanessa Colomar, his aide, and stepped outside. It was serious, she said. HP had put out a statement to the stock market saying they were slashing the value of the Autonomy sale by $8.8 billion because the accounts were dodgy and they hadn't known what they were buying. Colomar's usually unflappable demeanour had left her that afternoon.

Lynch grabbed Hussain, who of course was by his side, and both men left the meeting. It was indeed serious: the Americans were accusing Lynch and his management team of misrepresenting the accounts. HP had announced it had uncovered fraud at Autonomy after a whistleblower had come forward.

> *This individual provided numerous details about which HP previously had no knowledge or visibility. HP initiated an intense internal investigation, including a forensic review by PricewaterhouseCoopers of Autonomy's historical financial results. As a result of that investigation, HP now believes that Autonomy was substantially overvalued at the time of its acquisition due to the misstatement of Autonomy's financial performance.*

It had called in the regulators to start a civil and a criminal investigation into the matter: the British Serious Fraud Office, and the US Securities and Exchange Commission. It was also planning to sue. Lynch threw everything into his brown leather case and jumped in the back of his car to meet his public relations advisors at Brunswick.

Of the $8.8 billion write-down, HP was attributing $5 billion to accounting irregularities. Some former Autonomy staff members, it said, had made a wilful effort to push up the company's numbers, specifically to mislead investors and potential buyers. The press release ended ominously:

> *The company intends to aggressively pursue this matter in the months to come.*

The publication sent HP's already diminished share price plunging to a ten-year low. It had lost $100 billion in market value since 2000, and it fell by 12 per cent on the day of the announcement, representing a further $78 billion drop in market value.

In a sharp suit, Whitman addressed the rolling news channels. Staring down the barrel of the lens, she blatantly accused Autonomy of selling HP a pup. She said the company was smaller and made less money than they had been told. HP did its due diligence but when you are lied to, she later said, it is hard to spot these things. Whitman felt alarmed, disappointed and ultimately resolute, viewing the exposure of fraud as both necessary and deeply unsettling.

Schultz weighed in, explaining that it had taken so long to uncover the issues because critical documents were missing from the obvious places. He had had to look in every nook and cranny to piece together the information, he said.

The announcement was deeply sensitive and deeply political. HP needed a serious public relations campaign to hammer its message home – and so Project Sutton began, led by a man named Henry Gomez, who had run publicity for Whitman at eBay and worked on her campaign to be Governor of California. Concerned that she would get the flak for the Autonomy acquisition, Project Sutton was designed to protect and reinforce Whitman's credibility – and the business monitored the news coverage closely. The strategy was to get in front of the story and protect the people at the top. HP created a response team they aptly named the Truth Squad to keep a watchful eye on the media response to the write-down, correcting the coverage wherever necessary. The Truth Squad was also in contact with British government ministers.

There was one problem. HP did not immediately have the numbers to hand to back up the amount of the write-down which it claimed was attributable to fraud. It seemed to be shooting first and asking questions later.

LYNCH'S CHAUFFEUR-DRIVEN CAR swung into Holborn and then off London's busy main arteries into the elegant garden square of Lincoln's Inn Fields, where Brunswick, the famous City public relations firm, is based. For Lynch, the Brunswick offices became home to yet another war room, and the start of a bitter battle that would last until the end of his life.

After a long discussion about how to respond to the fraud

allegations, the small group of Autonomy executives and advisors who were present came up with one answer: We need to come out swinging.

That afternoon, Lynch accepted Channel 4 News's invitation to defend himself on TV. It was a unique decision. Usually, company bosses take time to think about these moments, and their answers are managed to the hilt. Yet Lynch was determined to be himself, and there was little time to work out set-piece answers to media questions.

Outwardly, Lynch was calm as he stepped out of the car at the Channel 4 studios for the pre-recorded interview, but in hindsight, perhaps sending a man who hated the media out to do a media round at a time of intense stress was a bridge too far.

Things rapidly came unstuck as he settled down with Jon Snow, the veteran British newscaster. Far from the opportunity he had hoped for to set out his stall, Snow went all-in, guns blazing, with an aggressive line of questioning about Autonomy's finances. He acted as if the fraud had been confirmed rather than alleged.

Lynch was shaking with anger when he walked off set and demanded that the tape be pulled. It was unfair and inflammatory, he felt, when nothing against him had been proved, to behave as if these claims were true. The producer summoned Ben de Pear, the then editor of Channel 4 News, from his offices. De Pear was used to being lobbied and threatened. Guests wanted to get interviews pulled all the time, it was an almost weekly occurrence. Lynch was immediately in his face about the unfairness of the interview. He reminded the watching journalists of Alistair Campbell, Tony Blair's infamous director of communications (often cited as the inspiration for *The Thick of It*'s Malcolm Tucker).

On this occasion, after watching the recording back with a lawyer, de Pear decided that Lynch had a point. That first exchange with Snow ended up being the dress rehearsal. Instead, Channel 4 agreed to re-do the interview on one condition. That it was live.

At 7 p.m., Snow's booming tones introduced the story to viewers: 'In the US, the FBI has opened an investigation into claims that a British company wilfully misled the American computer giant Hewlett-Packard about its finances before it was bought up.'

Wearing his usual navy jacket with an open-necked white shirt, Lynch settled into the interview chair opposite and refuted the accusations. He punched back hard in round two, laying a series of reciprocal blows on HP and its team.

'Autonomy has always been clear about its accounting. We've made sure it's always been transparent and open and easy for people to look at,' Lynch said, not mentioning past criticism of the company's finances.

'So they've made it all up?' Snow asked.

Lynch nodded his head vigorously, 'The business has been very badly mismanaged, much of the talent has left and that has led to the business being written-down. People are now looking for scapegoats. They don't want to own up to the fact that in a year they've destroyed value that was created over ten years.'

He went further, alleging the accusations were an attempt by HP to distract attention from 'some of the worst results in the company's history'. Lynch then raged that no one had phoned him personally to talk to him or explain what the hell was going on:

> *The normal process where you'd be warned, given a chance to understand, at the moment we are only getting the chance to see what they're saying, they're only saying the vaguest things, I've had a day to look at that and all that has done is reinforce my view that there is absolutely nothing here.*

It was not the only interview he did that day. And in the end, it was far from the worst.

Lynch had to speak to CNBC over in the US from their empty London offices, late at night. A security guard let him in. A cleaner was hoovering up the day's mess. Standing in the dark, under a lone spotlight, he stared into the camera with an earpiece to blast him the questions. For a deaf man, the situation could not have been less comfortable. He could barely hear anything, and he was unable to see anyone to lip-read. He was fighting to understand the myriad people chattering in his ear, while simultaneously fighting for his professional life.

Although it was difficult, his advisors felt it had to be Lynch himself doing the media interviews. The press needed to see the whites of his eyes. Their argument against HP was credibility- and personality-driven, so Lynch had to be front and centre. He was on the attack.

Like the HP team, the Lynch camp also came up with a name for their public relations strategy: Project Pacman, named after the classic 1980s computer game where a yellow circular character moves around a maze eating yellow dots. It was a case of eat or – like the weak piranhas that had once graced Autonomy's foyer – be eaten.

Lynch knew it was him against one of the biggest companies in the world, but he had deep pockets, and the brainpower to defend himself when others couldn't. He believed in the adage *If you throw stones at my house, I will nuke your village*, and would later describe the situation as like being the captain of a boat. You cannot control the weather. Sometimes there are big storms, he said, and you must keep sailing until you eventually come out the other side.

Lynch wrote an open letter to HP denying impropriety and demanding information. He did not really take HP or its claims seriously. He simply could not imagine that this unimaginably reckless, inefficient, bloated business, run by a vacillating leadership who had bought Autonomy for $11 billion just over a year before, could possibly come after him.

In any case, he was not going to take their behaviour lying down. On the contrary, in the face of the most damning allegations that he could be faced with, Mike Lynch was ready for the fight of his life.

PART FOUR
Mike Lynch vs The Law

TWENTY-THREE

A Law Unto Himself

Fraud on a grand scale; or relentless witch-hunt? That is the question in this claim against two individuals for many billions arising out of a corporate acquisition more than a decade ago.

– Mr Justice Hildyard, civil judgement, 17 May 2022

'*One of Britain's biggest technology success stories is now at the centre of a Silicon Valley storm.*' The radio announcer's voice seemed interminable, washing over Lynch as he listened. The segment went on, '*We launched an investigation, a forensic examination, and uncovered a whole host of very concerning accounting improprieties and misrepresentations . . .*'

Just after Christmas 2012, BBC Radio 4 broadcast a half-hour episode of *The Report*, presented by journalist Phil Kemp, which delved into the allegations made by HP against Autonomy. Lynch took part in it, claiming, once again, that the fraud allegations were a misunderstanding of the difference between US and UK accounting rules.

The programme said it found mixed reviews about the working culture at Autonomy and the quality of its technology:

> *We contacted more than 20 customers, several at the suggestion of Mike Lynch's PR team, to see if we could talk to them about how they use the software and what it did for their business. We said we wanted to be able to demonstrate it working for people listening to the programme and see its benefits. None of the companies we contacted were prepared for us to do that and most wouldn't give us a reason, although some said they couldn't comment on a third party's product. We spoke to a few clients who were happy with IDOL but were no longer using it. We also spoke to some who had bought it but had stopped using it when they couldn't make it work for them.*

The negative commentary within the programme stung. It felt like one blow after another, especially from the BBC, whose board Lynch had sat on for two terms, only leaving earlier that year. The programme concluded:

> *We may find out more about what to expect in the new year, when Hewlett-Packard files its annual report with the SEC, due any day. That's expected to discuss what HP executives knew about Autonomy, when they knew it, and what they planned to do about it . . .*

This media investigation was just the beginning. From the moment fraud was declared in November 2012, Mike Lynch's life – and the lives of all those around him – would be dominated by a series of probes and legal cases: expensive, interminable, stressful and intensely painful.

Lynch would wake up every morning feeling normal, then the weight of events would come crashing down on him. As the various lawsuits unfolded, there may have been victories on both sides, but there were no real winners, except for the lawyers, whose bulging wallets and groaning mantelpieces were testaments to the financial and professional awards reaped from the ordeal. The UK civil trial of

Lynch and Sushovan Hussain alone was estimated to have cost each side more than £2 million *a month* at its peak.

Lynch and Hussain always maintained their innocence, painting Autonomy as a plucky British David fighting the villainous American Goliath, which was on the hunt for someone to blame for its ineptitude. HP countered that this was nonsense. It made good on its promise to aggressively pursue the matter of the alleged fraud. Both sides dug in for the long haul.

The tangle of litigation which took place on both sides of the Atlantic takes some unpicking. The story of these curious cases, their Counsel and their outcomes could be a book all on its own.

In summary, there were four main proceedings in the UK.

The most important started in March 2015, and was dubbed by the media as 'the tech trial of the century'. HP launched a major civil case suing Lynch and Hussain for $5 billion in the High Court, accusing them of being the architects of a massive fraud. HP argued that it had been lured by an illusion, deceived by numbers artfully inflated to cast Autonomy in a golden light. Lynch counter-sued for £160 million, accusing HP of making statements that were damaging to him. It was a laughable and desperate move, HP said.

Mr Justice Hildyard, trying the case from March 2019, remarked that it might rank among the most drawn-out and intricate legal proceedings in English legal history: Lynch was cross-examined for twenty-one days; dozens of witnesses were called; over 36,000 documents were involved; and closing submissions were almost 5,000 pages long.

The second proceeding was the Serious Fraud Office (SFO) investigation launched in 2013, which it eventually handed over to US authorities in early 2015 because it felt there was insufficient evidence for a prosecution in respect of some aspects of the allegations. Quirkily, the SFO was an Autonomy customer, party to a contract worth £4 million.

A third case saw Lynch's legal fight against extradition to the US, which was hovering over him for years but officially got underway in 2019 when the US made the request. He wanted to stay on British soil, away from the jaws of the notoriously harsh US criminal justice system.

Finally, the fourth case in the UK concerned the British accounting regulator, the Financial Reporting Council (FRC), which started a forensic probe into Deloitte's audit of Autonomy's accounts in 2013 and finally reported in 2021. HP had also threatened a negligence suit against Deloitte, but the two companies settled in 2016.

Over in the highly litigious US, HP itself faced a barrage of cases over its botched Autonomy acquisition. It was sued by its shareholders, led by the Dutch pension fund manager PGGM, who called the deal 'reckless'. They settled in 2015. It was also sued by MicroTech, one of the resellers used by Autonomy, for the software it had bought from Autonomy back in 2010 to sell on to the Vatican Library, but that it never did. The most ominous of all the cases Lynch and Hussain faced, however, were the criminal charges brought by the US government, which said it was one of the largest frauds ever prosecuted by the United States Department of Justice. Unlike the others, which came with financial penalties, the criminal cases came with the threat of a prison sentence. In 2016, Hussain was formally indicted by the US Department of Justice for fraud. He did not fight his extradition and flew over for hearings from 2017. His trial started in 2018. Lynch's own would start in 2024.

IN NOVEMBER 2012, almost immediately after fraud allegations were declared, the FBI and the US financial regulator, the Securities and Exchange Commission, started investigating the matter in parallel with the British SFO. The US Department of Justice started pursuing former Autonomy leadership on criminal charges. The first to be targeted was Hussain. Lynch would follow.

Across the various trials on both sides of the pond, there are several legal figures who are important to highlight as, without their individual characteristics, traits and flairs, it's possible that the entire affair would have played out differently.

In New York, just a day after the news broke, Chris Morvillo, a prominent litigator at Clifford Chance, heard about the case. He smelt an opportunity, picked up the phone and called the firm's London offices. Was there any business to be done, he wondered, with this unfolding drama? As luck would have it, Lynch had already been in touch with the firm. Morvillo was hired, marking the start of his decade-long involvement in one of the most complex corporate fraud cases of the era.

Morvillo had an easy, kind manner and a good nose for a case, and was extremely popular among his peers. While US white-collar lawyers normally come with a good chunk of ego attached, Morvillo did not. He was someone who always brought out the best in people, who would take time to encourage and mentor junior lawyers and had an unfailing sense of humour, even when his clients inevitably lost theirs. He loved his work, and beyond it his passions were music, photography and theatre, but above all his family – his wife Neda and his two daughters.

Working alongside Clifford Chance were Reid Weingarten and Brian Heberlig from Steptoe; a firm headquartered in Washington, DC. Weingarten is about as big as it gets when it comes to names in the world of white-collar defence attorneys. A former public corruption prosecutor, he has represented an extraordinary array of people fighting infamous cases. Among them are Jeffrey Epstein, film director Roman Polanski and Lloyd Blankfein, the former CEO of Goldman Sachs who was sued over allegations that the bank had misled investors prior to the 2008 financial crisis.

Supremely well-connected, Weingarten is known for understanding the nuances of the law – the grey areas – and for possessing the rare ability to 'speak human' and connect with juries. You need flair in a US courtroom, and Weingarten has that in spades. Brian Heberlig was the perfect counterbalance to Weingarten's flamboyance. Measured, conservative, and methodical, Heberlig brought decades of experience as a top-notch white-collar criminal defence lawyer. Far less showy than his colleague, Heberlig was no less determined, forming a partnership with Weingarten that blended charisma with strategy.

For the prosecution, there was US Attorney Adam Reeves. With twenty-five years of experience investigating and prosecuting corporate fraud, Reeves was formidable. In 2019, he had been appointed First Assistant US Attorney, making him the top deputy in the office. Working alongside him was Robert Leach, known as Bob, a highly regarded government lawyer who had once served as chief of the special prosecutions section. Leach had spent nine years at the SEC, honing his expertise in financial regulation, making him perfectly suited to the intricacies of the Autonomy case. The prosecution team was meticulous, precise, and relentless. Reeves and Leach were determined to present their case with clarity and conviction, forming a powerhouse duo.

Presiding over it all and trying all the Autonomy cases in the United States was the legendary Judge Charles Breyer – known as Chuck. His illustrious experience included working on the Watergate team back in 1973, helping prosecute President Nixon's infamous group of 'fixers'. He is firm but fair, and he needs to be. His courtroom, the Northern District of California, has played host to Silicon Valley's most self-important gladiators over the years, including Elon Musk.

With a full head of white hair and his trademark bow tie, he has been through the proverbial court wringer over the years, which has sharpened his notorious sense of humour. When HP filed pages of redacted motions, for example, Breyer responded by issuing an order that itself was heavily redacted. A judicial mic drop.

AS THE PARALLEL proceedings unfolded on both sides of the Atlantic, the contrasts between the US and UK legal systems became increasingly pronounced. In Britain, the legal actors involved in the

Lynch cases appeared more restrained and traditional than their more theatrical American counterparts. At one point, Weingarten travelled to observe the British Autonomy hearings, reporting back to Judge Breyer with the wry observation: 'A lot of the Lords go flying around, and it is different than the way we do it'.

It's true. The British legal system is a very different beast to its US counterpart, a source of interest and amusement to both sides looking askance at how the other lot does things. British lawyers try to avoid the limelight. They say rather pompously, with a sly dig at their American cousins, that their role is merely to present the client's case and let the substance do the talking. Their personalities, they say, should not come into it.

The British Bar is a world steeped in tradition and formality, still reserved for those who fit a narrow, historically privileged mould, despite everyone's ostensible best efforts to push for diversity and inclusion. In certain circumstances, barristers still wear crisp black robes; judges wear wigs; they use archaic phrases like 'my learned friend'.

The judge in the UK civil case was Robert Hildyard – Mr Justice Hildyard to give him his full title – a through-and-through British establishment figure with an elegant turn of phrase, and a man at home in this intellectual and stuffy environment. Educated at Eton and Christ Church College at Oxford, the kind of singular traditions, formalities and centuries-old rituals that continue at the Bar would have been instantly familiar to Hildyard: he grew up with them. He is renowned for being perceptive, erudite, highly intelligent and very, very old school. Slim, bald and in his late sixties when the Lynch trial began, the ponderous judge has a habit of harumphing and peering severely through his steepled fingers when he is displeased.

He is an expert in business cases, and was also a member of the Financial Reporting Review Panel – ensuring that companies' financial reports meet accounting standards and regulations – further indicating his suitability to hear Lynch's civil trial.

HP was represented in its British suit by the elite firm Travers Smith, led by Toby Robinson and Andrew King. The lead barrister acting for the American conglomerate was Laurence Rabinowitz KC, known as 'Laurie' throughout the London legal world and one of the leading legal minds of his generation. In May 2025, he stepped up to become chair of the UK's Takeover Panel, an appropriate position given the time he spent looking at HP's takeover of Autonomy.

With Clifford Chance acting as Lynch's solicitors, led in the UK by Jeremy Sandelson, the entrepreneur's lead counsel was Robert Miles, then a Queen's Counsel but now a High Court judge, whose impeccable CV includes cases relating to Bernie Madoff, the Tchenguiz brothers and the implosions of both Lehman Brothers and Barings. Like Hildyard, Miles was part of a barristers' chambers named 4 Stone Buildings. The two knew one another well and were good buddies. Some mused that Miles got an easier ride than Rabinowitz in court.

When it came to his stellar cohort of lawyers, Lynch used to say that he was the patient and they were the surgeons: 'It's my brain on the slab, but I'm trusting you to operate.' He would treat them, to continue the hospital analogy, as consultants, but still get lots of different opinions about the prognosis and the best treatment.

He would often bring wildly ambitious thoughts to the table and the lawyers would have to say whether they would fly or not, trying to wrap the legal framework around them. It was very much a team effort. There would occasionally be times when Lynch would be in a difficult mood, there would be a disagreement, and the legal team would have to regroup later. He was never an easy man to work for at the best of times. Everyone was under a great deal of stress.

These were the characters who would take to the stage for a drama that would define careers and shape lives. Lynch's future lay squarely in their hands.

TWENTY-FOUR

Avengers Assemble

I think a lot of people at Autonomy were tarnished by the whole experience and what happened afterwards, a lot of people's reputations have been damaged, including their integrity.

– Matt Stephan, formerly of Autonomy's finance department, testimony 26 March 2024

While the lawyers were working their magic, Lynch went back into startup mode. There were far more interesting, more practical, more technological, more controllable and more fantastical things to think about than the ongoing Autonomy saga. As he was in the process of being fired from the software company, he immediately launched a new enterprise and set about regrouping his old team.

In the days when Autonomy's relationship with HP was crumbling beyond repair, Andy Kanter rang around members of the trusted group. It is time to hand in your notice, he said. Lynch was starting a new business called Invoke and he wanted his closest lieutenants on board. Kanter, Lynch and Hussain had been pondering it for a while, and now it was time to act.

While Lynch said the idea for Invoke went back 'to time immemorial', the actual formation took shape in summer 2012, shortly before Lynch's formal departure from Autonomy. He described the early shell as 'a PowerPoint and an idea', initially little more than a legal entity in the British Virgin Islands.

Some team members decided to stay on at HP. One was Stouffer Egan, who said he wasn't interested in continuing to work for Lynch, which was the alternative. Behind closed doors, Egan sparred with Nicole Eagan, Lynch's long-time ally, over influence, budgets, and power. He was tired of it. It was too much pressure, and he did not like the way Autonomy had been run. Derek Brown, Ian Black and Mike Sullivan also stayed under the new ownership. For others, the idea of independently reconvening outside HP was welcomed with enthusiasm.

Lynch had always started businesses, even within Autonomy, such as Blinkx, the video search business. They would sometimes start with a wacky brainwave. 'I want to see dinosaurs walk across my desk,' Lynch had told his tech team in 2011, setting them a new and intriguing mission: to step into the world of augmented reality, technology that blends the real world with the virtual, overlaying images, sounds or video onto what you see in your surroundings.

This was the start of Aurasma. It allowed you to hold up a mobile phone to a trigger image and watch it come alive on your screen, sparking content – a video for example. It was way ahead of its time. A couple of years later, *Pokémon Go!* would come along and do almost exactly the same thing. 'If you're truly going to interact between the physical world and the virtual world,' Lynch told *The New York Times*, 'you're not going to do that sitting in your bedroom at the keyboard.'

As the project grew and became more successful, Lynch would demo it at events while one of the developers, Graham Sills, was told to don the tech developer's uniform of a hoodie and jeans and stand in the corner. This meant Lynch could say 'this is down to him' and jokingly point out Sills in the crowd and blame or praise him, depending on whether the demo worked or not. Aurasma could be clunky, it could be glitchy, it could be slick or breathtaking. But it was early days, and that process was part of the beauty.

Aurasma's boss was a woman named Martina King. Lynch had found her quite by chance, at a Suffolk party. King had taken a step back from an extraordinary career, which had included running Yahoo in the UK, to raise her kids. She had never heard of Lynch when they met, but once the two got talking, they couldn't stop. She too was the daughter of Irish immigrants and they had an instant rapport, bonding over their mutual interest in tech. At their next meeting in London, they swiftly abandoned a Mayfair lunch and visited Autonomy's offices for a demo of Aurasma. King was hooked.

A straight-talking, warm and down-to-earth woman, King happily found herself back in a job, commercializing the product. It was one of the most inspiring and exciting opportunities she had ever had. She managed to build up quite a business, finding customers for the tech including Universal Pictures, who used it to advertise the film *Bridesmaids* in the British press.

The enterprise had so much potential that Lynch planned to spin it out from Autonomy, just like he had done with Blinkx. But it was not to be. Under HP, Aurasma changed, King felt. She did not think HP shared her vision and watched despondently while relationships with customers stagnated as the company became mired in internal politics. She found this all increasingly demoralizing. It made her next move a no-brainer.

'Now?' was all King asked when she got the call to join Lynch's new venture in 2012. 'Have you got any questions?' Lynch asked. 'Are we going to be sponsoring another football club?' she wanted to know. 'No, we're not,' he said, which she greeted with some degree of relief. That was it. King didn't need anything more – feeling that being part of the team held exciting promise, and the guarantee that Lynch would look after her was enough.

Jack Stockdale, one of Lynch's key technologists, had left Autonomy before the sale to HP to take some time out. His phone rang as he was halfway down to Brighton, preparing to go out sailing. It was Suzanne Howarth, who had run HR (among other things) at Autonomy since the early days. 'Mike's doing this new thing called Invoke . . .' she said. 'OK, Suzanne!' he replied, and immediately turned around and drove back to Cambridge.

The band, as Lynch put it, was all back together. There was Vanessa Colomar, Sushovan Hussain, former Autonomy CTO Pete Menell, accountant Lisa Harris, Martina King, Emily Orton and Charlotte Golunski, also formerly of Autonomy. From the US, Nicole Eagan joined too, tasked with keeping her ear to the ground in Silicon Valley, to make sure Lynch's investments stood out from the crowd. Unwisely, given the circumstances, Lynch boasted loudly about the number of people who followed him out of the door of HP after he was fired.

Andy Kanter was an exception. He wanted to take a six-month break and ended up working in hospitality for the next few years, before eventually heading back into the Lynch fold.

The newly regrouped team moved to a different premises in Mayfair, the area of London which Lynch always loved, and took a small space back in the St John's Innovation Centre in Cambridge, where Autonomy had begun. The plan for Invoke was simple: to invest in and commercialize new, exciting, homegrown AI technology.

The new venture was one way that Lynch kept his sanity, despite the failure of the HP deal. It was a way of proving himself, as his reputation took a beating in the face of the fraud allegations and the onslaught of litigation. Proving that he could rise from the ashes was part of restoring his hurt pride. It gave him back the control he had lost completely after the sale of Autonomy. It was a way of proving his ability to spot and create winners.

There was a sprinkle of patriotism to it too. Lynch constantly asserted the pre-eminence of British technology. He also bemoaned the UK's sluggishness and ineptitude at spinning technological innovations out of university labs. His pet theory was that British companies had to be aggressive, or they'd be left behind and crushed by the big US software giants. The Brits simply don't have the same leverage and power, so they need to (as usual) take guns to knife fights.

Lynch and his team had been around the block. They asserted they knew what they were doing and wanted to do it again, to apply all they had learnt from Autonomy. They had a simple formula: find a great idea, bolt on the right people plus the investment, and turbocharge it with sales and marketing. People who worked for Lynch are not always complimentary about his character, but it's beyond doubt that he always had an uncanny ability to build a strong team, like a jigsaw puzzle, piecing together compatible strengths and spotting gaps.

The model itself was unconventional. Unlike a traditional venture-capital- or Dragon's Den-style model, where random businesses could approach the team for investment, Invoke would build core technologies in-house or acquire them early, then scale them with heavyweight capital – 'build the jet engine first, then buy Boeing,' as Lynch put it. So Invoke's portfolio of companies were all handpicked or even created from scratch by Lynch or others, run by people from his team or by those they personally knew and parachuted in. He had never lost the habit of collecting good people.

The US prosecutors saw it differently. They claimed that Invoke was a witness-tampering scheme, pointing to the number of former Autonomy staff on its books and the stakes they were being given in new companies as a way in which Lynch was controlling people who should have given evidence against him, rewarding them for their loyalty.

'Lynch finds $1bn pot of gold to spark new wave of technology', proclaimed a headline in *The Times* on 9 February 2013. The article ran on:

Britain's best-known technology entrepreneur is plotting a comeback after raising a $1 billion fund to fast-track the development of some of the country's most promising companies.

It was not true. There was not $1 billion sitting in a bank account waiting to be spent, and Invoke would never go on to invest anywhere near that sum. Lynch was, as always, giving it a marketing gloss. 'I wouldn't say it's untruthful,' he later said. 'If you hear Carlsberg saying, "It's probably the best lager in the world", then I think that we don't assume that there has been a full scientific study [undertaken] before that claim is made, but it may well be the best lager in the world.' Invoke followed a draw-down model, meaning the funds were pledged but not yet invested.

The reality was that after HP made accusations of fraud at Autonomy, it became hard to raise significant money. Companies were very afraid of the reputational risk of being associated with Lynch and his team. Lynch complained that the Ontario Teachers' Pension Plan, along with American private equity firm Warburg Pincus, were considering investing $500 million and $400 million respectively into Invoke, but didn't because of the allegations that had been made against him.

Nevertheless, he persisted with the $1 billion claim, even making it onto TV on CNBC. 'When we all started, no one would give us money or take our phone calls,' he joked to one newspaper. 'Now . . . we raised the Invoke fund in a couple of weeks. The problem is, we don't have the brains of 22- to 24-year-olds anymore.' It all sounded very plausible, but it was yet another example of his free and easy relationship with the truth. In the end, it did not really matter. Invoke might not have had $1 billion in a bank account, but it created far more than that out of the businesses it spawned over the next decade.

Meanwhile, the trend of Britain losing its biggest and brightest tech to foreign acquirers continued. In 2016, ARM Holdings was sold to Japan's SoftBank for £24 billion. The Cambridge-founded company, which designs chips for iPhones, would later go public again, but on Wall Street, not in its old London home. Another FTSE 100 company, Aveva, one of Britain's oldest software companies, was bought by France's Schneider in 2022.

IN THE EARLY days of Invoke, Lynch would bring his eldest daughter Esme to strategy meetings, and the team remember her brilliance, even as a young girl. They recall heady days of working and playing hard. Yes, the legal proceedings were ongoing, but the day-to-day felt normal. On top of the busy day job, Hussain led cake-baking competitions and charity fundraising days to boost morale.

Even in that post-Autonomy world, working with his hand-picked favourites, Lynch continued to be a challenging boss, yelling at people: 'You've ballsed it up. If you'd have done it my way it would have been easier!' What wasn't ballsed up, though, were the artificial intelligence companies Lynch and his team picked, created and backed, which all became runaway successes.

The first came from Cambridge, where the Invoke team began its trawl for ideas. They spoke to Bill Fitzgerald, the ever-curious polymath don at Christ's who had sparked Lynch's initial fascination with Thomas Bayes. Along with another academic, Dave Excell, he was using machine learning to look into patterns of behaviour. The enterprise became an Invoke-backed company: Featurespace, a virtual lie detector. When you see someone's body language, you can discern what they are thinking and feeling to a greater or lesser extent but, when someone is doing things digitally, that is harder. If someone is playing games online, how do you know if they are cheating?

In 2008, the tech turned commercial after the gambling company Betfair asked Featurespace to try to beat fraud attacks by thinking like its customers. Distinguishing between normal and unusual activities, Featurespace proved it could accurately detect genuine player behaviour and uncover new types of fraud. After Aurasma, Lynch asked Martina King to pick up the mantle as Featurespace's chief executive in 2012. It branched out to be used in tackling rising financial crime and then both credit-card and online-payments fraud, as well as scam detection. Lynch would remain a non-executive director for a decade.

Not long after the investment in Featurespace, in 2014, Fitzgerald died of cancer. He had given King one mission: to make the business as commercially successful as he was academically, to build value in the business in order to support the family he left behind – his wife, three sons and their families. King, always a popular leader, did them all proud.

There were other companies too. Sophia Genetics, which made personalized medicine, really captured Lynch's imagination. Using the tech was like reading over a poker player's shoulders, Lynch said. It spun out of the Federal Institute of Technology in Lausanne in 2011, and used algorithms to analyse DNA, speeding up the diagnosis of cancer and other hereditary diseases.

There was one more company that would prove a chart-topping success – yet another venture that was ahead of its time. Lynch's patience for legal matters was wearing thin. Embroiled in legal documents, he was well aware that much of the work he was doing could be sped up by computers. Automating the endless paperwork done by endless numbers of 'twits in suits', as he called lawyers and bankers, sparked the idea for another Invoke company: Luminance.

Autonomy had already bought several legal information management companies over the years, so Lynch understood how tech and the law fit together. Luminance was a leap forward using AI, spun up by three techies he had kept close to: Graham Sills, James Loxam and Adam Guthrie. They partnered with the legendary legal firm Slaughter and May, who had acted for Autonomy in its sale to HP, to develop the tech.

Luminance's product could read and understand long, dense legal documents, speeding up the rate at which companies could do due diligence, a somewhat delicate issue, given HP's cursory review of Autonomy's numbers. At its 2016 launch, Lynch announced that it would put artificial intelligence in the workplace, where its impact would be most felt. Not even a decade later, as AI threatens traditional white-collar jobs, his prediction has come true a thousand-fold.

Luminance, Featurespace and a third company called Darktrace were all AI companies backed by Invoke and run by women, extraordinarily unusual in the male-dominated tech world, and a far cry from the situation at Autonomy. Lynch insisted it was in no way intentional. It was, he added, simply the result of being gender blind.

'SHHH, NOT A sound,' whispered Lynch to his co-conspirator and friend, Albert Read. Read stood just as he'd been instructed, hiding behind a curtain while standing on a chair in the dark in the billiards room at Loudham, holding a piece of string.

It was Halloween, and as usual Angela had gone all out to provide a joyful party for family friends and their children. American Halloween traditions had been imported to Suffolk, and there were games and decorations, spooky lanterns and lights strewn around the garden, where children were running around and shrieking excitedly.

Crowds arrived from London to mingle with the Suffolk neighbours; there were groups trick-or-treating around the farm cottages, tramping through fields in the crisp night, across to the woods festooned with lights and terrifying illuminated masks hanging from the trees.

Lynch was never one to rest on his laurels. Even as the legal web spun and tightened around him, he pressed on with Invoke – striving to appear unfazed, to maintain a sense of normality, to keep business ticking over. Business certainly helped, but also bolstering him was the unwavering support he received from those back home.

Plenty of people in Suffolk stayed very loyal to Lynch throughout his legal ordeals. In 2014, he was made one of the Deputy Lieutenants of the County of Suffolk, a largely honorary and ceremonial role in his adopted home which gave him even more letters to sign after his name (DL). Suffolk and his alternate life in his rural idyll provided some breathing space.

One Christmas, Lynch dealt with the overhang of the fraud accusations head on. Guests arriving for festive drinks were greeted by an unusual centrepiece among the sparkling lighting and decorations: a giant inflatable elephant. It was, Lynch chuckled with his untouchable humour, the 'elephant in the room'. These parties continued, and Suffolk friends would ask in the usual way how Lynch was coping, but they didn't pry too much. They offered support where it was needed, but they kept business and friendship firmly apart.

This attitude was far from universal. A crisis can knit people together or explode relationships, but there was no such thing as 80 per cent with Lynch. People were either 100 per cent a friend or 100 per cent an enemy, and that became a problem as more details about the fraud accusations emerged. Many just did not know what to make of it, especially given the questions around the company's accounts, which had been circling for years. Those friends who dithered fell by the wayside. Lots of his 'friends' in the City and in politics distanced themselves from him. The annual summer party at Loudham became thinner and the number of financiers attending noticeably diminished (which wasn't a bad thing, some Suffolk friends remarked wryly).

Others, like former politician Lord Deben, redoubled their support. He understood the pain of being in the spotlight from politics, and helped Lynch to fend off unfriendly media attention. Angela encouraged local friends to write to their MP about Lynch's case. But on the whole, the Lynches let people act as they pleased and otherwise just carried on as usual, life structured around the rhythm of the seasons and the calendar of holidays.

Back to the Loudham billiards room. Lynch loved the theatre of Halloween. He had led the children around the Hall with only a candle illuminating his face, and Albert Read had been (quite literally) roped in to assist Lynch with an elaborate prank. The dark room he was in, hiding atop the chair behind the curtain, was to look as if it were empty – but the string he was holding was attached to a gramophone.

He had to hold the thread high in the air for about twenty minutes and, as soon as the children walked in, yank it to trigger the old-fashioned gramophone to leap into life and start playing eerie, scratchy music. The children duly screamed and fled in abject terror.

Lynch grinned and released Read from his duties, giving him the nod of a job satisfactorily done. It gave Read a glimpse of what it must have been like to work for him – of his charisma and single-mindedness. Read had needed to hold on to the thread at all costs.

Just as Lynch did during those uncertain years.

TWENTY-FIVE

Stouffer and Sushovan

Although he acknowledged it might be crazy, Egan maintains the view Hussain is a highly ethical person . . . and Egan thought he was massively under the spell of one of the most powerful human characters on the planet [Mike Lynch]. Egan thought Hussain got screwed into doing something, but that Hussain would never do something self-beneficial.

– *Stouffer Egan, US witness statement, 20 May 2014*

In the run-up to the 2016 referendum over Britain's membership of the European Union, Lynch messaged Patrick Jacob, his Suffolk friend, and asked him out for lunch in London. The pair were slap-bang in the middle of an argumentative flurry of texts about the upcoming vote, and Lynch wanted to take it offline.

While the final result was very far from a landslide, Britain narrowly voted to leave the European bloc – 51.9 per cent to 48.9 per cent. It created an ideological chasm between friends and within families across the country.

Lynch was firmly in the 'remain' camp, even donating £100,000 to the campaign for Britain to stay a part of the EU. The matter was a long-running but good-natured battle between him and Jacob. The spat was made even more frustrating by Lynch's communication style. His kidnap-style notes were, as usual, hard to decipher. His brain always seemed to leap ahead of his hand, which left his written English to friends in a terrible state.

The pair met in the traditional environs of Wiltons in London, one of those few restaurants that Lynch could tolerate with his hearing aids. And they went at it. While they were having a full-on row, they never lost their tempers or their respect for one another. It was the kind of deeply affectionate debate you can only share with someone you really like, even when your opinions diverge. Jacob chalked up a minor victory, even winning Lynch over on a few of his points.

Not long after the Brexit referendum, there was another announcement regarding sovereignty. 'Autonomy is coming home, even if football isn't', reported the *Financial Times* on 8 September 2016, in a reference to England's dismal performance in the European Football Championships.

With far less fanfare, five years after the disastrous sale to HP, Autonomy had been sold once again. This time, it was back to a British company which specialized in legacy technology – Micro Focus International – for $2.5 billion in cash.

The sale was triggered by major changes at HP announced in 2014, when Meg Whitman decided to split the giant in two. HP's woes had continued post-Autonomy. It had lost its position as the world's leading supplier of PCs to China's Lenovo in 2012, and more changes were needed. The new companies were Hewlett-Packard Enterprise – known as HPE – aimed at business services, and HP Inc, aimed at consumers and focusing on printing, printers, laptops and desktops. Whitman took the helm at HPE and spun off its software division, which included Autonomy.

This second sale aside, there were also several developments in the tangle of litigation around Autonomy.

In April 2016, HP settled claims it had asserted against Deloitte for their role in auditing Autonomy's accounts. At the same time, Deloitte signed an agreement with the US Justice Department which stated that the Deloitte partners involved would cooperate fully with the criminal investigation. Then, on 15 November 2016, there was another, far more personal, blow for the Lynch camp. Stouffer Egan had officially turned against him.

Egan had stayed on at HP after the 2011 sale. Despite Lynch's attempts to tempt him away, Egan knew he could not work with his old boss any more. He loved his former team. They were tight after a decade working together, building up the software business from its tiny beginnings, and he always admired Lynch – but he needed to move on.

Alas, it was not to be. Soon after Lynch's departure, first HP executives, and then the FBI, came knocking on Egan's door. The pressure became too great for him, and he revealed his version of what had gone on inside Autonomy in astonishing detail.

First, in 2016, Egan confessed to taking part in fraud at Autonomy. The US financial regulator publicly announced that he had agreed to pay a fine of $923,000 to resolve charges against him for illegally inflating the company's sales figures. A year later, there was a further shock announcement, this time from the US Department of Justice. Egan had struck a deal with US prosecutors and was going to actively testify against his former Autonomy colleagues in exchange for swerving criminal charges.

The terms of the deal were subject to the successful completion of the case against Sushovan Hussain, which was gathering pace. Egan was not allowed to give any opposing evidence or arguments, or he risked being prosecuted immediately, with no chance to defend himself. Egan's decision to turn wasn't unusual – these types of deferred prosecution agreements (DPAs) are another way in which the legal systems in the UK and the US differ. They are common in America, where prosecutors agree to suspend (or 'defer') criminal charges, in exchange for cooperation with ongoing investigations or the payment of fines. The defendant must acknowledge their wrongdoing that led to the charges. It is typically seen as a way of recognizing the seriousness of an offence without experiencing the full consequences of a criminal conviction.

Critically, DPAs are principally used as a way for American prosecutors to get to other perpetrators. British lawyers are far more dubious about these agreements, which they feel undermine the credibility of witnesses who are only testifying to try to save their own skin, although the UK Serious Fraud Office launched a DPA regime in 2014, as an alternative to prosecution and to encourage more companies to self-report wrongdoing.

In any case, Egan's DPA certainly led US prosecutors a step closer to Lynch and Hussain. Speaking out against them felt like an enormous act of betrayal, both for him and especially for those watching in horror back in the UK as this all unfolded. Hussain, Pete Menell and Lynch had become Egan's best friends over the years, like family. Not any more. His warts-and-all testimony from inside Autonomy was explosive. And there was no doubt who was to blame for the fraud. He described Mike Lynch as one of the most powerful characters on the planet. In contrast, Hussain was, Egan said, a highly ethical man operating under Lynch's spell.

Lawyers' notes from the time read:

> *Egan saw Hussain push back on Lynch's unethical ideas. Egan didn't think he was particularly privy to those conversations, but Egan saw Hussain be worked by Lynch just as hard as the rest of management was worked.*

Egan claimed he himself was also mesmerized by the CEO and flattered to be worthy of working with him. Now outside the fold, he painted a picture of a business that would do anything in order to hit its sales numbers in each quarter, describing Lynch as a tough, demanding and incredibly smart boss.

Egan's was a lurid tale of a mismanaged company whose sales were being pushed up by backdated deals, including crafting fake email trails to mislead the auditors and the sketchy involvement of resellers. Lynch would later say cuttingly that Egan was always his best friend – but only when he was asking for more money.

Egan told prosecutors about many deals where Autonomy had crossed the line, including the 2011 attempted contract with Prisa, the publisher of Spanish newspaper *El País*, when Hussain had backdated a reseller sale to make the deal fall into a previous quarter. Egan also described a rogue transaction signed in August 2010, related to the US Department of Veterans Affairs. Autonomy was going to miss its targets if it did not land a sale with the American government. Lynch emailed Egan and the team in his typical fashion: 'We cannot act like muppets on a deal of this size . . . break the rules and do it right.'

Later, Lynch claimed it had been a particularly rare $70 million deal, which was the reason he was so insistent on its success. It was the same old story. As it was a government contract, Autonomy had needed to partner with a government-approved supplier, so, Egan testified, he had organized a deal with a friendly reseller. So far, so good. But he also did a side deal, so that Autonomy would be responsible for finding an end buyer and ultimately paying the money back to the reseller. The use of the reseller was a delaying tactic to make up for the shortfall in sales numbers until the government contract came through. If it ever did. Filetek, the reseller, was just holding the bag on Autonomy's behalf.

If it all sounds messy and complicated, that's because it was. The transactions Egan was describing were fudged and deceitful. The prosecutors from the Department of Justice went one further, alleging that the fraud was not just present in one deal here and there, but that it was an orchestrated scheme. They accused Autonomy of thirty such dodgy deals with resellers between 2009 and 2011, worth nearly $200 million in revenue.

Much later, despite Egan's testimony against him, Lynch would tell friends he could see a way back to a reconciliation with his former colleague and friend. While others found it hard to forget his treatment of them, he would not bear a grudge for the long-term.

EGAN'S BEAN-SPILLING PROVED pivotal to Sushovan Hussain's case. On 10 November 2016, the former Autonomy CFO was indicted on fifteen counts of fraud. He consistently pleaded not guilty, but it made no difference. To the devastation of his wife and two daughters, a bewildered Hussain was soon on his way to California to face a jury on criminal charges.

When it came, the Department of Justice case was swift and brutal. Hussain and his co-conspirators felt they were above the law, prosecutors said, claiming he had an attitude like a James Bond villain or a mafioso. Prosecutors had dug up all of the stories from Autonomy's past, about meeting rooms named after those Bond villains, schools of piranhas in the office and parody sales videos where Hussain and others dressed up as members of the mafia. These jokes had come back to bite them, hard.

Hussain's trial began in February 2018 in the enormous California Northern District Court in San Francisco. Friends from as far back as his Cambridge days went out to America to support him and sit through some of the long, boring days of testimony. It was a year after Donald Trump had begun his first term as president, and some worried that there might be more than a little prejudice against the British Muslim man.

The usually gregarious Hussain was advised to stay quiet and not to smile by lawyers during the trial. Displaying a poker face and dressed in a demure suit, he was at odds with the relaxed San Francisco vibe. To the seated jury, he seemed remote and cold – far from his true personality. Judge Chuck Breyer, then aged seventy-seven, was clear from the outset: the fact that HP could have acted differently in their acquisition was not an excuse for any fraud that existed within Autonomy.

For the prosecution, Bob Leach's opening was simple. He said that Autonomy's growth had been slowing since the financial crisis of 2008 and so Hussain and others started to fiddle with the numbers to make Autonomy's sales growth look better than it was. Hussain was, the prosecution said, the man really in charge of Autonomy's sales. The transcript reads:

> *Hussain backdated contracts in order to bring revenue into a particular period. He pretended that Autonomy had shipped goods it hadn't really shipped. He started buying things that Autonomy did not need and did not use so the sellers could pay their debts to Autonomy and so Autonomy could continue to recognize revenue on deals with them.*

Hussain's lawyer made the case that he was not working alone on the accounts – there were more than 100 people on the finance team across the United States and the UK, many of whom checked the accounts, collected the money and made sure that everything was done properly. The argument was that US and UK accounting systems were different and that the experts at Deloitte had given Autonomy's numbers the rubber stamp.

Hussain did not take the stand to defend himself. Nobody ever heard him speak to give his own version of events. For the watching jury, the accounting story was complex and dull, even if they could understand a modicum of what was going on. Judge Breyer himself declared the affair 'soporific'.

Chris Morvillo, Lynch's attorney, was sitting in the second row of the courtroom taking it all in, watching and learning from Hussain's experiences. A roster of key witnesses took to the stand, including Cathy Lesjak, Mike Sullivan, Dave Truitt, Daud Khan, Leo

Apotheker, Mark Geall and, of course, Stouffer Egan. It was tense for them, facing their old employer across the courtroom and giving answers that could see him thrown in jail.

Egan acknowledged personally approving payments, writing misleading emails, and being less than forthcoming with colleagues. Under cross-examination, he admitted these deals helped inflate sales figures and, at times, contributed to company targets, though he denied directly benefiting through bonuses. Hussain would 'die on the hill of a deal' and he was aware of and at times approved or ignored the questionable arrangements, Egan claimed. Hussain instructed him not to put side deals in writing and insisted that revenue recognition policies were tightly controlled.

It was not a total mea culpa from Egan. The former US CEO's tone was one of partial contrition: he admitted to misleading behaviour but also positioned himself as a pressured subordinate, trying to navigate an intense corporate environment. He acknowledged that Hewlett-Packard was paying his legal fees and that he had strong incentives – both legal and financial – to cooperate with prosecutors and support the tech giant's position.

William Frentzen closed for the prosecution by saying that this was not an HP conspiracy to 'get' Hussain, but asserted that he was representing the US government, which was prosecuting a serious fraud:

> *This is like a guy getting struck by lightning repeatedly over the course of two and a half years. It does not just happen. This is not just happenstance. This was a scheme. This was a plan. This was orchestrated to pump up their numbers, make the quarter, every quarter, no matter what, and then eventually as you saw it was unsustainable. Mr Hussain knew that the deals were bogus, each and every one of them.*

At the end of April 2018, Hussain was convicted on all counts of fraud. It was one of the largest frauds the DOJ had ever prosecuted, and a 'massive victory for the victim company, our community and for the American people,' gloated John F. Bennett, the Special Agent in Charge of the FBI's San Francisco Division.

The sentencing recommendation from prosecutors, issued in May 2019, was utterly damning. Prosecutors alleged that while Hussain might not have made a fortune from Autonomy, he was still holding out for a substantial pot of gold from Lynch because of the shares he had in Invoke businesses. Lynch was dangling $58 million of hush money over him to buy his silence, they claimed:

> *Hussain, completely undeterred and accepting no responsibility for his years of crime, looks forward to an unearned and undeserved payday in Lynch's enterprise the minute he steps out of prison.*

Government lawyers called for Hussain to serve twelve years behind bars.

A startlingly long list of friends, family and colleagues wrote strong letters to Judge Breyer ahead of the sentencing to call for leniency, in praise of his character, telling the story of a devoted, reliable and hard-working family man. One schoolfriend wrote: 'I can tell you that if everyone was like Sushovan, we would be living in a better world. A world of true brotherhood.'

On 13 May 2020, Hussain was sentenced to five years inside the medium-security section of FCI Allenwood, a federal prison in Pennsylvania. He was also hit with a fine of $10 million, the value of his Autonomy shares when it was sold to HP, though he had made substantially less after tax. HP was jubilant, releasing a statement:

> *That Mr Hussain attempted to depict the fraud as nothing more than a misunderstanding of international accounting rules was, and still remains, patently ridiculous.*

For the Hussain family, always believing in his innocence, it was a terrible shock.

Granted leave to appeal and bail, Hussain continued to be restricted to travel within northern California, barred from places from which he could flee (like bus stations and airports) and with a GPS tracker wrapped around his ankle. Lynch and the Invoke team paid for him to live in a $7,500 a month San Francisco penthouse apartment, where he had to regularly return to charge up the battery on his ankle tag, restricting his movements still further. He lost his appeal and, on 26 August 2020, his five-year sentence was upheld. Throughout his case, the US Justice Department had been cajoling and tempting Hussain to testify against Lynch, to flip as Egan had done, in exchange for leniency. He flat-out refused, and the two men continued to speak as often as they were able.

The cost of all of this litigation was adding up, even before proceedings against Lynch himself took any real effect. The $100 million pot from Autonomy's directors' liability insurance, which had been set aside to cover the legal fees, was vastly depleted. All these lawsuits became a black hole for cash; a bottomless pit lined with paperwork and legal bills. Lynch bought some Invoke shares back from Hussain to help him pay his legal fees. Prosecutors again alleged this was hush money.

With Hussain in prison, the odds against Lynch stacked higher and higher. It was clear that American prosecutors had him in their sights and they were not going to go away. At this stage, the tide turned in terms of just how seriously Lynch took it all. Before Hussain was put away, he had been telling friends that the whole thing was just ludicrous and would have to stop.

But now he had to step up his efforts to fight it off.

TWENTY-SIX

Keep It Civil

I'm not skipping like a lamb, but I am upright.

– Mr Justice Hildyard, 20 June 2019

It was early 2019. After being battered by snow and heavy winds, London had sloughed off its cold and dreary winter and was emerging into a hopeful spring.

A year after Hussain's trial ended and almost eight years after the sale of Autonomy, the UK civil trial led by HP against Lynch and Sushovan Hussain finally got underway. It would rank as one of the longest and most complex in English legal history. Rather than losing their liberty in the process, the pair faced losing a fortune and what was left of their reputations.

When they make a film of this, Lynch said, he would be played by Patrick Stewart, referencing the very bald actor who starred as Captain Jean-Luc Picard in *Star Trek: The Next Generation*. It was apt. Robert Hildyard, who tried the case, has something of Spock about him; he's cool, dry and detached, and bald with pointed ears.

It was an unusual trial in many ways, not least because of the looming uncertainty of a possible US criminal trial for Lynch, and

Hussain's recent US trial, which almost overlapped. Most of these commercial cases typically settle well before they reach court, but not this one. Lynch was trapped. Settling at this stage, with the size of the financial penalty HP was after – $5 billion – would have been impossible. On top of that, with the increasing probability of the US trial coming to fruition, a settlement agreement would not have sent a particularly good message to any American juror who might be tempted by a sneaky Google to find out more about the British tech entrepreneur.

Lynch was still publicly, vocally and regularly proclaiming his innocence. His team had set up a website called Autonomy Accounts, which published updates on his trial and set out his arguments against HP. In private, he told friends there may have been a few deals that perhaps warranted quibbling about, and there had been some occasions when Autonomy may have sailed 'close to the wind' or 'pushed the envelope' – by now a well-worn phrase in Autonomy circles – but, he would say, it was nothing serious. In the face of a mountain of witness statements and insurmountable evidence against him and the business, he seemed to have somehow genuinely convinced himself he had done nothing wrong.

Just days before the High Court trial began in late March 2019, US prosecutors unveiled new charges against Lynch. In this way, the two proceedings in the US and UK moved uneasily in parallel, intertwined yet jostling for independence, both judges extremely aware of the other but determinedly treading their own path.

As a pre-trial hearing for Lynch approached in California, Mr Justice Hildyard voiced concern over the potential for showboating US prosecutors to inflame matters in the UK. 'My particular perspective,' he said, 'is to safeguard this process and ensure that it is both fair and not destabilizing to anyone.' Indeed, Hussain's sentence was finally announced in the US smack bang in the middle of the UK trial. Yet, because of the strange way in which these things work, his US conviction was not admissible as part of the UK proceedings. It was another elephant in the courtroom. Everyone knew about it, but it couldn't be used or considered by the judge.

On 25 March 2019, the global media circus joined the two sides gathered in a courtroom of the Rolls Building, built in 2011 to house the business disputes which London regularly hosts. Intended to be a sleek, modern, high-tech outpost of the High Court, in reality it lacks the imposing majesty and grandeur of its older siblings. Instead, it is a functional, drab and uninspiring space, furnished with melamine desks, bland office chairs and microphones. Some have called it 'the court for eastern Europe', given the number of litigants from the former Soviet bloc who bring cases there.

On that first day, Lynch, in a show of bravado, smirked at the proceedings and settled into the public gallery among the press and some of his team to watch HP's opening remarks. Pretending to shrug off the seriousness of the situation, in his self-deprecating way that always won people over, he joked to those around him about the number of documents he would need to take in over the nine-month trial. He mused out loud about whether his eyesight would cope.

Taking notes, he would occasionally exhale loudly, showing flashes of irritability and frustration. Slipping back into his charming facade for the reporters later, he told them with false bravura that the morning in court had been like watching paint dry. The arguments were certainly well-rehearsed by this stage.

Kicking off the trial on behalf of HP, a fiery Laurie Rabinowitz did not mince his words. It was inconceivable that Lynch, a 'controlling and demanding individual', could not have known about the erroneous reporting, given the interest he took in even the most trivial aspects of Autonomy's business. For the defence, Robert Miles made the case that Lynch was merely HP's scapegoat when the company had a serious case of buyer's remorse over its purchase of Autonomy.

Just as the arguments had a tired familiarity, so too did many of the witness statements which were heard for the second time, after Hussain's trial. The list of people appearing in the witness box ranged from Autonomy insiders to Leo Apotheker, Stouffer Egan and a new star turn by Meg Whitman, not present for the Hussain affair, which drew flagging reporters back to the courtroom. For those who did not appear, some of the cross-examination transcripts from Hussain's US criminal trial were also used in the UK.

Inside the courtroom, there were files upon files of evidence and trainee lawyers scurried to get the required papers for the round robin of witnesses. The trial drew on millions of emails and memos and transcripts – the trial bundle alone was made up of 36,000 documents. Ironically, they could have probably done with Autonomy's technology to go through it all.

Witnesses who testified in both trials reported a harsher ride in the UK than in the US, because the questioning was far more forensic. Unlike in America, where a witness starts by fielding friendly questions from their own side, when they take the stand in the UK they walk straight into the bullets of an aggressive cross-examination. There are also different rules in the US and the UK about how witnesses can be prepared to testify. In both jurisdictions, lawyers can explain the process and help the witness understand what to expect, but only in the US are the parties allowed to rehearse their statements or conduct mock cross-examinations.

As a result, Hildyard found the US witnesses tricky to unpick. They had discussed their evidence with either HP's lawyers or the US prosecutors so often that the judge felt like he was being treated to a received and then rehearsed version of events, rather than the witnesses' actual recollections.

But as striking as the names on the stand that were present, were those that were absent during the UK civil trial. The biggest hole was left by Hussain – then by Andy Kanter, Steve Chamberlain, Nicole Eagan and Pete Menell. Kanter and Eagan had originally submitted witness statements and were due to be among those called by Lynch but, shortly before they were due to take the stand, Lynch's lawyers said that they would not appear, and their witness statements were withdrawn.

As a result, HP's lawyers could not cross-examine them. Hildyard raised a severe eyebrow at their no-shows. It seemed as if Lynch was deliberately keeping his top team well away from proceedings.

IT WAS A long, long trial which required a great deal of patience. Almost halfway through, Hildyard reassured the court: 'I'm not skipping like a lamb, but I am upright.'

The moment everyone had been waiting for came at the end of June 2019, when Lynch himself entered the witness box. Dressed simply in a white shirt, navy suit and a striped blue tie, he maintained his nonchalant air. In front of him was a notebook with a few scrawled words of warning: 'be calm and polite' and 'microphone on', so he didn't inadvertently say out loud something he'd regret and have it blasted around the room. But maybe it wasn't necessary. Somehow, Lynch managed to remain calm, courteous and polite throughout the subsequent weeks.

In his flat, nasal and unflustered tone, he spent twenty-one days being cross-examined throughout July, in a gruelling verbal boxing match with Rabinowitz. Two razor-sharp minds going head-to-head four days a week, crawling through the evidence together, debating every point. Throughout this period, Lynch was subject to 'purdah', a type of legal isolation which meant he was not supposed to discuss his testimony with anyone.

If there was ever any doubt about Lynch's brilliance, it was quickly dispelled when he had his month in court. He appeared to have a photographic memory for the documents he was shown. This wasn't always to his advantage. His supporters contested that he had spent so long looking at the relevant information surrounding the allegations that he *appeared* to have a finer appreciation for the details of what had happened inside Autonomy than he actually did.

Despite the overhanging threat of the US criminal proceedings, he kept up his unnatural cool. He had answers to everything and, even if they did not always stand up to scrutiny, he was eloquent and measured. There was no real gotcha moment, no moment of breaking the witness which every barrister hopes for.

At the start of his cross-examination, Lynch conceded that he now knew of some examples where he believed someone had behaved improperly at Autonomy, but he dismissed this quickly as a normal phenomenon when running a multinational company. He was given the chance to throw Hussain under the bus at one point, but he stayed resolutely loyal. Asked whether his Chief Financial Officer would have done anything behind his back, he replied: 'I don't believe Mr Hussain would have engaged in any improper conduct.' Rabinowitz probed: 'Behind your back, is the question.' Lynch replied: 'In front of my back or behind my back. I don't believe that he would have done anything like that.'

He gave lengthy answers to questions which were peppered with analogies, to the extent that he was told to slow down and wait for questions instead of blithely making statements. There were some missteps and characteristic blagging amid the show of confidence. When it was put to him by Rabinowitz that he was literally making things up on the spot, he would allude to unidentified documents that he assured Hildyard would support his statements, but which in the end were never produced.

Lynch was on the stand for so long that the judge remarked it was 'a very strange feeling', when his testimony had finished in August, to look over and not see him in the witness box. He had not disappeared from court, though. Unusually for someone in such a complex trial, he was present every single day – not just for the big set-piece witnesses.

In contrast, apart from for the glitzy appearances, British reporters did not bother coming to court. Many news organizations had got fed up and lost interest by now; many had fallen out with Lynch or been burnt by him in the past. There was one exception. The online publication *The Register* kept the diligent journalist Gareth Corfield attentively across the story. Corfield frequently found himself the only reporter watching proceedings in the Rolls Building.

The trial finally ended in January 2020. Then there was a terribly long wait – almost two years, in the end, as the judge weighed up the evidence, looking at where the truth lay on a balance of probabilities. An appropriately Lynch-like way to assess a situation.

WHILE LYNCH WAS fighting one legal battle in the UK, he was also battling to physically stay in the country, fending off ongoing US government prosecutors' attempts to bring him to America to face the same criminal proceedings as Hussain had. They wanted his extradition but, to do it, they had to get the permission of the British Home Secretary.

Lynch's British legal team argued that he should be tried in the UK and were determined not to put him on a plane to America. To take on his extradition case, Lynch tested and probed a litany of lawyers, in the way that he always did with people, getting the full measure of them, finding their foibles, their strengths. It was obvious to everyone, especially Lynch, that there was a big battle ahead and he wanted to work with someone who had the staying power for the fight. Picking the right people at this stage mattered more than ever. Finally, he hired Alex Bailin as his barrister.

Known as 'smooth' and 'wildly clever', Bailin, a King's Counsel, specializes in financial and business criminal cases. 'Everyone,' his Matrix Chambers web page proclaims, 'wants him on their side'. His most high-profile cases have included the public inquiry into the murder of Alexander Litvinenko; the extradition of billionaire Oleg Tinkov; and the businessman Robert Tchenguiz's battle with the Serious Fraud Office. He is an extremely charming man, but you know you are in trouble when you have to call on him for help.

Getting to know Lynch in an exclusive private members' club in Mayfair, Bailin confessed that he had studied maths at Cambridge and that he had been at the university around the same time as his new client. 'What went wrong?' Lynch asked the bemused Bailin, pondering how this bright, scientifically minded man had ended up as a twit in a suit.

Over in San Francisco, Chris Morvillo, Reid Weingarten and Brian Heberlig were not optimistic of thwarting extradition. They were absolutely sure that Lynch's day in a California court would come, it was just a matter of when and how. Thus, as the possibility of being sent to the US came ever closer, Lynch picked another battle: with the US–UK extradition treaty itself, which he argued was fundamentally flawed. His attempt to fight his extradition would not go well for him, he claimed, because it wasn't designed to go well for him – he went full conspiracy theory, arguing that the whole system is pitched against defendants in the UK.

The issue Lynch was pinpointing was a change made to the extradition treaty between the US and the UK in 2003, in the wake of the 9/11 attacks. The process was made quicker and easier, to emphasize the closeness between the two nations. Yet it has faced severe criticism for the perceived imbalances in how it is applied – in short, many argue that the US government gets who it wants from the UK, but the UK government does not get the same cooperation in return.

The best-known example of this perceived imbalance, at least in the UK, is the death of Harry Dunn. In August 2019, Dunn, a nineteen-year-old British man, was fatally injured after being hit by a car being driven on the wrong side of the road in Northamptonshire, near RAF Croughton. The woman behind the wheel was an American, Anne Sacoolas, whose husband worked at the airbase. While she admitted that she was at fault, she fled the UK, claiming diplomatic immunity. Sacoolas was charged with causing death by dangerous driving in December 2019, but the US State Department rejected an extradition request from the UK. To many in the UK, including Lynch's supporters, it seemed grossly unfair.

Lynch had some cause for hope. Back in 2010, then-Home Secretary Theresa May had blocked the extradition of Gary McKinnon, an autistic British man accused of hacking into US military and NASA computer systems, citing human rights concerns. She also changed the extradition Act in 2013, introducing a 'forum bar' which allows UK courts to block extradition if they believe the trial would be more appropriate in the UK. That change was meant to address concerns about fairness and protect individuals from being sent abroad unnecessarily when the alleged crime has strong British ties.

This was the core of Lynch's argument. That Britain was the forum in which he should be tried. There are big differences between the American and British justice systems – the US system can dish out much harsher penalties, and the US penal system can be much more brutal. America is also more reliant on people, such as Stouffer Egan, turning into cooperators, admitting their own involvement in a crime to obtain immunity. US prosecutors have also been known to try to drain people's legal funds in order to squeeze them into accepting such DPAs.

It was not just the civil case that Lynch needed to win to try to halt the extradition. Almost a decade on from the disastrous sale of Autonomy to HP, his star and profile had fallen fast, and the court of public opinion had long turned against him. It was a bewildering and often lonely time. When veteran tech journalist Jonathan Margolis offered the *Financial Times* a soft story about Lynch's interest in the psychic ability of dogs, he was told the newspaper did not want anything to do with Dr Lynch.

A public relations campaign was needed. Lynch and his friend Patrick Jacob went for a walk in Staverton Thicks, an ancient oak and holly forest in Suffolk, where they came up with a strategy to complement what the lawyers were doing. Uncharacteristically, Lynch listened to Jacob, who offered to support him finding and funding the correct advisory team to work with. As boutique PR firms pitched for the job, Lynch set out the conundrum to potential companies thus:

> *Imagine there's a cave with a dragon inside and the dragon is HP. Anyone who gets anywhere close, ends up getting burnt – so your task is to figure out how you can get into the cave and not get fried alive like everyone else.*

Lynch and Jacobs eventually plumped for Audley Advisors, run by Sir Michael Lockett, an eminent establishment figure renowned for his organization of high-profile events for the royal family. His powerful and discreet organization boasts that it helps clients 'overcome really complex challenges'. Under Chris Wilkins, once Head of Strategy and chief speech writer to Theresa May during her time as prime minister, a team was pulled together, overseen by a determined Jacob.

One strategy they devised was codenamed 'Make Mike Matter'. The idea was to boost his profile and credibility by pushing out messages about Lynch's entrepreneurial and scientific expertise, and his importance to the British tech sector. The firm filmed a series of leadership videos for the Invoke website, and Lynch authored blog posts with his reflections on the latest tech trends. They did not make much of an impact, and even made him look more of an outlier – forced to push out information through his own channels rather than making a splash in the mainstream media.

Lynch and his PR team also turned to sympathetic company and political leaders to drum up support. Lynch considered trying to get signatures from the bosses of every FTSE 100 business, bashing the extradition treaty, 'explaining' to them, in the way he had of thinking he knew better than everyone else, the perils they were running by doing business in the United States, but he was persuaded that very few were likely to sign.

He also met influential figures: newspaper bosses, editors and politicians. On one occasion, Lynch went to see Tony Blair in his office to discuss the founding tenets of the extradition treaty, which had come into being on the former prime minister's watch. On particularly pugnacious form that day, Lynch started sparring with him. His advisors rolled their eyes – he was impossible to control.

Such lobbying was made difficult by the revolving door at the top of Britain's Conservative government, and while there was sometimes sympathy and support in private, few politicians or business leaders wanted to put their head above the parapet to speak up for him. Advisors scratched their heads, perplexed and frustrated, as they found that even those who had remained close to Lynch did not want to stick by him publicly.

Lynch even tried to draw on his connections in the security services. Audley helped to organize a series of dinners to discuss cyber threats to national security, inviting key figures from that world. While the events were well-attended, Lynch was furious that none of these high-level contacts stepped in to help his cause when it came to extradition.

Part of the problem was Lynch's difficult reputation. He had rubbed many people up the wrong way over the years, across the media, the City and in business. Many saw a reputational risk in being linked to him. Others saw him as a lost cause; there was a sense of fatalism around the outcome of the case.

On 5 February 2020, Lynch submitted himself for arrest, handing himself into Charing Cross Police Station in Central London before facing an initial extradition hearing at Westminster Magistrates' Court – just a formality. He was released on £10 million bail.

Not long after, on 15 March 2020, his mother died. She had long been suffering from Alzheimer's, which made her erratic and ill-tempered. Friends all said Lynch was close to her and many remember her visits to Cambridge, so many years before. On 23 March there was an added complication when Prime Minister

Boris Johnson announced that Britain was entering Covid-19 lockdown, causing unprecedented delays and complications in all facets of British life.

IT WAS OVER a year later, on 12 January 2021, that a letter signed by the handful of people who did publicly support Lynch appeared in *The Times*. It was signed by four former Tory cabinet ministers: Andrew Mitchell, David Davis (who had also supported Lynch during his civil trial), Lord Maude of Horsham and Lord Deben; along with Sir Vince Cable, the Liberal Democrat former business secretary; and from the business world Sir John Rose, a former head of Rolls-Royce, and Marcus Agius, a former head of Barclays, who had chaired the BBC board while Lynch was on it.

The letter warned that the government had surrendered sovereignty over extraditions, and that Lynch's case could set a dangerous precedent: 'The government cannot stand by as another Briton risks being delivered like this to the US justice system.'

Nevertheless, the process to send him to America ticked on. And so it was that in February 2021, yet another British legal battle began. This time, Lynch stood in front of District Judge Michael Snow in a last attempt to remain on British soil.

His lawyers tried everything. Lynch's medical conditions meant he would not cope well with prison life, they argued. They said he had laryngospasm and sleep apnoea as well as complex gastroenterological problems which required strict personal hygiene. The defence called Joel Sickler, a witness in the Julian Assange extradition case who works on prisoner advocacy, to describe what life was like in an American jail. Asked if a portable bidet was a possible solution for the gastroenterological distress, Sickler responded:

> *He's going to sit in it for an extended period of time. Then he's going to have to dispose of it, and somehow clean it, and he's going to have to*

> *bring it back to his dormitory, put it in his cubicle under his bed. He's not going to be a popular inmate doing that day in, day out.*

It was anything but glamorous. It was gritty, and specific, and human, and would have been humiliating for someone with less pride than Lynch.

Alex Bailin, Lynch's barrister, said that the Serious Fraud Office had reserved its right to prosecute him in the UK, if his extradition to the US were blocked, so he could still face British criminal charges if the civil court went against him.

> *What is clear is that a decision in Mr Lynch's favour by this court would not be an automatic get-out-of-jail-free card . . . The SFO might decide to prosecute him depending on their view of . . . the judgment and he would vigorously contest this on British soil.*

In the event, Lynch lost his fight and began a long wait for the final decision from Priti Patel, the latest Home Secretary. Theresa May's changes to the extradition Act had limited the Home Secretary's powers to say yes or no – they are now only allowed to consider specific legal matters, such as the rule that a person should only be tried for the crimes for which they have been extradited, or the impact of the death penalty. 'What are the odds of her not signing [the extradition warrant]?' Lynch asked advisors. 'If you win the civil case, then 50 per cent,' they replied.

In reality, no one will ever know for sure what difference the civil judgement had on Priti Patel's decision. However, given the legal constraints, in the end there was little she could do.

TWENTY-SEVEN

Poppy from Accounts

We need to rein her in; she's just a salesgirl.
She's just Poppy from accounts!

– Mike Lynch

Tall, dark, striking and immensely clever, Poppy Gustafsson looks and acts nothing like a tech-bro boss. In the pale, male and sometimes stale world of UK tech, she has always stood out.

At Autonomy, she was 'Poppy from accounts' – or Poppy Prentis, as she was before she got married. After studying maths at Sheffield University, she had trained as a chartered accountant at Deloitte and then taken the well-trodden path over to Autonomy, where she worked for Sushovan Hussain. She became pregnant in her early thirties, just after the sale of the company to HP, and left to have her child.

On maternity leave, her phone rang. It was Suzanne Howarth, Autonomy's HR head, calling her exactly as she had called Jack Stockdale, asking when she was planning to come back to work and if would she like to join Invoke. 'Yes!' she said. It was an exciting offer; Gustafsson had heard that Lynch and Hussain's top team were reconvening to spot fast-growing tech investments, and she was keen to rejoin the fold.

Soon, she started to spend more and more time on one business: a cybersecurity company called Darktrace, where she took on an increasingly prominent role. And it was here that the problems between her and Lynch really started.

OF ALL THE companies which were born from Invoke, Darktrace, which launched in 2013, was the one which meant the most to Lynch. It was his redemption business after Autonomy, proving that he could achieve success twice, critical to restoring his pride, boosting his profile and bolstering his legal case. And like all great passions, it came with a good deal of pain. It was not initially his favourite company from the new round of investments. He was far more interested in Sophia Genetics, the company investigating the medical applications of AI.

Just as with the founding of Autonomy and the question of John Snyder's involvement all those years ago in Cambridge, the stories of Darktrace's beginnings differ and are surprisingly controversial. What is clear is that Darktrace's founders consisted of a mixture of (literal) spies, tech nerds and experts from Invoke. And that no one person can take all the credit for the idea.

It appears that a former customer of Autonomy, a member of MI5's cyber defence team named Steve Huxter, came to Invoke with the germ of a concept: he saw a massive problem with cybersecurity and thought it should be approached differently, but he didn't have the tech or the business expertise to make it happen, which is where Invoke came in.

The cybersecurity problem that Huxter (and other experts) had spotted underpins the premise for Darktrace: that all of our systems have already been infiltrated, and that there's no point trying to put a wall around a business. Hackers are everywhere. Instead of trying to keep them out, we need to shift focus. Computers must learn what 'normal' looks like for a business and respond autonomously to anything that deviates from it, much like how the immune system instinctively responds to infection.

Standing at a whiteboard, Huxter sketched out the idea to Sushovan Hussain and Pete Menell. They summoned tech whizz Jack Stockdale, asking him if building something like this was possible. He got to work. Soon, Thomas Bayes was back in play. Darktrace's technology was based on recursive Bayesian estimation – where the probabilities of events are continually revised in the light of new information.

Lynch, always a fan of 'spooky stuff', would later explain Darktrace's functionality in his usual brilliant analogistic way. He said that companies' tech systems should not be treated like castles with moats, that it is hopeless to bolt the doors and windows and hope for safety. Instead, he claimed that the new digital world was like a city where terrorists – cyber attackers – roam about everywhere: on the tube, on the buses, inside all our established infrastructure. Spotting anomalies in patterns of behaviour was the most effective way of pinpointing planned attacks.

On 29 March 2013, Stockdale wrote the first line of code and demonstrated the technology on the Invoke office printer. The whirring back and forth of this bog-standard machine is an example of a system with a regular pattern, because it is only used in office hours. It triggered an alert when it spotted an anomaly, and Darktrace was quickly born.

As for the name, one legend has it that Invoke kept two flip charts in its Mayfair offices for staff to brainstorm. They were scratching their heads for something that might work for cybersecurity. Eventually two words scrawled on the adjacent pages stuck: DARK and TRACE. Pete Menell insisted on using *Minority Report*, the 2002 sci-fi film, to inspire the look and feel of the business.

In September 2013, Invoke announced its investment in Darktrace to great fanfare. Lynch told the press that Invoke had ploughed 'up to' $20 million into Darktrace. Actually, it had invested £10,000 in exchange for shares and funded the rest with £6.6 million in loans until 2015. Lynch and Hussain did not make direct investments, but Darktrace paid Invoke, including Hussain and Lynch, for management advice.

They pulled in some top names. Sir Jonathan Evans, the former director general of M15, joined the company's advisory board. Not long after, in January 2014, Andrew France left a senior position at GCHQ to become the chief executive. And despite ongoing legal shenanigans, Rob Webb KC, the former Autonomy chairman, accepted the role as the Darktrace chairman in August 2014. He never minded a bit of noise. Hoxton Ventures and others put money in and, in 2015, Summit Partners, KKR and other investors came on board, eventually valuing the company at $100 million.

Early on, there was a disagreement within the upper echelons, and the business split between two factions: the Invoke camp versus Huxter and France. Eventually, the two spies handed in their resignations while Hussain and Lynch were on holiday one summer. To try to keep the former spooks sweet, in case they tried to take swathes of the team with them, Hussain and Lynch offered them some Darktrace shares as they departed.

Darktrace had a strong commercial plan from the start. This was crucial. Lynch used to say that the reason Britain doesn't have many successful technology businesses was because the country cannot compete against the marketing machines of Microsoft, Salesforce, Oracle, Google, HP and Dell. 'That is how it works, that is the game,' he would say. 'Everyone in the UK says they want the next Google, and then you start putting some numbers on the board, and they start calling you aggressive.' Darktrace would prove to be a home run, although there were plenty of bumps along the way.

Its first big win was a deal with Drax, the energy company, which became a loyal customer. This was the sale that would prove the concept, and it was then that Lynch started to take a real interest. His presence in the Darktrace offices was often signalled to staff by his dogs rootling around in the bins. Hussain and Lynch had joined the board in 2015 as non-executive directors. Gustafsson was the chief financial officer and in 2016 became the co-chief executive alongside Nicole Eagan, Lynch's former chief marketing officer from Autonomy.

As the pressures from the fallout of the Autonomy sale grew, Lynch became more and more irate and more and more unreasonable to deal with. Within Darktrace, he was always using his 'get the dog off the sofa' strategy, a Lynchism for a power play, a way of showing he was in charge and asserting his authority. It was exhausting for the team.

In 2016, Hussain stepped down from the Darktrace board when his criminal charges came through. This meant that Gustafsson was spending more time with Lynch, and their relationship was souring by the day. They had not known each other well at Autonomy, so it was an unpleasant voyage of discovery on both sides. Lynch loathed not being in charge and would belittle Gustafsson, humiliate and try to control her. The young leader would not tolerate some of his behaviour; he felt she was ignoring the voice of experience.

One day, he rang her up to berate her because the office internet was not working. 'It is not fucking acceptable!' he yelled, and swore at her repeatedly down the phone. Gustafsson hung up and refused to take his calls until later. There was nothing Lynch hated more than this kind of insubordinate behaviour. Eventually, she deigned to speak to him, telling him in no uncertain terms that she did not like being spoken to in that manner. She just would not fall into line.

The tension between the two became an open secret. It was a fissure that would become a gulf. It didn't help that Gustafsson's public star was rising while Lynch's was waning fast. In 2018, when he was formally accused of criminal conduct by the US government, Lynch followed Hussain and stepped down from the Darktrace board. At the same time, for the same reasons, he stepped down from his government advisory role. A year later, a fund chaired by the former US vice-president Al Gore pushed him off the board of Sophia Genetics because his presence was a 'distraction'. In 2019, just as Lynch's achievements were being discredited and undermined, Gustafsson was made an OBE for services to cybersecurity. It all grated.

As the British court case got underway, with the added pressure of Covid thrown in for fun, Lynch began to feel he was losing his grip on Darktrace, and he didn't like it. This sent him into a spiral of paranoia about and irritation towards those who were running it day to day, mainly his by-now-nemesis Gustafsson.

Lynch never did things by halves. He was all or nothing, so inevitably the court cases were at the front of his thoughts. But he kept trying to drive the car while sitting in the back seat, irritated by the strategy Darktrace was pursuing and not afraid to make his feelings known. He thought it was underperforming, that the company had not released a new product for too long or published regular enough press releases about its achievements. 'If this hadn't happened to me,' he told everyone who would listen, 'Darktrace would be worth much, much more than it is now. It should be Britain's next ARM', a reference to the Cambridge chip megalith whose designs feature in every iPhone.

DARKTRACE'S CAMBRIDGE HEADQUARTERS looked over the St John's Innovation Centre, where Autonomy started life. It also boasted a deluge of former Autonomy staff members, and there was something of the Autonomy culture about the place, not least because of the intense emphasis on sales and Lynch and Hussain as co-founders. The links between the two companies were unavoidable, and the public fallout from the Autonomy scandal soon started blowing back hard on the cybersecurity business.

The US Department of Justice subpoenaed Darktrace in 2018,

asking for information about the hiring of former Autonomy staff and the shares issued to Invoke. It was an issue that Darktrace would come up against again and again. The company was almost always mentioned in the same breath as Autonomy, if not in the same newspaper articles. As a result, there were many who would not invest in the business or join it because of its links to Lynch. Darktrace executives felt very strongly that separating from him, forging an independent path and identity of the company's own, was the right thing to do. As the UK civil trial started, it was preparing to launch on the public markets.

So, Darktrace started to try to distance itself from Lynch. Lynch was hurt by this. Rightly or wrongly, he felt that he had made the product and the business such a success and he was upset at being shut out. On top of the perceived personal and professional slight, Lynch felt Darktrace's attitude towards him was also unhelpful for his defence in the trial.

The company was meant to be a validation strategy for him, to show his critics, HP and the whole world that he could once again achieve stratospheric success with a homegrown British technology business in a very short period of time. But by putting clear water between Lynch and Darktrace, his former colleagues and friends neutered that idea. People involved in the company were forced to pick sides between Lynch and Gustafsson. It tore some in two.

Things came to a head when Darktrace floated on the London Stock Exchange in April 2021. It meant a final separation from Invoke and Lynch, a huge change in the way the company operated. The co-CEO arrangement with Nicole Eagan was severed, and Gustafsson moved to the helm. By this time, Amber Rudd – another former Home Secretary who had preceded Priti Patel in the role – and Alan Wade, the CIA's former chief information officer, sat on its advisory board. Lord Willetts, former Minister of State for Science, and Sir Peter Bonfield, former boss of BT, were among the non-executive directors.

In the run-up to the float, the hangover from the links to Lynch and Autonomy continued. The prospectus sets out starkly just how much of a problem Autonomy posed, listing risks of money-laundering and reputational damage. Darktrace struggled to find a top-tier bank to work on the floatation, as the likes of Goldman Sachs and UBS declined, with the trial still ongoing. Instead, two small banks called Jefferies and Berenberg picked up the job and did it with aplomb.

Then, Covid came along. Taking a company public is hard. Taking a company public when you can't meet people properly is even harder. At this point, Darktrace was a sizeable entity with over 4,700 customers in over 100 countries and more than 1,500 employees. Sales had bounced from $79 million in 2018 to $199 million in 2020. And it was going to get even bigger.

In the end, it launched with a bang on Friday 30 April. At one point on the day of the float, Darktrace shares jumped up by more than 44 per cent. At the close, its market value had soared from £1.7 billion to £2.2 billion. Constrained by Covid guidelines, the Darktrace team gathered outside a pub, umbrellas glistening in the Cambridge rain, to celebrate. Only allowed to sit in socially distanced groups of six, it was all a bit of a damp squib; adrenaline turned to relief which turned to exhaustion.

Lynch sucked any remaining joy out of the situation that weekend, when he sent a long irritable email to a long list of people, criticizing Gustafsson for not emailing him to thank him for the float's success. However, a new dawn was beginning for Darktrace as a listed business, and he could not ruin the mood for long. He no longer had the authority.

Ideally, he would have gone for long dog walks with Gustafsson and told her what to do with the company, but public businesses have fiduciary duties to their shareholders. The team was not allowed to meet up with Lynch privately or give him the special treatment he would have liked, and so it became easier to pull the business away from the conundrum they saw him as. Most of the time.

They could not shake off his shareholding. At the float, Darktrace paid Invoke £1,200,000 and ended the advisory relationship between the two firms but, at this stage, the Lynch family owned almost 18 per cent of Darktrace, the bulk of it in Angela's name.

Success has many fathers and failure is an orphan. The phrase could have been written for Darktrace. Lynch became totally obsessed with its founding story – always a vital part of an entrepreneur's fable, the how-I-made-it fairy tale crafted to inspire, show innovation and underscore the founder's resilience and vision.

Darktrace was the second successful technology business that Lynch had worked on and he wanted the credit, to wave it under the court and the public's nose to prove his worth. Gustafsson was repeatedly described as 'co-founder' in the media and it riled him that she was given such important status. He felt completely airbrushed out of the company's history, like she was getting the accolades for his work.

In fact, the Darktrace prospectus – as close as you'll get to an authorized history of the company – does not name one founder:

> *[Darktrace is a] collaboration of cyber experts from various government intelligence backgrounds and mathematicians who were experts in machine learning.*

Gustafsson is described as having 'joined the Group as an employee with effect from November 2014', something she has never challenged, but every time she was named as a co-founder in the press, it set Lynch off. In December 2021, it got to him to such an extent that he published a blog on the Invoke website titled 'The Creation of Darktrace', where he set out his own version of its history.

It had been almost two years since the civil trial hearings ended, and there was still no word of a verdict from Hildyard. The immense stress of the lawsuit, the continued uncertainty, was taking its toll. In the blog, Lynch wrote that he had come up with the idea for

Darktrace years earlier at the BBC, when he had seen first-hand how staff had looked up the salaries of celebrities and leaked them to the press, something others there at the time do not recall. He also made sure to diminish Gustafsson's role by comparison:

> *Darktrace's founding product and positioning were created in the early days within Invoke.*
>
> *A few months later in February 2013, an accountant from one of my previous companies who was, luckily for us, returning to work part-time after the birth of her first child joined DVL [Darktrace Ventures Limited]. Over the years that person, Poppy, had an impressive growth trajectory that would lead her to becoming the company's CEO.*
>
> *In June 2013, Jack [Stockdale] and the Invoke technology team reviewed the latest product and Invoke decided it was time to form the company. After a few near misses with a number of dubious names, I came up with the names Darktrace and the Enterprise Immune System.*
>
> *Poppy filled out the relevant paperwork.*

The story of Gustafsson taking over the business at the expense of Lynch became a major issue among some at Invoke, who said being around her made their skin crawl. On 9 November 2022, Lynch wrote a letter to the Darktrace board complaining about how the company's founding story was being portrayed. The letter was sparked by an interview Gustafsson gave to the *Mail on Sunday*'s legendary business editor Ruth Sunderland just a week or so beforehand. Lynch was a founding investor, Gustafsson said, but now Darktrace was a standalone business and 'he doesn't get involved. I don't see him'.

In his missive to executives, Lynch accused Darktrace of creating a fictional account of the period around the company's early days, insisting that Invoke's involvement was far more than just seed investment. He understood Darktrace's desire to distance itself from him, he wrote, but it must not be done 'at the expense of the facts'.

No formal response to his letter is recorded from the Darktrace board. In a sign of their irritation with the Darktrace team, the Lynch family started selling off its shares. Also in November 2022, they and the Invoke team publicly undermined the company by voting against Gustafsson's £12 million pay packet, which included £10.7 million in long-term share awards linked to the IPO.

The City and the press were broadly unaware of the tension behind the scenes between Lynch and Gustafsson, and so the Autonomy story continued to dog Darktrace. Hedge funds started circling the tech company, much as they had around Autonomy in the wake of the 2008 financial crash, raking over the links between the businesses and betting that the price of Darktrace's stock would go down.

Matthew Earl, a trader nicknamed the Dark Destroyer, turned on the company. His business, Shadowfall Capital, was best known for exposing the Wirecard scandal. On a call to investors in 2022, Earl made some damning claims about the culture at Darktrace, the number of former Autonomy employees who worked there, its accounting practices and the product. Then, in 2023, an American short-seller called Quintessential Capital Management published a paper called 'Autonomy 2.0? The dark side of Darktrace', which ripped into the business. It drew many comparisons with Autonomy, including questioning the integrity of Darktrace's accounts.

The pressure on Darktrace to prove it was whiter than white meant that it ended up taking the unusual step of employing Ernst & Young (EY), one of the four biggest accounting firms in the world, to look over its books. The auditor gave Darktrace a clean bill of health to the market and the regulator, but the company remained under a huge amount of scrutiny and – worse – mistrust.

By December 2022, tensions across the Darktrace board had made it a difficult place to be for Lynch's supporters and friends. Vanessa Colomar wanted to step down from her seat representing Invoke, and Lynch asked his friend and supporter Patrick Jacob, a former investment banker, to replace her. In private, shareholders continued to murmur that any links to Lynch were 'unhelpful' and depressing the share price.

IN CONTRAST TO the continued noise around Lynch, Loudham Hall was silent during Covid. Planes stopped flying and cars stopped passing. The family locked down in Suffolk, along with their housekeeper, six months' worth of food and various other supplies. While most of the staff worked from home, the hall's stock-keeper Mark Gilbert kept some freedom. Still permitted to work outside, he would stride out into the fields looking after the herds, feeling as if he had the whole farm to himself.

In truth, the prospect of Lynch's extradition was unsettling for everyone at Loudham, both the family and those who worked there. It made the place feel stagnant, preserved in aspic until a decision was reached. It was such a Mike house that the prospect of a life without him made everyone doubt the future. Yet, as the strain of the long legal fight continued, Loudham provided some moments of levity. Esme and Hannah's silvery pygmy goats, Milly and Tilly, had their adorable kids, which delighted the family.

Lynch wrote to his friends and supporters on 8 January 2021:

> *With a pandemic raging it is difficult to be very optimistic, and yet there are reasons to be hopeful. The government, with Brexit behind it, is looking ahead and keen to create a new identity for 'Global Britain' as a scientific and technological superpower. I obviously welcome this, and am helping where I can both directly, and through the portfolio businesses.*

Given his vastly reduced influence, it's hard to read the last line above as anything more than self-aggrandisement. Lynch also noted that Mr Justice Hildyard had not yet come to a conclusion with regards to the civil case, which had finished exactly a year before:

> *While this is stressful, it is also an assurance that he is giving the evidence as much consideration as is needed.*

He most certainly was.

TWENTY-EIGHT

Come Fly with Me

One of the tragedies of the case is clear: an innovative and ground-breaking product, its architect and the company will probably always be associated with fraud.

– *Mr Justice Hildyard, civil judgement, 17 May 2022*

On 6 January 2021, England entered its third national lockdown. That same grey winter's day, the verdict of one of the most damning investigations into Autonomy emerged from the driest of quarters: the British accounting regulator, the Financial Reporting Council.

Raking over the accounts from a decade earlier in a 2019 disciplinary tribunal, the FRC slammed Deloitte with a £15 million fine for its poor audit of Autonomy's numbers, and for failing to act with integrity and objectivity. This addressed one of the big mysteries surrounding the fraud: how financial statements, despite being questionable, were regularly signed off by the auditors.

The regulator's report found that Deloitte's relationship with Autonomy was far too cosy because it was such an important account for the Cambridge office of the business, its only FTSE 100 listed client. Richard Knights, the 'modest bookkeeper', as he described himself in that infamous medieval-pasta missive to Lynch and Hussain, should have asked for more evidence from Autonomy and kept a greater degree of distance and professional scepticism, the FRC said. Nigel Mercer, too, was found wanting, particularly for not correcting a misleading letter sent to the Financial Reporting Review Panel.

The tribunal concluded that Deloitte, far from being the watchful guardian of financial integrity, had slipped into complicity through repeated and serious lapses in professional scepticism. What made the case so grave was not simply a few poor calls, but a consistent failure to uphold professional standards.

It expanded upon a litany of errors. Autonomy's plans on how to account for its disguised hardware sales cried out for an explanation. It looked as if their misallocation as a sales and marketing cost was made under pressure.

It also drew attention to how the value-added reseller (VAR) sales in Autonomy's accounts, which had not been closed, came to happen. Lynch had repeatedly obfuscated, with persuasive conviction, that prosecutors had misunderstood the differences between US and UK accounting requirements, which had different rules for when a sale could be clocked onto the books. The FRC did not agree.

Knights was barred from membership of the Institute of Chartered Accountants for England and Wales for five years, and fined £500,000, while Mercer was fined £250,000 and received a severe reprimand. Sushovan Hussain was later banned from the body until 2038.

Mercer and Knights disagreed with the findings, arguing that the accounting was always a question of judgement. They believed 'they had acted professionally, diligently and in good faith', adding, 'we are grateful for the full and unwavering support of Deloitte in this matter.' There was a powerful fog of technical complexity around Autonomy's products, and their deals involved bespoke bundles, cross-border elements and fast-moving digital contracts. Each transaction had just enough documentation to sound plausible, and Deloitte often had to audit under tight timeframes. In that environment, judgement calls became blurred, and Deloitte leant towards giving their client the benefit of the doubt. This was unfortunately just the latest in a series of blows to trust in UK audit companies.

The FRC judgement allowed Lynch to heap further blame on Deloitte, who remained one of his key scapegoats. In one of his regular letters to his supporters, Lynch said that the FRC findings were troubling because CEOs should be able to rely on their auditors for independent, accurate and fair advice.

There was one good thing about the result, he said: at least it showed the UK could deal with complex commercial and accounting disputes itself, without involving American prosecutors. As the somewhat circuitous line of reasoning to link the affair to his pending extradition showed, the FRC ruling did not remotely draw a line under Lynch's legal problems. Indeed, a year later, another verdict followed which would have further-reaching implications for everyone linked to Autonomy, especially Lynch.

AFTER A SERIES of frustrating delays, on Friday, 28 January 2022 – to coincide with Priti Patel's deadline to decide whether to sign the warrant for Lynch's extradition – Mr Justice Hildyard delivered his findings. Everyone involved in the case was hastily summoned to the Rolls Building and waited apprehensively for the outcome. Had Lynch committed a fraud or was HP trying to blame him for their expensive mistake?

The lawyers were confused. Normally, they get advance sight of judgements under embargo, to check for any glaring errors. Not this time. No one knew what to expect.

Unlike his regular attendance during the trial, Lynch did not turn up to court for the verdict, to the disappointment of the waiting photographers. He and his advisors gathered in PR firm Brunswick's offices, with someone in court feeding back to them.

Everyone on Lynch's team thought the civil trial had gone very well. As always, he wanted to know what his odds were of winning. Pretty strongly in favour, he was told. Similarly, HP felt it had probably gone against them, given some of the remarks from the judge during the trial. Hildyard put everyone out of their misery very quickly.

At the end of what he called 'an exceptionally onerous case', the judge found in favour of HP. The US company had substantially succeeded in its claims, and Hildyard believed that Lynch and Hussain had orchestrated a fraud at Autonomy. Its sales over the relevant period from 2009 to 2011, he found, were overstated by almost half a billion dollars.

The outcome left Lynch's, Hussain's and Autonomy's reputation in tatters.

Months later, in May 2022, Hildyard's full 1,650-page judgement landed. This combed through each of the queried transactions in forensic detail and broke them down one by one. 'Fraud on a grand scale; or relentless witch-hunt?' was the elegant question the ponderous judge posed at the start of his mammoth judgement. By that time, everyone knew the answer.

It was a tragedy, Hildyard said, that Autonomy, with its innovative and ground-breaking product and Lynch as its founder, would always be linked to fraud. Yet his judgement went beyond Lynch and Hussain. He found that the company was run by a 'cabal' which included Andy Kanter, Steve Chamberlain, Nicole Eagan and Pete Menell, all of whom pulled various levers to push up the company's sales numbers.

Brent Hogenson, Hildyard found, had been fired because Lynch and Hussain were trying to prevent an official investigation into illusory and improper reseller sales. Resellers helped the business to plug shortfalls and allowed Autonomy to recognize income before a sale to a customer. Hildyard recounted how Lynch and Hussain would keep a close eye on sales and, if a shortfall came up, use a reseller to cover it up with no questions asked, usually at the very end of the quarter – it was almost exactly the same conclusion the FRC had drawn.

Autonomy's hardware sales were not for promotional purposes, Hildyard said, but to enable the company to hit its financial forecasts, thereby deliberately misleading the financial market. There was absolutely no business justification for them, and the idea they were for marketing was a pretext to mislead the audit committee and Deloitte. The final judgement damningly stated that 80 per cent of original equipment manufacturer (OEM) deals in the relevant period, representing over $250 million in revenue, were misclassified. The 'Hogenson Episode', as Hildyard called the US accountant's whistleblowing, had provided further support for the judge's conclusion that both Hussain and Lynch knew that the VAR sales were 'illusory and improper' and were determined to dodge any investigation that would reveal this.

Interestingly, whether HP did its due diligence correctly was irrelevant to the case, Hildyard said: 'It would be beguiling but wrong to think that the answer could be "caveat emptor" [Buyer Beware].'

HP might have succeeded in its case, but there was a kicker for the American company. The judge said that the American giant might still have bought Autonomy, even had they known the true financial picture. Furthermore, he found that HP was aware of some of the sales mechanisms inside Autonomy, including that it was selling some hardware, although not the scale of it. No one knew that. Meg Whitman, he said, 'fell in with HP's corporate antipathy to any culture other than its own' and, whatever she said, saw Autonomy like an 'unwanted stepchild'. He dismissed Joel Scott's whistleblowing as 'largely self-serving'.

He was also scathing about the state of HP, calling it an ailing institution, saying it was fractured in 'silos' with intra-division jealousies, poor cooperation and overall direction, and short-term focus.

In contrast, he said, Autonomy was 'energetic and driven by entrepreneurial zeal, with little formality or adherence to strict process'.

Hildyard concluded by estimating that the amount owed to HP would be substantially less than the $5 billion they were seeking. The exact figure would be decided at a much, much later date. It meant yet more waiting and uncertainty.

THERE WAS A cacophony of responses to Hildyard's full judgement. Lynch's press team issued a statement calling the outcome 'disappointing' and stating his intention to appeal.

Some Autonomy insiders felt the judge had done a thorough job. They described an 'addiction' that developed within the business. A startup is all about 'go, go, go' and the excitement of the vision. No one wants to fail the quarter. A former senior staffer said: 'Of course we could have done, but we started not wanting to. If you can catch

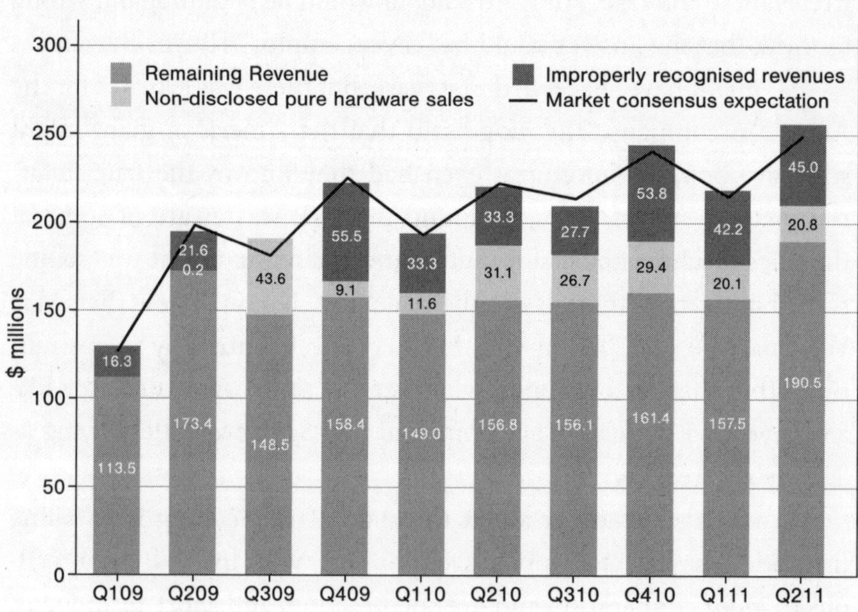

it at that early stage, it's relatively easy to fix but once it becomes ingrained, it is a big problem.'

Some of Lynch's friends fell by the wayside, expressing disappointment at what was revealed by the evidence. Others argued that Lynch might have pushed the envelope or sailed close to the wind – euphemisms which kept being applied to Autonomy's accounting – but they believed that he did not realize he was doing anything seriously wrong. Others countered that the fraud outlined wasn't particularly 'bad stuff'. They believed that it might have crossed a line, but it was not an orchestrated scam. Or they blamed HP for needing a scapegoat for the chaos it was in at the time.

There were those who believed everyone was 'at it' in the business world, especially in the fluid software sales game, and that Autonomy's only mistake was getting caught. Lynch was a victim of tall poppy syndrome, some said, an ingrained British bias against success. It did not help that he looked like a James Bond villain and played up to that persona, they shrugged.

The judgement was far from the end of it. Most importantly, the 'quantum' – how much HP would be awarded – was yet to be ruled on. Meanwhile, the verdict sent Darktrace's share price plunging by 15 per cent as Nicole Eagan, now the company's chief strategy officer, was named as a member of the Autonomy 'cabal'. Darktrace was forced to update the stock market to deny any links to the proceedings.

Later that evening, on the same day Hildyard released his summary findings and a few short hours before the midnight deadline for her decision, Priti Patel picked up her pen and signed the warrant for Mike Lynch's extradition to the United States.

It was never said out loud, but some of the lawyers involved suspected that Patel wanted to at least have an overview of the judge's findings before she made her decision to send Lynch to the US. But Lynch was prepared for it by this stage. He took it in his stride – as he did every knockback, to his credit. On to the next challenge.

Lynch's legal team applied for permission to appeal the Home Secretary's decision, but this was rejected by the High Court in April 2023. At Loudham Hall, staff were summoned to a brief meeting: 'The news will break shortly that Mike is off to America and that is all we know at the moment. He could be gone for a very long time.'

Lynch's lawyers sent him for a medical exam days before he flew out to the US, to see if it might throw up anything that might be useful, amid the ongoing mayhem, in delaying his extradition. There was only one outcome of any significance.

'Good news!' he told a friend at dinner afterwards. 'I'm high-functioning!'

FOR A MAN who'd spent many years traveling in the efficient comfort of a private jet, Lynch's journey to the US, against his will, was always going to be difficult. But if the day of the event was tough, the evening and night would prove even worse. In London, on a sultry early summer morning, myriad families with young children dangling behind them excitedly trundled their suitcases around Heathrow Airport, ready for holidays. People hurried through security departing on routine work trips. Groups of friends met for an early drink ahead of celebratory adventures. It was business as usual.

Lynch, wearing handcuffs and chains, boarded a large United Airlines commercial passenger plane bound for California. A baseball cap bearing the logo of the San Francisco Giants – coincidentally Judge Breyer's favourite team – was placed on his head by the US Marshals to shield his identity. They also draped a coat around his person to hide the chains.

The fifty-eight-year-old knew it could be the last time he would see England for decades, if ever. He was looking at more than twenty years in US prison. In the weeks before this unwelcome day, he had spent his time bidding farewell to the people and the life he loved, avoiding watching films and television programmes with storylines around jails. This aversion would continue for the duration of the trial.

Lynch sent an email to friends:

> **The pressure of taking on a fight of this magnitude takes a tremendous toll on me and on my family. As I leave Angela and the girls behind, I ask you to put your metaphoric arms around them. Their ordeal is no easier than mine, and it is for them that I keep fighting.**

He thought about how the whole saga had hung over his daughters, who were now on the cusp of adulthood, and how young they had been when it started. At that time, he had explained it to them through a story, a picture-book version of the HP debacle: 'Daddy sold someone a plant,' he'd said, 'and they failed to water it, and it died – and they're trying to blame Daddy for that.'

Lynch had said goodbye to his homes: to Chelsea and to Loudham Hall, to his painstakingly restored working water mill. He had gone to give the wheel a turn, savouring again the sense of achievement at having restored it, and of peace in his environment. He had walked the dogs, and had been absolutely convinced that they knew something was afoot. For the lifelong dog lover who regarded them as family members, those goodbyes were particularly painful – they would certainly not be able to visit nor live to see his release, if the worst happened.

When friends came to wish him well before the flight, they noticed that Lynch's usually eagle-sharp eyes were fuzzy and unfocused, allowing the stoic mask to slip a little.

And now the day had finally come. As he prepared to face the might of the US legal system in person for the first time, Lynch dressed smartly in a suit with an open-necked shirt. The Metropolitan police, to save his blushes, met him civilly round the corner from his Chelsea home. No scene was made for nosy neighbours, nobody was escorted in handcuffs from the front door into a squad car. They even apologized to Lynch for the very early start.

The Americans extended no such courtesies. After the UK police escorted Lynch through the corridors of Britain's busiest airport, he was handed over to US guards, who put cuffs on his wrists, chains around his waist and walked him onto the aeroplane. He boarded first, and was led to the very back row, hidden from view of the rest of the passengers. It was a process designed to intimidate. Lynch found the psychology of it bizarre and unsettling – he called the US legal system horrific, but full of perfectly decent individuals.

This was a contradiction he would face time and again.

The eleven-hour flight between London Heathrow and San Francisco International Airport marked the end of a twelve-year fight for Lynch, and the beginning of the final round. This was the one he needed to win. But could he?

Lynch's mind whirred as scenarios and strategies ticked away, and London's familiar suburbs grew smaller out of the plane window and then vanished. As he had repeated to himself and his teams again and again, there was a 0.4 per cent chance of acquittal in his circumstances (per numbers from the respected Pew Research Center, in federal criminal cases in the US, only about 0.4% of defendants who went to trial were acquitted in 2022).

0.4 per cent between him, and the rest of his life.

PART FIVE
Improbable Odds

TWENTY-NINE

Hello, I'm Stephen

Innocent until proven guilty, they say. Bullshit.

– Stephen Chamberlain

Back in 2005, on only his second day at Autonomy, Steve Chamberlain got an early glimpse of the unpredictable journey his career would take at the idiosyncratic Cambridge software business. 'Grab your passport, you're booked on a flight to Dallas this afternoon,' he was told. Autonomy had bought yet another business, eTalk, based in Texas, and someone from finance needed to go and sort out all the paperwork. That someone was him.

Before Chamberlain could say 'call-centre products', which is what Autonomy was buying in the Lone Star state, he was on his way to the US.

He rang his wife in a panic to break the news that he was off to the other side of the world in just a few hours' time. She patiently packed him a bag, dug his passport out and drove them to the office with a kiss and a smile. It was all fine. Karen was proud of him, and she always had his back.

Vice-President of Finance at Autonomy was Chamberlain's first major in-house accounting job. He was only thirty-three when he took it on – and it proved quite a different beast to working within the staid environs of Deloitte, where he had spent six years. He soon learnt that this kind of split-second decision-making was not unusual at Autonomy, but it made the job far more exciting than being stuck in an office. It was dynamic and fast-paced, offered international travel and there was something unexpected around every corner. Even if it was often a headache.

The company was worth $200 million when he joined, growing quickly. Only three years later, Autonomy was ranked one of the UK's biggest companies, moving up into the FTSE 100 for the second time in its history. At that stage, Chamberlain would find himself overseeing finances for a blue-chip British business worth billions of dollars – a huge, frenetic job.

The Chamberlains' children, Ella and Teddy, were four and two years old when their father started at Autonomy; and Chamberlain did not want to miss out on any of their key moments because of work. His role only required him to travel five or six times a year – not nearly as much as some colleagues – but he felt a twinge of sadness at saying goodbye to his young family each time he wheeled his case out of the door.

Being a father was important to Steve. During the regular working week when he was in the Cambridge headquarters, he'd make sure he was home as often as he could be to read them a bedtime story and tuck them in. Often that meant leaving the office a little early and working again once the kids were in bed, but he was always 'on'. His team never doubted his commitment to either his work or family and they knew he would always answer his emails.

The Chamberlains' happy home life mirrored his own growing up. A sweet, chubby, blond-haired child, Steve (as he was always known) was born in Marston Green, just outside Birmingham, in 1972. The eldest of three, he had that natural sense of responsibility which comes with being an older brother to two sisters, and which was encouraged by his early jobs: an early morning paper round and the back-breaking repetitive task of wheat-picking in the summer.

The family moved to Cambridge when Steve was eleven, but when he finished school he went back to his roots to take up a place at university, studying mechanical engineering at the University of Birmingham. As the first person in his family to get a degree, everyone was inordinately proud of him.

The Chamberlains may not have been wealthy, but Steve's parents, Grenville and Liz, whom he adored, financially supported him as best as they could throughout his studies. On top of their support, the young student worked a range of jobs to supplement his income while he was in Birmingham; he worked in a betting shop, and he cleaned the student halls of residence, doing even the most menial and disgusting tasks, like emptying out ashtrays and scrubbing the toilets. Hard work mattered to him. He was never a particularly ambitious man, but he was always proud of paying his own way and he always, always had a job. He knew that when he left university, the financial support from his parents could not continue and he needed a steady, reliable career. And so, the world of chartered accounting beckoned – about as steady and reliable as it gets.

In 1996, a mutual friend introduced him to Karen. Chamberlain was out for a Christmas party with the local football team he played for. The football lads were in high festive spirits and the drinks were flowing, but once he laid eyes on Karen, that was it for Steve. They got married in July 1999 and, before long, they had moved in with Karen's parents, with a mind to save up for a deposit on their own house.

A good job at Deloitte followed. This is where Steve Chamberlain came across Autonomy for the first time, when he worked on auditing their books. Through this, he got to know the finance team and Sushovan Hussain, Autonomy's personable CFO, who started asking him to consider joining the company. Chamberlain was keen on the idea, but as he had been reviewing Autonomy's numbers, he needed to take a year-long break from Deloitte before he was allowed to make the move, conforming to strict rules which are meant to prevent any potential conflicts of interest.

Once this cooling-off period was over, more than eighteen months later, he duly took the Autonomy job. With his can-do, responsible attitude, he was popular with his team from the get-go. Lynch described him as a good bloke: always reliable, he was the kind of person who got on with everyone. Affectionately nicknamed 'Grumpy' by his friends, his cheeky, everyman sense of humour made him approachable and well-liked by everyone around him.

Many years later, several colleagues swore that he would never do anything deliberately wrong.

AFTER CHAMBERLAIN'S BAPTISM of fire at Autonomy, zipping out from Cambridge to Texas, he got involved in several other deals.

These included the acquisition of Michele Bettencourt's Verity in 2005 for $375 million, Zantaz in 2007 for $550 million and Interwoven in 2009 for $775 million. There was a lot of money at stake and Chamberlain was right in the weeds when it came to undertaking due diligence ahead of each new acquisition, which took months. To examine the books closely, and to get to grips with each company's financial model, was a detailed and painstaking process. It is important to remember this, Chamberlain said with feeling, when you consider how HP handled the acquisition of Autonomy – he did not feel the US giant took enough care in its research.

Chamberlain was not close to Mike Lynch. They spoke infrequently during the seven-year period that the accountant worked at Autonomy. They'd see each other around, and at the legendary Autonomy Christmas parties when Lynch would make polite conversation with Karen, but in Chamberlain's words: 'He was the CEO of the business, was not really interested in finance, and so our paths rarely crossed.' Chamberlain certainly wasn't a part of Lynch's Inner Circle of trust; instead, Hussain was his main point of reference, because Chamberlain was the CFO's number two. But as with others, the Chamberlains had been guests on board the Lynches' luxurious yacht, and Karen was later invited on board by Angela while Mike was unable to travel and Steve was caught up in the furore around Autonomy.

Sitting in the finance department, Chamberlain was not involved in the strategic direction of the business. He never spoke to City analysts; his job was to be presented with a commercial rationale, and to execute it. The specific mandate of his job became important in subsequent years, but he always insisted that he was someone employed to implement a vision, not come up with the vision himself. He was paid well – £140,000 a year – but this was hardly a super-league figure at Autonomy. As well as dealing with the sporadic due diligence around Autonomy's hungry acquisitions, Chamberlain's role was to integrate the new companies into the parent company. There were over a hundred people in the finance team, both in the UK and the US. It was a difficult and demanding role, overseeing a growing group of reports, dealing with international operations and managing taxes.

His day job also involved dealing with Deloitte's quarterly reviews of the company's books, trying to make sure that all was as it should be. He was their primary Autonomy contact, the person Deloitte went to with queries, for tracking audit progress, and for ensuring they received documents in a timely manner. Deloitte's job was to challenge and question Autonomy's finance department. Chamberlain understood this because he had been on the other side once.

Auditors would come into Autonomy's open-plan office, and be given a conference room to work privately, but they had access to every employee and free rein to look at any documents they wanted to.

During his time at Autonomy, Chamberlain faced some challenging situations, partly because software accounting is notoriously difficult and sales would happen up until the very end of the quarter when there was often a sudden whirlwind of activity. Customers knew they could get a better deal if they held out until that period, when the salespeople were desperate to hit their numbers and get their bonuses. His job was also tricky because new strategies were constantly introduced by the executive team. Autonomy was not a company to rest on its laurels and Chamberlain had to move with the shifting currents.

A particularly problematic period came in 2009, when Chamberlain was told about Autonomy's new strategy to sell discounted hardware, presented to him and others as an attempt to build goodwill with customers and ultimately to sell them more of the company's expensive software.

Deloitte, the auditor, was informed about the sales, and they were well-known in the Autonomy finance department. Poppy Gustafsson, at that point working under Chamberlain, said the finance team always interpreted hardware sales as genuine efforts to maintain customer relationships and generate further software sales, exactly what they were told at the time.

When the first big hardware sales push happened, which made up a whopping 20 per cent of sales in the third quarter of 2009, Richard Knights (the Deloitte partner) was pushing for proof that the hardware sales were intended as a marketing strategy. He had outlined to Chamberlain and Hussain exactly what evidence they needed to provide to pass Deloitte's checks – in turn, Chamberlain told Mike Sullivan, then leading the sales push, exactly what he needed to produce in order to make the numbers work.

But Chamberlain pushed back hard on Deloitte's asks too, emailing Hussain on 16 October 2009 that 'battle lines have been drawn' with the auditor, which was uneasy about the way Autonomy executives tried to allocate the sales:

> **The key issue with the auditors seems to be around the use of the word IDOL. Strong organic growth and strong organic IDOL growth – to them the former includes**

> **hardware sales and the latter does not . . . While we may find a way to get there on organic growth through allocations they are going to really struggle with including hardware within the description of IDOL product or IDOL organic growth. Battle lines have been drawn.**

Eventually, Knights agreed to the allocation of the hardware as suggested by Autonomy, as a marketing expense. This amounted to a gold stamp of approval. Nothing to worry about. Chamberlain could move on.

Deloitte was not the only check-and-balance the finance department at Autonomy had to face. There was also the audit committee. The disclosure of hardware sales was a point of discussion within these meetings, latterly chaired by Jonathan Bloomer and attended by Chamberlain. In the published accounts, hardware and software sales were bundled up into one figure. That was fine, Bloomer always said; the company was not attempting to hide anything. It just didn't make sense to separate the sales out, because no one considered hardware as a separate part of Autonomy's business. Had the percentage of sales hit a higher figure it might have been different, Bloomer argued. Although those in the City trying to make sense of the finances begged to differ.

For Chamberlain, managing the accounts was complicated further by the presence of resellers, the middlemen who took on some of the Autonomy sales. Under global accounting regulations – not the same as those used in the US – a sale can be counted once the purchasing party takes on the risk for it. Each reseller signed an Autonomy standard contract to say they understood this point. Another tick in the box on his side to say everything was OK.

With all of this in play, the complexity of managing the accounts meant that things sometimes had to be juggled around. This happened in 2010, when Autonomy was negotiating a $4.5 million deal with the Financial Services Authority, the UK's City watchdog. It did not close by the end of the quarter, and so Autonomy did a deal in a hurry – as it usually did – with a friendly reseller from a different time zone who would pick up the contract and allow Autonomy to recognize the sale. This time it was Capax.

As the clock ticked towards midnight on 31 March 2010, Capax slipped in to 'pick up' the FSA transaction. It had the advantage of being based on the East Coast, five hours behind London time. Capax was offered a 10 per cent commission once Autonomy closed the FSA deal; it was not getting involved itself.

This time was a little different though. There appeared to be some faffing about over whether the revenue should really be booked in that quarter. Chamberlain wrote to Cynthia Watkins and Matt Stephan in his team on 8 April 2010, *after* the quarter had closed, when things were *not* supposed to change, telling them to defer $4.3 million in revenue.

> **I apologize for the constant changing of your numbers. Powers greater than me are making these decisions, and while I understand them, I know they will be causing you a lot of pain. I will make sure this is remembered when it comes to sorting out Q1 bonuses.**

Four days later he emailed again: 'We have had to make further changes to your numbers'. He told them the revenue *did* need to be recognized after all. The Capax/FSA sum was back in. Much later, in August 2010, Autonomy finally won that contract with the FSA. The money Capax owed was waived. It was another example of how Autonomy used VARs as shells to accelerate revenue recognition and hit targets, regardless of real sales or risk.

So, in all of this, Chamberlain was caught in the middle – he had to relay constantly shifting numbers to finance staff who were trying to close the books and finalize the accounts, while the executive team was still reshaping the financial picture behind closed doors.

There was also the difficult question of the 'marketing assistance fees', or MAFs, which Autonomy was doling out to its resellers. In theory, MAFs could be legitimate payments to support promotional activities, such as funding events, training or co-branded materials. In fact, they were another way that Autonomy could inflate its revenue, used to pay money to its resellers, so they could appear to purchase software without actually taking on real risk. Chamberlain did sometimes push back on this practice, as in this email to Stouffer Egan in 2011:

> **Stouffer – let's be very clear here. I have no wish other than getting my $9m. I have not agreed any MAF. Any MAF will need Sushovan Hussain to be onboard. From my perspective he owes me the $9m.**

Chamberlain did not decide what sales to make, or who they were being made to, or how they were structured – all the details would be sent to him afterwards. Furthermore, he was always doing his job in real time, rather than anticipating what was happening nine months down the line. He regularly chased companies for payment if none was forthcoming. Finally, his work with the sales numbers did not finish at the end of each quarter. There was then the unenviable job of working through some of the deals afterwards, to judge where they should be allocated, which was often less black and white. Sometimes the criteria for revenue recognition would depend on other information, like whether a customer was creditworthy. Close and sensitive judgement calls like this were left to Hussain.

Everyone said Chamberlain did this monumental job diligently, but that perhaps he did not always ask as many questions as he should have. One of his team, Matt Stephan (also previously of Deloitte), said he seemed to take the view that the finance team were like troops in an army – that the general (in this case Hussain) told them what to do and that the accounts team just followed orders.

When the explosive news of the sale to HP emerged, Chamberlain was involved in the flurry of due diligence and was interviewed by KPMG as part of the process. Everything seemed to pass without a hitch.

OSTENSIBLY, THE FRENETIC Autonomy chapter of Chamberlain's life closed in 2012, when he left the company, not long after the HP deal had gone through. Chamberlain had made around £500,000 from the sale, a substantial sum which meant that he had enough money to purchase land owned by Karen's parents after their deaths, and to start building their forever home from scratch.

He wanted a career change. The preceding years had been hectic, and at times the workload had been too much to handle. He didn't really want to work for another Mike Lynch company either. It was time for a fresh start. As such, in March 2012, Chamberlain took on the role of CFO at another Cambridge tech company, Sepura, a designer and manufacturer of secure digital radio communication systems. There, things went well. Until they didn't.

Just eight months later, the explosive HP allegations surfaced and, after the shakedown of Lynch and Hussain, all eyes turned to Chamberlain, with day-to-day control of the accounts department. He never wavered in his conviction: he had done nothing wrong. In fact, he was so convinced that he was innocent that he started writing a memoir, detailing his experiences in the aftermath of the Autonomy fraud allegations. As the US Department of Justice investigated Hussain before turning their attention to Chamberlain himself, he documented what was happening in his life, in his own words.

Writing a book was a typical Steve Chamberlain response to events. He was a precise, orderly person, exactly what you'd expect from an accountant – it was part of why he'd chosen the profession in the first place. Given the conflicting reports and the swirl of sensationalism around the Autonomy story, he wanted to lay out the facts clearly; to share his experiences exactly as he interpreted them. More than anything, he wanted to prove his innocence.

In 2013, Chamberlain was interviewed by the accounting watchdog, the FRC. By April 2015, when the civil lawsuit against Lynch and Hussain was filed in the UK, Chamberlain had appointed lawyers to work for him on both sides of the Atlantic. Flak and blame were flying around, and he quickly realized that he was smack bang in the middle of the danger zone.

The gravity of the situation was becoming clearer as the months passed. By July 2015, everything had come to a head. The stigma surrounding the HP allegations was too much, especially with a full-time job, and Chamberlain resigned from his CFO role at Sepura while on holiday in Canada, moving to a less intense role as the Head of Integrations. Taking a step backwards at the company felt like a practical defeat – suddenly he was reporting into someone where previously everyone had reported into him. It wasn't long before he decided to leave altogether.

But where could he work now? He was offered a CFO role elsewhere, but his legal counsel had advised him against US travel and the offer was soon revoked. He felt helpless: 'I literally had nowhere else to go. No one would employ me with those charges hanging over me.'

Eventually, he was offered the job as the CFO of Darktrace. It was another Mike Lynch company, but it was one where Chamberlain was already known and liked, and where the stain of the HP allegations wouldn't be an automatic barrier to his progress. Besides, he didn't really have any other options. The only place he could get a job was around people who were sympathetic to his case, who were prepared to accept the reputational risk of the allegations.

The Chamberlain family kept up hope that in time things would settle down, and in the meantime Steve threw himself into the Darktrace job, along with an unpaid role at his beloved local football team Cambridge United. He described how he felt during this time, as his reputation was dragged through the mud:

Innocent until proven guilty they say. Bullshit. I have never been treated like an innocent person during this last 12–13 years. These claims were made and they get believed. People start whispering behind your back, chatting to others, armed with even less facts than HP and the DOJ had. It is one of the saddest characteristics of human nature. We are fascinated by gossip, taken in by rumours and do very little of our own fact-finding to support what we hear.

Then, in November 2016, the US prosecutors made their first move, charging Hussain. They asked Chamberlain to testify against his former boss, but he refused. Chamberlain was extremely fond of Hussain and watched in horror as he was found guilty and handed a lengthy custodial sentence. There was a healthy dose of racism in it all, he felt:

The CFO of a UK company who allegedly defrauded an American giant in Trump's America. He also happens to be of Bangladeshi heritage and is a Muslim. A crook? No. A motivated and driven person who was pushing hard to grow a successful FTSE 100 software business? Yes.

The US prosecutors were emboldened after the Hussain verdict, Chamberlain felt, and they set their sights on their next victim: him.

There was no new evidence, no sudden revelations in Sushovan's trial. They were simply able to convince a jury that Sushovan was guilty, beyond reasonable doubt. Now they thought they had a chance of convincing a jury that I was also guilty. However, I was not the prize they

> *were after. They wanted the big guy, they wanted Mike Lynch and this conviction gave them the encouragement they needed to indict both Mike and myself.*

On 29 November 2018, in his own words, 'shit got real'. Alongside Lynch, US prosecutors charged Chamberlain with fourteen counts of fraud. He was once again asked to turn on his former boss, to testify against Lynch in exchange for leniency, offered the same kind of deal that had wooed Stouffer Egan. Again, he refused, insisting that he'd rather face twenty years in prison than tell lies.

A FEW CHOICES faced Chamberlain at this point. The most pressing was whether he should attend the American hearings and trial voluntarily, or whether he should refuse and stay in the UK to fight extradition. The choice wasn't a simple one.

In hindsight, it's clear that the gravity of the situation was rather lost on Chamberlain at the time. He later reflected how he naively thought that heading to the US and fighting his case in person was the simplest and therefore the best course of action. He saw it as straightforward: he was going to prove he was innocent. He would just tell them his side of the story and then it would all be over. He did not realize he was entering the jaws of a legal system which encourages plea bargaining, where it was highly unlikely that he would come out untarnished. One thing he did believe was that the structure of the US/UK extradition treaty was weighted against him, sharing Lynch's opinion on the matter:

> *In layman's terms: so long as the US make an application and have some grounds, then the UK effectively hands over its citizens. There is no robust legal challenge or detailed consideration of the evidence, just an assumption that the US are acting in good faith. There's the*

problem. I have seen with my own eyes that the political motivations underpinning their system mean that objectivity and fairness are not the core values they should be in these situations.

On 3 February 2019, Chamberlain travelled to the US for the first time. As someone charged by the government, he was treated like a criminal every step of the way.

Ahead of this, among many other witnesses three accountants who worked for him out in the US had given evidence to the US grand jury – a legal body of citizens that reviews evidence presented by prosecutors to determine whether there's enough evidence to formally charge someone with a crime. Chamberlain called them the 'three amigos'. They backed up Brent Hogenson's whistleblowing testimony. Chamberlain did not blame them for speaking out; two were fired in the incident and one, he felt, was under immense pressure from US prosecutors.

Yet they, like so many other witnesses, had had their memories 'refreshed' by the prosecution to fit a narrative, Chamberlain felt, believing that it would be virtually impossible for anyone to recall the events of so many years earlier with anything approaching accuracy, and that selective emails were being shown to witnesses to create a storyline with enough credibility to convict him. He was furious:

Photographic memory or total recall are very rare. The US prosecutors were highly skilled at presenting an email and providing their own background and context to the events leading up to the writing of that email. Given a set of 'facts' and presented with an email, it is very easy for a witness to create a false memory. There may be elements that they recall but the human mind allows others to fill in the blanks for us. The only way to combat this was to assemble all of the emails from the relevant time period and place the email being used by the government back into its original context. Only then could you begin to properly understand the email.

He was fighting a losing battle, and he felt like nobody was listening to him. One way he found to clear his head, and to retain an element of control over his life, was through running. He became more and more dedicated to the pastime as the various legalities proceeded, sharing his long trails on the sporting app Strava, as well as creating a running blog to document his achievements and drum up sponsorship for various charitable causes. He even completed the Cambridge half marathon in March 2019.

Chamberlain was never cross-examined in any of the Autonomy trials, so the only evidence of his conduct during his time at Autonomy was in the form of his contemporaneous emails and the testimonies of others who worked with him. This was a source of frustration to Mr Justice Hildyard, overseeing the UK civil trial, who was trying at length to understand what had gone on within the business. Chamberlain did not give a witness statement to the London court and Lynch did not call him to do so, saying it was to be expected that he would wish to remain silent, given the pending charges he was facing in the US. Hildyard felt he had no choice but to make a judgement on Chamberlain's conduct, despite his absence. 'Dr Lynch told me he did not know whether there was any reason why Mr Chamberlain could not have given a statement,' Hildyard wrote.

The pressure within Darktrace to distance itself from the Autonomy debacle intensified and Chamberlain's position soon became completely untenable – the company could not have its CFO actively accused of fraud. With great reluctance from both sides, he was placed on administrative leave at the end of 2020. His regular 5 km runs started to get longer and longer, reaching up to 30 km.

Chamberlain had quite the fiftieth birthday present in 2022, when the case against him got even worse. In his mammoth judgement, Hildyard found that Chamberlain had been a central character in the Autonomy machine and that he was part of the core management team – part of a 'clique' which was responsible for pulling the 'levers' behind the fraud at Autonomy. He was, Hildyard said, an 'energetic aide de camp', having day-to-day control of the accounts department. It did not bode well for him and only served to fuel the case of the circling US prosecutors.

There was a period of instability while he went back and forth to San Francisco to face his accusers for various pre-trial hearings, as Lynch's extradition proceedings dragged on and on. The logistics of all this travelling became a pain. Once, when he was summoned for an in-person appearance before the trial began, this time for jury selection, Chamberlain rushed to the US embassy in London to collect his travel documents. Dutifully, he did not open the envelope containing his paperwork, which was intended for border control to handle.

When he got there, there was a pause. 'You're Ukrainian?' the guards asked him quizzically. Chamberlain sighed. The American embassy's administrative staff had written the wrong birthplace on the vital forms he needed to enter the country – a mess-up on the computer drop-down menu, perhaps, with Ukraine just a click away from United Kingdom. Several tedious hours later, he was eventually free to pass, but it created an unwelcome layer of stress.

There was also the expense of the trips. Comfortable, the Chamberlains took nice holidays and were putting the finishing touches to their new home. Yet, compared to the Lynch family, they were financial minnows. Chamberlain had considered asking if some of the in-person court appearances could be done remotely, so they didn't have to keep shelling out for flights and hotels. He decided against it in case the judge thought he couldn't afford to keep up his long-distance commute and he was told to permanently stay put in San Francisco, away from Karen and the children.

The Chamberlains gritted their teeth. Before every trip, Steve would make his way to the US Embassy in London and, before every trip, they felt a twinge of fear that something could go wrong. Their new home was still unfinished when the trial date loomed. There was no kitchen yet, and Chamberlain worried about how the subsequent months would impact Karen and the kids in an incomplete house. The children were now older than when the whole debacle started, young adults, meaning Karen would be alone for the majority of the time.

Under this immense stress, running had become a complete obsession, and Steve put himself through harder and harder paces with longer and longer routes. Along with his daily circuits, he tackled official races and challenges which lasted for several days, like the Great Lakeland 3Day, a three-day mountain running event held annually in the Lake District; and the Spine Race, a non-stop 268-mile endurance race held along the Pennine Way, a hiking trail in England and Scotland. He suffered painful blisters, but they were the experiences of a lifetime.

Ultimately, though, Chamberlain could not run away from the inevitable. When he went to San Francisco for the trial, he and Karen would be separated by thousands of miles and an inconvenient time zone. She'd spend her evenings wondering what was happening over in California and staying up late to hear from her husband. She couldn't quit her job and come over for the trial to support him for months on end, because they couldn't afford it. This became a source of sadness for them both, especially Steve: 'It broke my heart to hear her talk of many an evening crying alone sat in a chair.'

As the big date for the trial approached, Chamberlain remained convinced, despite the many misgivings of others, that it would all be over soon.

He never really doubted that he would be coming home.

THIRTY

San Francisco

I'd had to say goodbye to everything and everyone, because I didn't know if I'd ever be coming back.

– *Mike Lynch*, The Sunday Times, *27 July 2024*

Lynch stared out the window, watching London disappear behind him, thinking once again about his chances of acquittal, running the odds over and over in his mind. The data points did not look good.

There was nothing in the way of special treatment from the US officials accompanying Lynch on his flight from London to San Francisco, down to their refusal to uncuff him when he needed to use the bathroom. Overnight, Lynch had been thrown unceremoniously into a very different world, one where he was no longer in control.

It was like being dropped into a scene from a Hollywood thriller. He was being treated like a dangerous criminal – he had always joked about being a mafia boss, but not in this guise. It wasn't, he'd tell people dryly afterwards, as if he was some kind of Olympic boxing champion either – he physically couldn't run, and in any case he had nowhere to run to.

Trying to get comfortable in the cramped seat, wrists clamped together, he remembered hundreds of past trips, when Autonomy was riding high and he was at the apex of a thriving transatlantic business. His latest was a humiliating and exhausting journey. He was still feeling the pain of failing to avoid extradition, the humiliation of a British political elite that had seemingly abandoned him, and the disappointment that his connections with security services had been completely ineffective in preventing this outcome.

Yet, as always, worries about what was to come next were partially soothed by practicality. He had a saying, which he repeated again and again throughout the trial: this was the 'first tiger on the path'.

If you're facing multiple problems along the way, they are like tigers along a path. You need to worry about tiger number one, not tiger number four. He went over and over the next steps, his next move; tiger number one, getting bailed in San Francisco and heading to New York where he would meet his crack legal team. Talk about taking a gun to a knife fight – led by Reid Weingarten, Chris Morvillo and Brian Heberlig, this was more of a bazooka.

Sitting at the back of the plane on the long flight, Lynch nevertheless started weighing up how he'd cope serving time in a US federal prison. Age and his health conditions gave him a poor assessment of the odds. He firmly believed he wouldn't leave prison alive if he was sent down like Hussain had been. Close friends disagreed, telling him that he wasn't dead yet. But it all weighed heavily on his mind as the plane approached San Francisco, and the old prison island of Alcatraz loomed into view. It was Thursday, 11 May 2023.

HIS LAWYERS HAD been making all the arrangements for his arrival. Lynch was due to head to New York the morning after he landed, following some perfunctory admin in San Francisco. He'd be based in New York to be near his East Coast legal teams and much closer to his family in England. Restrictions on his daily life while in the US would be minimal.

An energetic Jonathan Baum, one of Steptoe's brightest young lawyers, was sent to greet him. He had flown over from Washington DC and, as instructed by his boss Reid Weingarten, had booked a room for Lynch at the Four Seasons hotel. With his usual confidence, Weingarten had reassured Baum – who had young children and whose wife was pregnant – that it was all taken care of, and the job was going to be straightforward. Lynch would be released when he got there, Weingarten told Baum; he himself had thrashed out the details with the courts and the government.

It felt a bit like an errand. Baum was effectively going to collect Lynch like a high-value parcel and was there to make sure everyone was happy and that the paperwork was in order. Baum said the process would be swift, and wrapped up by about 4 p.m., knowing that working days in the court don't stretch much past five, and they needed to have this all sorted before the close of play.

But Judge Breyer had a surprise waiting. The welcome party would not be taking place at the Four Seasons that night.

Lynch was escorted from the plane straight into a cell on the top floor of the San Francisco courthouse, where US marshals put people as a stopgap when they are moving them from jail to hearings.

Baum walked past the row of offices to the tiny rooms which served as holding pens. Behind a thick glass window, still wearing handcuffs, was Lynch. 'Hi, I'm Jonathan,' Baum said. 'Very nice to meet you,' Lynch mouthed back at him, the sound of his voice dulled by the barrier. Platitudes over, it became swiftly apparent that Lynch could barely hear a thing. It was not just the glass – compounding an already painful indignity, Lynch's hearing aids had been confiscated as he sat waiting for the next part of the day's drama to unfold.

Baum's first task was to reunite Lynch with his hearing aids, which was duly done after an urgent request to the judge. But the logistical problems were only just beginning. Morvillo and Baum went into the courtroom with Lynch to take care of the necessities, but it was swiftly apparent that this was no mere perfunctory bail hearing. Ignoring the deal which had been struck with the UK government over the conditions of Lynch's extradition, Judge Breyer had weighed up the odds and concluded that Lynch's unwillingness to cooperate with the US justice system – his long years of fighting his extradition – meant he posed a serious flight risk. He set out a series of strict and very complicated conditions around Lynch's release. Everyone's jaws dropped.

For Lynch and his lawyers from the East Coast, a flight to New York became a distant dream. Breyer would not let him out of San Francisco, or for that matter, his house. He would have to pay for his own round-the-clock armed security detail, be fitted with an ankle tag and only be allowed to leave house arrest for a few exceptions: religious services, medical examinations, court appearances or to see his lawyers. Adding insult to injury, the bodyguards with guns that *he* employed and bankrolled would need to be authorized to shoot him if he tried to flee. It seemed slightly farcical.

To add to the drama, the judge had ordered that Lynch would be transferred to a tough local jail, Santa Rita, over the Bay Bridge in Oakland, until these arrangements were finalized. Oakland has its fair share of violent crime, and entrenched issues with gangs and drugs. Santa Rita jail, one of the largest in the US, has a nasty reputation for holding drug dealers, crackheads and gang members. It did not normally play host to middle-aged British software entrepreneurs in chinos, accused of fraud.

Lynch was transferred to the medical wing of the prison and given jail clothes to wear. It was deemed to be safer, and the most suitable spot for this unusual prisoner. While their precious cargo was at least settled somewhere for now, his lawyers panicked about what they should do next.

Baum's and Morvillo's minds first switched to the problem of finding round-the-clock armed security, two people on duty at any one time, so everything would be in order to present to the judge the next day. Hastily, searching through contacts of contacts, they pulled a million-dollar team together. Getting people to watch Lynch round-the-clock was expensive; finding people who were armed was even more so; finding some who would also be willing to shoot him was one step beyond.

When the lawyers rang various security companies, the voices on the end of the phone puzzled over the legality of shooting their client. They were used to protecting the billionaire Silicon Valley tech-bro types, not threatening them. Baum had some unlikely contacts in this world from a previous case and, when he tracked down someone who could help, convinced them in legalese that the judge's court order ironed out the unusual shooting part of the contract.

Then there was the question of money. When the next morning came, Lynch had to pay an exceptionally large $100 million bond to stay out of jail, which he did using $50 million of his Darktrace shares. These were part of the few assets he could get his hands on immediately; Morvillo explained to Breyer that Lynch's 'approximate net worth is in the range of $400 to $450 million,' noting that many of his assets were 'encumbered' as a result of the ongoing matter. Back home, the share certificates in his and Angela's names were hurriedly sought by his lawyers, who flew to San Francisco and handed them over to the court. Now, a day and a half after leaving London in chains, he was exhausted.

His lawyers optimistically tried to arrange for him to stay in the Four Seasons as per the original plan, but the luxury hotel did not take too kindly to the idea of having an armed guard standing outside his room in the corridor. It made him persona non grata. They found a likely Airbnb later that day, but the same issue came up: nobody wanted to host the entrepreneur with his gun-toting companions in tow. The Lynch travelling circus was moved on once more.

A refuge eventually presented itself. A suitable home was up for rent – a bigger one, in the fancy Pacific Heights neighbourhood.

Lynch was able finally to settle into his new life, under house arrest, in San Francisco. 'It did not go as I expected, Your Honour,' Morvillo said in court, with his usual upbeat manner, now facing the alarming, unexpected prospect of being separated from his family for months, 'but I'm privileged to be here.'

PACIFIC HEIGHTS, WITH its large homes and famously steep slopes, is where you live if you're *somebody* in San Francisco.

High above the tumbling onslaught of downtown life, the illustrious neighbourhood houses heavyweights including Nancy Pelosi, the former speaker of the US House of Representatives; Peter Thiel, the billionaire investor; and Larry Ellison, the Oracle founder who Lynch had crossed swords with all those years ago. One slice of the area is locally known as Billionaire's Row, featuring storeyed mansions with Victorian architecture and big windows, which qualify as historic by US standards.

With a view of the city to the front and the Golden Gate Bridge to the back, Lynch's spacious four-storey home was in a prime spot. It was also a familiar area for Lynch. He'd rented houses here in the past for extended working holidays with the family, with Autonomy's old American office a ten-minute drive away. At times he'd spent up to three weeks a month in the city. He was on home turf.

House arrest could have been a bleak, isolating experience. But because of how specific the bail conditions were, Lynch had companionship all day – the armed bodyguards watching him. As it happens, one of these bodyguards was to become a significant part of Lynch's life and prove to be an unexpectedly good cop for the Lynch family: Rolo Igno.

Igno has an open and young-looking face, an all-American warmth. He's the kind of person who suits the California sunshine. When he was a police officer, he had given none other than Meg Whitman herself a speeding ticket – a fact which never failed to make

Lynch chuckle. He had worked as personal protection for some of the billionaires in the area, accompanying them on work trips, or holidays.

Igno was happily working at the family business when a former colleague called him to ask if he'd be interested in helping put together the team on a highly unusual job: a billionaire who'd got in big trouble with the law was paying them to make sure he himself didn't escape. It was the most peculiar gig Igno had ever been asked to work on.

Knowing the other guys on the rotation, and the lack of travel, made it an appealing offer. Igno agreed, and within days started to bond with his new roommate.

It was a big house; the armed security lived downstairs, while Lynch occupied the upper floors. It took a few days for the security staff to realize that Lynch was not a flight risk – that they didn't have a mobster or cartel boss like El Chapo on their hands. Rather, this somewhat out of shape, clever Brit liked to ask genuine questions about the guards' families, and was about as far as could be from the stereotypical biohacking hoodie-clad Californian tech CEO, in both appearance and character.

Early into their time together, Igno watched as Lynch huffed and puffed up some of the infamously steep streets in the Pacific Heights neighbourhood, slightly concerned about his ability to reach the top. Lynch turned to him and said, breathing heavily: 'You know you don't really have to worry about me running from you?' 'I got you, Mike,' Igno replied with a smile. Unlike Chamberlain, Lynch was unlikely to be running anywhere.

Igno was with Lynch from six in the morning to six in the evening, four days a week, week in, week out. Whether Lynch had to attend a doctor's appointment, a trial hearing or the lawyers' offices, Igno was there. Every time Lynch needed to go to the bathroom in the courthouse, Igno would accompany him and wait outside.

He had such a positive effect on Lynch's mood that Angela even asked him to spend more time at the house, beyond his professional mandate. From being merely a bodyguard, Igno soon became part of the Lynch Inner Circle. After a while, a trusted crew member from Lynch's prized yacht, Sasha Murray, was brought over to act as a kind of housekeeper for the unusual house-share. Hers was another welcome and friendly face.

When he was not working full-pelt on his trial, Lynch turned to his beloved jazz music to keep himself occupied, practising the saxophone. It was a bit like lockdown all over again. One day a flight simulator was delivered, and then a treadmill. The security team joked that Lynch was trying to get fit and plot his escape, which made him laugh. With Igno, he was his charming everyman self. He would chat about life and family and was genuinely interested in the views of the security team when it came to politics. After these discussions, Lynch assured everyone back home that Trump was a dead cert to win the next election.

There were several moments of human bonding – nothing extravagant, but always genuine. During that most American of all occasions – the Super Bowl – Lynch ordered food, and the guys mocked him for his lack of sports knowledge while he poured chilli flakes onto his pizza.

Soon, there was another extremely significant new face in Pacific Heights. Lynch's daughters, Esme and Hannah, were worried that Lynch was lonely in his new home. This fear led to the purchase of a sharply intelligent Shetland sheepdog rescue named Faucet. He became Lynch's favourite dog, and was given special treatment, flouting previously well-enforced rules for Lynch canines, such as no sleeping on the bed.

The simple routine of looking after Faucet gave the long days in San Francisco a comforting rhythm, between morning walks, mealtimes and afternoon strolls. And just as the new dog provided a warm sense of normality, so did visits from old friends and associates, such as Rohan Silva, who had worked with Lynch in government, and his Suffolk friend Patrick Jacob.

Michele Bettencourt and her wife met Lynch and Angela for dinner a few times during that first year, at a more welcoming Four Seasons. There'd be a table in the back for the two couples, with a table elsewhere in the restaurant for the security team. The meals were always under pressure because Lynch was on the clock, needing to be back home in time for his evening curfew. When dinner was running late, Lynch became nervous and anxious, and suddenly the reality of the situation would come to the fore all over again. The Bettencourts would send him home and bring dessert back with them.

This was the lighter side of life, but, inevitably, preparation for his trial was Lynch's main preoccupation, and he ran his legal team with an iron fist. Video calls dominated Lynch's days, given that his top-tier lawyers were based on the East Coast, and there were early mornings to compensate for the time difference between San Francisco, New York and Washington DC.

This might not have been the life he had been promised upon his extradition, but it was at least extremely comfortable. At Christmas, Angela bought an eight-foot tree, which was bedecked with lights and candy canes while Igno and the security guys helped to decorate the house, so it felt more like a home. In a picture of domestic normality, Lynch carved the Christmas turkey. His cousins thoughtfully sent cards and gifts in brightly wrapped paper, making sure Lynch knew he wasn't forgotten, and that his family was raising a glass to him from across the pond.

STEVE CHAMBERLAIN CELEBRATED Christmas with his family too, but at home in England. Unlike Lynch, he was able to travel back and forth to the UK because he'd surrendered voluntarily to the US authorities. This was far from the only difference in their circumstances.

As the trial approached, Chamberlain's San Francisco home was a one-bedroom Airbnb downtown, with a sofa bed for visitors. He spent his free hours going on long runs, sometimes up to three, four or even five hours at a time, not about to abandon the activity that he had found such solace in over the prior few years. He would take adventurous routes, posting them on his Strava account, taking in sketchy parts of the city people cautioned him against running through alone.

It was during this pre-trial period that he started writing down every detail of each day religiously for his book. This, and the daily running, helped to keep his mood measured and focused. Chamberlain surprised himself with his ability to plough on with the practicalities of the situation. He even joked that he wished he knew the secret of how he kept on such an even keel because, if he did, he could bottle it and make a fortune.

But the Chamberlains did not have a fortune. This became a problem when it came to funding the lawyers needed to defend him and pay his living expenses in the US. Lynch had set aside a pot of money to cover his former employee's fees, and Chamberlain carefully rationed his time with his lawyer, always trying to keep within the fund's limits.

In comparison to the Lynch legal juggernaut, which was six times the size, Chamberlain's was made up of just three people. Chamberlain saw himself as part of this and threw himself into the task of prepping for trial in whatever way he could, treating it like his full-time job, determined to prove his innocence. He knew how high the stakes were, and was driven to avoid the fate of his former boss, Sushovan Hussain.

Then, the money ran out. This became an entrenched issue as bills racked up. It was a massive source of stress for Chamberlain, and created tension within the legal teams, which only increased as time went on.

Chamberlain's US attorney was Gary Lincenberg at Bird Marella, a boutique firm comprised of about fifty lawyers. A former federal prosecutor, the accomplished litigator now specializes in defending white-collar cases. He is a cool, confident man, who speaks quickly and with purpose. He gives the impression of someone who doesn't suffer fools gladly, and he likes to get to the point.

Chamberlain and Lincenberg were very different characters, with very different backgrounds, but the US lawyer really liked and trusted his client, who he felt was one of the most honest individuals he had ever represented. He seemed genuinely outraged at his impending trial.

Chamberlain, Lincenberg thought, was the kind of man who kept his nose to the grindstone – he was loyal, committed to doing his job and unafraid to speak his mind. Chamberlain believed in doing what was right, even if it ruined his life. And it did. For a decade, his choice not to testify against his former bosses upended everything: he lost his job, spent years under indictment and risked going to prison in a foreign country.

And if an American jury convicted him, he was prepared to face that. Very few people have the backbone, the ethical conviction, and the strength of will to follow that path and stand their ground against all the odds.

But Steve Chamberlain, Lincenberg felt, was one of them.

THIRTY-ONE

Setting the Stage

As to the sales video and as to James Bond and then there was some analogy about piranhas . . . I think that's all excludable because its probative value is, to me, outweighed by its prejudicial effect.

– Judge Chuck Breyer, pre-trial hearing, 21 February 2024

Sushovan Hussain was released from his time in a Pennsylvania prison just a few months before Lynch's trial began in March 2024, and he immediately started helping the legal team as much as he could with their preparations.

Ever the optimist, Hussain took his strange prison experience in his stride – after all, life inside a US jail was better than being in a UK equivalent, he told friends in his Pollyannaish way. Initially in solitary confinement, bound by Covid regulations, he read and read, including some old favourites such as *Pride and Prejudice*, which kept him distracted. As did endless walking and doing press-ups.

When Covid took hold, Hussain had asked Judge Breyer to trim his sentence. He argued that he had already been restricted to the Northern District of California for years, when he entered the country to prepare for his trial, and the pandemic meant he had not been able to see his family. Breyer ruled that there were no 'extraordinary and compelling reasons' to do so. Hussain stayed put.

In normal times, medium-security inmates in FCI Allenwood were allowed to use the gym, make ceramics, play music and watch TV, while outside there is basketball, a running track, a football pitch and a courtyard. When Hussain finally met his fellow inmates in what was sometimes jokingly dubbed a 'federal holiday camp', he discovered an anthropologist's wet dream. Everyone was informally divided up by their crime or their caste into what is known in prison slang as a car.

Hussain was part of the large Muslim car, and he was 'accepted' by other contingents, including the white supremacists, marked out by the swastikas tattooed on their calves. The prisoners were unified in ostracizing the 'snitches' and those inside for child molesting or sexual offences. There were only a handful of other European white-collar crime guys inside. They were the outliers. The roost was ruled by an Italian mafia boss who had been in there for a long time.

Just as he had been at Autonomy, Hussain was well-liked by those around him. Always a whiteboard guy, he taught astrophysics, his hobby, to other inmates, and his popular classes were structured across ten-week semesters exploring subjects such as black holes and Newton's theory of relativity.

Even after he was released, Hussain still proclaimed his innocence, and believed in Lynch's and Chamberlain's. He made himself available to Lynch and Chamberlain's lawyers, seeing it as his duty to help them in whatever way he could. Andy Kanter did the same and both were an immense support. Hussain had seen many of the same witnesses and documents during his trial and he was perspicacious enough to realize which strategies had worked for him and which hadn't, not to mention having had several years in prison thinking over events at Autonomy. His time behind bars had not soured his affection for Lynch and, despite the prosecution's hopes he might turn on his friend and former boss, he never did. In times where others would have just moved on with their lives, he showed more loyalty than ever.

YET HUSSAIN AND his guilty verdict presented a major conundrum for the defence teams. Clearly, as the chief financial officer, it would have been easy for them to throw all the blame for any accounting improprieties at Autonomy onto him. Any juror doing some illicit research into the case would soon discover that Hussain had already been convicted and sent to prison for the same alleged crime only a few years earlier.

In the end, Lynch's lawyers trod a neutral and sometimes uncomfortable path over Hussain's involvement. The position they decided to take was that Lynch was not the ultimate decision-maker, but rather the person who gathered all the facts about the deals and presented them to Hussain, who then held the final authority on whether revenue could be recognized in financial accounts. Lynch was no accounting expert, they argued, and so he relied on Hussain, in good faith, to make the right calls.

They would not go on to say that Hussain had done anything wrong or acted improperly. At the same time, they didn't feel compelled to fully endorse every one of his decisions. This position allowed them to argue that Lynch had no reason to believe Hussain had acted improperly – but if he had, it was not his responsibility. The lawyers didn't want to concede any wrongdoing at Autonomy, but they also recognized that some elements of the government's case, such as the backdating of contracts, looked extremely suspicious. As a result, they were careful not to go too far in defending every action that Hussain had taken.

The shadow of Hussain was also difficult for Chamberlain, who of course was much closer to the accounting than Lynch. There were decisions that his team needed to highlight as having been Hussain's, but there was also a need to defend the overall accounting culture at Autonomy and not point the finger too much. It was a tightrope walk for Lincenberg.

Hussain aside, the relationship between Lynch and Chamberlain (or lack thereof) was one Lincenberg could use to his advantage, emphasizing that his client was not part of the Lynch Inner Circle, that the two men did not work closely together and in fact rarely crossed paths. It would serve both men well as a line of defence. One was making the big decisions and taking care of the bigger, more strategic picture while travelling almost constantly; the other was an innocuous lower-level employee in the accounts department. Lynch wasn't an accountant, and Chamberlain reported directly to someone else. Why would they know what one another was doing? The prosecution was effectively running two totally separate trials at once.

The two defence teams needed to collaborate, though. Turning on one another in court and playing the blame game would help no one and they avoided it at all costs.

The stress of the trial preparation was compounded by tragedies at home. Shortly after the extradition flight came some shocking news. Lynch's brother Richard, who had long struggled with mental health problems, had overdosed and died at his home in Essex. Being in San Francisco, Lynch was unable to attend the funeral. He had supported his brother, giving him work and funds over the years, but now there was nothing more he could do.

There were further bad tidings from home a few months later, this time from Loudham. Mark Gilbert, the farm's long-standing stock-keeper, had been taken desperately ill with necrotising fasciitis, also known as the flesh-eating disease. He was playing golf one Friday afternoon and, by Saturday evening, was gravely ill. The Lynch family did not hesitate to step in and help, financially supporting him through his illness. This was life-changing for the Gilbert family, who was thus able to put food on the table and fuel in the car, not to mention support Gilbert's wife, who has multiple sclerosis. Their future, with Lynch away and Gilbert's illness leaving him scarred and walking with a stick, had felt very uncertain.

Finally, in December 2023, there had been another blow, once again from Darktrace quarters. After Vanessa Colomar had stepped down as Lynch's chosen representative on the company's board in December 2022, he had turned to his old friend Patrick Jacob to ask if he would take the role instead. Jacob reluctantly agreed, as a favour to Lynch. In reality, there were fewer and fewer people Lynch could trust at this stage of his legal proceedings to do that kind of role for him. Eyebrows were raised within Darktrace at Jacob's unusual appointment; it looked a rather desperate move on Lynch's part.

Jacob was on his way to the Darktrace annual general meeting when Andy Kanter rang him. He had heard rumblings that things might not be as smooth as expected: 'There's been a whip round,' Kanter said. 'KKR, one of the investors, has got some friends and relations together to get you off the board.' On arrival, Jacob shook his fellow board members by the hand: 'You're not going to vote against me, are you?' he asked directly. They would not look him in the eye, offering mumbled denials. This shiftiness irritated the typically straightforward Jacob, especially when he was summarily voted out of his seat, just as Kanter had warned.

Justifying the decision, Darktrace's backers said they wanted to boost the board's independence. Jacob's Invoke role and his overt links to Lynch were perceived as 'governance issues'. Behind the scenes, the schism between Lynch and Darktrace management was continuing to painfully deteriorate, and they wanted to get rid of him as quickly as possible – to shake off his needling about the company's strategy.

It was yet another humiliation from Lynch's favourite business, a final sucker punch against him, knocking him out of position. Lynch no longer had a seat on the Darktrace board. They did not want him near the business. The company let it be known that the trial was a noisy distraction which was holding Darktrace back. Its share price was lower than its peers, which Darktrace felt was down to Lynch's damaged reputation. Darktrace executives banged the same drum again and again: they had to do what was right for the company, what was right for the shareholders. If that meant pushing Lynch out, then so be it. Later the Invoke holding fell below the 10 per cent it needed to be represented, and Lynch officially lost the right to appoint a director.

Meanwhile Lynch's family had gone on selling their Darktrace shares, held in Angela's name. Their ownership share continued to fall until December 2023, when it was just under 5 per cent.

But, back in San Francisco, there were more immediate worries to contend with.

BY FEBRUARY 2024, a veritable host of lawyers had decamped to the city for a final month of frenetic preparation ahead of the trial. Representatives from both firms defending Lynch – Clifford Chance and Steptoe – set up a base in the latter's office, coincidentally in the same development as Autonomy's former San Francisco offices, squeezing into whatever space there was, and working long into the night.

Being away from their families for so long was brutal for the defence. For four long months, Chris Morvillo stayed at a hotel a short fifteen-minute walk from the office, and a five-minute car ride away from the courthouse. He missed his wife, Neda; he missed his daughters and his dog and his home in New York. The rest of the troops were housed in Airbnbs dotted around the city.

During the trial, Morvillo was the good cop, personable and accessible. He kept an open line of communication with the prosecution, which meant he sometimes got advance notice of witnesses. Adding to his air of warmth, he wore cheap, plastic reading glasses in a variety of bright colours which he seemed to need to buy more and more of each week, as he lost them in the busy chaos. Vibrant blue was his favourite. At one point the jury wondered if his spectacles were a code for something; perhaps the different colours sent secret signals to his team?

Brian Heberlig played the tough-guy bad cop in court. Backstage, his office was papered with news articles which spelt out the unlikelihood of a win – the long odds of 0.4 per cent. He found them motivational. 'He is one of the clearest lawyers I've ever encountered,' Judge Breyer said. 'Even with my common cold, what he said to me resonated.' Finally, Reid Weingarten was the ringleader, the consummate storyteller, the one who would get the jury onside and would spin the story of Lynch and his meteoric rise from a human angle.

Just as he did at Autonomy and in all his business dealings, Lynch liked to have absolute control over the people working for him. He was paying for the best of the best of the best to work on the case, full-time, and he expected nothing less than perfection. Lynch would demand the undeliverable, asking lawyers to prepare for court scenarios they couldn't yet predict. He'd sit with his feet up on their desks and bark orders, much as he did back in his offices in Cambridge all those years before.

Many of the rank and file found Lynch hard to handle, smiling grimly that this drive and determination explained his power and wealth. He was a nightmare to deal with. He would regularly fall out with Morvillo, the two would snipe at one another like an old married couple and stop speaking, such was the level of irritation. He would also go toe to toe with Weingarten, and disputes between the pair would combust into blazing rows. Lynch knew how to push everyone's buttons.

As important as the legal team was the jury. There was much discussion over the sort of people who would be most likely to back Lynch, about whether his wealth and success would make him a target of hate or jealousy. In the end, they decided to push for a college-educated group as much as possible, and it was indeed a highly educated bunch, including some software types, a person who worked in investment banking, a doctor and a law student.

While Lynch was keeping his foot hard on his lawyers' necks, he also wanted to keep his finger on the jury's pulse. He had a smart strategy to win the case: trying to understand what the jury was making of it all as it unfolded, working out which way the wind was blowing on a daily basis. To do this, he needed some fake jurors who would give their honest opinions on the proceedings.

Laughing at a professional jury consultant's $200,000 proposal to put a panel together for him, he sent his team out hunting for a couple of totally random 'ordinary people' who would sit through the trial and feed back their views on the affair. Bringing an accounting fraud to life – making it interesting – was no easy task for either side; it was essential to find out how it was all landing with the everyman.

Igno helped out, contacting a neighbour of his cousin's to be part of this curious focus group of two: one of them loathed Lynch and one of them liked him. Once the trial got underway, after each day in court, Jonathan Baum would interview them for about half an hour each, taking note of their feelings about the latest twist in the trial, then he'd whizz a detailed summary around by email.

The reports from these 'real people' watching in real time were an eye-opener. They proved either remarkably insightful or demonstrated how the jury had likely completely missed the point. Sometimes their views would spark alarm at how quickly a judgement or sense of mistrust could be formed. 'I don't know what he did, but he definitely did something, so I'd convict him,' one shadow juror said of Lynch, without a flinch of hesitation.

Morvillo loathed and dreaded these daily write-ups from Baum. It caused even more work, as Lynch would send the summaries to Angela and together they would question one thing or another based on the candid comments. Unlike during the civil trial, overseen by an expert judge, these inexpert opinions from laymen were all-important.

*

LYNCH AND ANGELA were becoming more of a team as the trial prep continued. She supported him through the ongoing pain of his chronic medical conditions, which were exacerbated by the mental pressure of this final trial. The decade-long debacle over the HP sale had taken a toll on their relationship, which they'd kept behind closed doors. There were several rumours that Lynch was having affairs.

Personally, Lynch remained steely and level-headed with those around him. He gave the impression of a confident, controlled man, but he would sometimes drink too much at lunches and write notes to those close to him, expressing his struggles. Wildly out of character.

Everyone involved with the trial needed an outlet for their stress and frustration.

Chamberlain had running. He and Lincenberg would meet every Sunday to work out together, then sometimes go for a pizza afterwards.

To give everyone a break, the trial was held over a four-day week, with no court on Fridays. Morvillo and his colleagues would go for dinner on Thursday nights at the same restaurant, week in, week out. (In yet another odd coincidence in a story full of them, and unbeknown to either side until after the trial concluded, one of the shadow jurors worked in that restaurant's bar.) Every time, Morvillo chose the same wine – the evocatively named Sea Smoke Pinot Noir. It became the lawyers' lucky vintage, so much so that chaos arose when the overworked group was told one Thursday evening that it was out of stock; they had drunk it all. To avoid any future panic, the sommelier started ordering it especially, and normal life shortly resumed.

Left lurking in the wings were spies. Real or fictional, all of Lynch's 'spooks' were off limits for the duration of the trial. Any references to James Bond films from the Autonomy days were struck out. There was a fear that a jury might be in danger of believing that Lynch genuinely thought of himself as a wannabe Bond villain, as he'd often joked.

Weingarten wanted to elaborate in his opening remarks on Lynch's fabled relationship with the intelligence community. The secrecy around it would explain a lot, he said, because some of the important work Lynch was doing was during 2011. But Breyer saw through this, ruling references to the spies out of his opener. It might appear prejudicial, he said, persuading the jury of Lynch's importance to the US government or to the achievement of world peace or something equally crucial to humanity's survival.

In the end, there were no spoof videos, and just the briefest mention of the piranhas.

THIRTY-TWO

Deal or No Deal

I needed to look myself in the mirror every day of the rest of my life and had I lied it would have been difficult. Yes, I could have flown home . . . but as a guilty man. No, this is a fight I must take on: win or lose. No deal.

– *Stephen Chamberlain*

San Francisco can be grey, rainy and miserable. Thick fog rolls in from the Pacific, shrouding the Bay area. But on 17 March 2024, the eve of the trial, the sun shone and it felt like spring. It was a day which could have heralded a fresh start for everyone involved, and their families.

In the early evening, shortly before sunset, the prosecution tossed Chamberlain and Lynch a hefty curve ball in the shape of a deal – a plea bargain. If they just admitted their guilt, the prosecution offered, their sentences would be cut and the trial would be scrapped. A simple word – guilty – and they would be home with their families far sooner than they could have hoped, without having to go through the pain of the drawn-out process looming ahead.

Lynch was really tempted, and his lawyers were exploring the conditions of the offer. While he played the crusading victim in public, in private he was always pragmatically weighing up the odds. Given the previous verdicts, he was unlikely to win the trial. On top of that, his health was poor, and he feared prison. The potential length of his sentence could eat up most of the rest of his life.

It was not the first offer Lynch had received. In fact, wranglings over these deals had been a source of great frustration to Morvillo. Lynch would stipulate strict conditions to take a deal with the prosecution and then, when Morvillo managed to hit the target set by his client against the odds, Lynch would withdraw. 'I quit,' Morvillo finally said after one of these protracted and ultimately thwarted negotiations. Only to turn up again the next day.

Chamberlain received the offer from the prosecutors in writing at 7.21 p.m. and was given a deadline of 10 a.m. the following day to deliver an answer. For many people considering such an important offer, a sleepless night might have followed. The idea sounded appealing: admit wrongdoing and you could be on a plane home.

Not for Chamberlain. It was an offer that held no temptation for him. He spoke to Karen who, as always, backed him all the way. With a sense of rising indignation, and a doubling-down on his resolve, he felt the prosecution's assumptions about his character had been flawed from the start.

They assumed that they could flip him. They assumed that he would testify against his former bosses, and that he would submit a guilty plea purely to save his own skin. They could not have been more wrong, he thought grimly.

For him, a stint in prison was preferable to admitting something that he did not believe to be true. He felt he needed to be able to look himself in the mirror each day for the rest of his life, and if he lied he could not have done that. Of course, a plea deal would have meant a flight home, but for him it would have meant returning as a truly guilty man – not for his alleged crimes at Autonomy, but for his cowardice in misrepresenting the truth of the matter. It was a fight he needed to take on, regardless of the outcome.

Chamberlain had good reason to feel like he wanted to fight the case on his terms. The HP debacle had dominated his life back home in Cambridge. It had caused him to lose out on jobs that required travel to the US, it had cost him his job at Darktrace, it had even forced him to resign from his unpaid role at his beloved Cambridge United, managing their accounts.

He had volunteered to hand himself over to the US authorities. He had complied with all of their wishes. He wanted to put an end to all those years of turmoil in the way he felt was honourable. He had been dragged into this mess, and he would be damned if he didn't find a way out of it that he and his family could be proud of.

And so he gave his answer quickly. There was no way he was going to take the deal. Not even a call to Chamberlain from one of Lynch's close friends and allies could sway him. Karen was proud of his strength, but not all his friends were so certain it was the right choice. In frustration and pain, one later called it the single most stupid adult decision they had ever witnessed in their entire life.

Back in Pacific Heights, this meant Lynch's opinion on the agreement did not matter. A condition of the deal was that it had to be accepted by both parties for the defence to make it valid. Because Chamberlain had almost immediately decided to turn it down, it was automatically dismissed.

It's curious, how this particular aspect of the affair unfurled. The two men, Lynch and Chamberlain, had spent so little time together at work all those years before. One was the big boss, the other further down the ranks. Yet when they found their fates chained together there was no power imbalance. If one said no, the other could do nothing.

Chamberlain had made his decision. One that meant Lynch had no autonomy to make his. The preparation was finished, the offers refused, and the stage set. One of the biggest criminal fraud trials of the century was on.

THIRTY-THREE

Trial of the Century

A reasonable doubt is a doubt based upon reason and common sense and is not based purely on speculation. It may arise from a careful and impartial consideration of all the evidence or from lack of evidence.

– Judge Charles 'Chuck' Breyer, 3 June 2024

On Monday, 18 March 2024, Mike Lynch strode purposefully into the massive twenty-one-floor courthouse for the first day of his trial, accompanied as always by one of his bodyguards. The thin smattering of hair left at the back of his large domed head was now mainly grey, but his expressive eyebrows remained resolutely dark, his face remarkably unwrinkled. The portly man was dressed in a dark blue suit and a blue tie with horizontal stripes, his thick neck bulging out behind the shirt collar. He gripped his soft brown leather briefcase in his right hand, swinging it by its top handle as he marched.

In contrast to his former boss, Steve Chamberlain took the bus to court each day. His lawyers put it down to a quirky British love of public transport.

Once everyone was settled, it felt a bit like Groundhog Day. Lynch and Chamberlain's criminal trial was a hotchpotch of the British civil trial and the Hussain trial: it included much of the same evidence and many of the same witnesses – Stouffer Egan, David Toms, Mark Geall and Daud Khan would all find themselves telling by now familiar stories; it took place in the same courtroom; and even featured the same prosecutor, Adam Reeves. This time, though, there were different defendants, a different jury and a new defence team.

'Calling criminal action CR-18-0577,' the clerk said. 'USA versus Michael Richard Lynch and Stephen Keith Chamberlain.' The lawyers introduced themselves, the judge instructed the jury and soon it had all begun.

Once inside the courtroom, Lynch sat quietly, twiddling his pen, eyes staring forward, mouth set. He was listening intently, trying to take everything in, paying close attention, trying not to let his hearing loss get in the way. He wanted to follow the arguments being made by both sides, but he was also already prepping to take the witness stand, running through scenarios in his head.

AMERICAN JURY TRIALS are theatrical, about showmanship and storytelling. The opening remarks from both sides set out their stall for what's to come, but as Lynch always said, real life is not so binary.

For the prosecution, Reeves painted a picture of the calculated, tyrannical Dr Lynch, who ruled his business empire with an iron fist, a dominating, controlling overlord. He was desperate to sell his business, tempting HP executives with a fairy story of success based on false accounts. It was a tale, Reeves told the jury, which was built on feet of clay. Lynch had orchestrated a 'multi-year, multi-layered fraud' which was calculated to woo a buyer.

Over the course of an hour and a half, Reeves argued that Lynch started his deception as soon as he met HP's bosses in their Palo Alto headquarters in 2011, when he misrepresented Autonomy as a 'money-making machine'. Lynch's control of Hussain in all of this meant Lynch himself did not leave any fingerprints. Chamberlain's job was to do deals that did not make any sense, and he lied to the auditors, argued Reeves.

The challenge for the jury, Reeves warned them, would be understanding a volley of jargon as they faced an endurance test, hearing about software accounting. Indeed, making the story comprehensible and engaging was the major challenge faced by the lawyers on both sides. To quote the Deloitte auditors from a decade before, a strong story, a strong narrative and some 'wordsmithing' were needed.

This was always, always, Lynch's forte.

For the defence, Weingarten stood up and told the jury about *Mike* – simply '*Mike*' – a successful man who was approachable, relatable and even (sometimes) likeable. The first-name moniker was very deliberate. The cornerstone of a character sketch of a tech everyman, a visionary in Silicon Valley where top founders are always known by their first names. The likes of Bill (Gates), Steve (Jobs), Mark (Zuckerberg) and Elon (Musk) were this man's peers, it implied. It strengthened his image before the jury as the kind of entrepreneur Americans love to idolize, one those in the Bay Area are especially familiar with.

This rebrand was a sharp about-turn from the days when he wore his Cambridge PhD like a badge of honour, 'Dr Lynch' proudly emblazoned across press releases and signatures. Now, stripped back to *Mike*, he traded academic prestige for a calculated return to the working-class roots he'd once worked so hard to outgrow. And in the hustle culture of San Francisco, that down-to-earth makeover played well.

Just Mike, the successful businessman from humble beginnings, a startup guy who was most comfortable at home eating cold pizza at 2 a.m. while inventing something, a CEO who was not interested in the finer details of running a company, especially not the accounting. Yes, of course he was a hard-charger with a bit of an edge, Weingarten said, but that's how one gets on in the business world. The jury shouldn't blame the man for having exacting standards.

And why would Lynch commit fraud? Weingarten sowed seeds of doubt in the jury's ear. Lynch knew that he would have to hand over the accounts to HP when Autonomy was bought and so it was preposterous he would have done that had he known they were fraudulent. He would have been found out straight away. In addition to that, he was a wealthy man who did not need or want more money. Why would he risk his life, liberty and reputation for the sake of lying about some hardware? Lynch was a strategy guy. There was nothing he hated more than living quarter to quarter in a relentless three-monthly cycle he considered 'the bane of Western economic systems'.

Turning to HP, Weingarten claimed that the tech giant had rushed the Autonomy deal and was now nursing a serious case of buyer's remorse. The due diligence took a mere nine working days, he calculated, less than a day for every billion spent. If HP had taken the time, they might have found everything they complained about before ever putting pen to paper.

Then came Weingarten's mic-drop moment, the grand finale of his speech. At the end of the day, here's the deal, he said: 'Mike Lynch is not Superman. He's not perfect. He's not a saint, but he sure as hell ain't no criminal. He ain't no crook. He ain't no fraud, and you're going to be satisfied of that.'

Lynch's team had picked out two strong and simple lines of defence. First, there was the 'good faith' defence, arguing that the CEO was entitled to rely on the credible, competent people who he employed to look after the details, including the blue-chip company Deloitte, which had signed off Autonomy's numbers, and the audit committee which was staffed by top professionals. Lynch had trusted that they would pick up on any problems, and that was totally normal.

Second, there was the 'just business' defence. Lynch was just doing business at Autonomy, as they might have at any other software company. He and his team were just conducting normal, everyday business deals and the American government was trying to criminalize them and make an example of them. The jury was encouraged to cut the guy some slack.

As for Chamberlain, Lincenberg argued that Autonomy's VP of Finance was a mere pawn in a battle between two titans: HP and Lynch.

As the trial continued, the defence lawyers pushed the line that it should never have got as far as a criminal court in the first place. 'This is why God made civil cases,' Weingarten laughed. Given the outcome of the UK's civil trial, the joke was close to the line. But the jury should have been unaware of what had happened in a London courtroom just two years prior, having been instructed not to do any research about the two British men.

The persuasive rhetoric from Reeves and the electric Weingarten started the trial with a bang, but it quickly stuttered to a whimper as the first witnesses took to the stand. The month of March passed, marked by appearances by people from Autonomy's accounts department whom Lynch had never met. The number crunchers told the tale of Hussain micromanaging sales, trying to ensure the company hit its quarterly targets. The jury was thrust into stultifying boredom. One juror fell asleep.

Early in the trial, there was another unexpected twist when Weingarten collapsed with a stomach infection, the lingering effects of a cancer which he had beaten a couple of decades before. He had not been at his best for a few weeks, and this shock event meant he had to fly back to New York for treatment and follow the remainder of the trial from his hospital bed.

Lynch had lost his star player. More than that, it meant the lawyers had to start a mountain of work from scratch. Weingarten had been due to cross-examine the most important witnesses, who now had to be divided up among the team. Worse, Weingarten was not a computer guy. Instead, he wrote his notes, his thoughts, his musings about his strategy on pieces of paper. He had stacks of file boxes with seven or eight individual folders inside, each representing a topic to grill the witnesses on. When something occurred to him, he would scrawl a note to himself in Sharpie and chuck it into the boxes. His colleagues could not make head nor tail of most of it and lost months of preparation time for critical witnesses.

The most critical came on April Fool's Day, of all days, when – for the first time in this entire tumultuous affair – Autonomy's first whistleblower, Brent Hogenson, took the stand. Hogenson, now retired and living in Panama, was the government's top witness, and his first day giving evidence was devastating for Lynch. He described how he came to the point of raising official concerns about the accounts. There were a few things which made him suspicious, he said: the way that sales were being counted, bills which had little chance of being settled. Old invoices are like milk, he told the jury; the older they get, the more they start to smell, and Autonomy was far too smelly. Then, of course, he was fired.

After hearing Hogenson's story, the shadow jury was convinced that Lynch was guilty. But this did not last long.

When it was the defence's turn, they were well prepared, roaring back with a story of their own, picking apart Hogenson's credentials and his supposedly benevolent motivations. Heberlig, in charge of the cross-examination, made him out to be a bad manager who had fluffed dealing with a million-dollar payroll fraud, who had let a financial qualification lapse and who had later wiped his computer under suspicious circumstances.

Lynch's team made a big play about Hogenson's multiple applications to join an official whistleblower programme, which would mean claiming a share of the compensatory funds from Autonomy, presuming there were convictions. He was on the stand for almost three days. By the end, the shadow jury was unanimous. Hogenson's credibility had been utterly destroyed.

ON 26 APRIL, there came a financial windfall for Lynch which more than helped pay the mounting legal bills.

Slap bang in the middle of the trial, Darktrace was sold for more than $5 billion to Thoma Bravo, a well-known US private equity firm, netting a fortune for its founders. It created dynastic wealth for some of its shareholders. Brokering the deal? Frank Quattrone's Qatalyst, the same company which had sold Autonomy to HP.

The Lynch family netted around £300 million, Hussain more than £100 million, Nicole Eagan £69 million, Jack Stockdale £26 million and Poppy Gustafsson £34 million. It was not the first foray into this story for Thoma Bravo. In 2016, the firm had approached Meg Whitman about buying HP's software division, which included Autonomy. They had been in talks with Darktrace the year before the trial, but media leaks put paid to the deal at that stage. The private equity business pulled out, irritated by the information getting into the public domain and blaming Darktrace. Some at Darktrace in turn blamed Lynch, suspecting he wanted to kybosh the deal, or even that Whitman had rung up her contacts at Thoma Bravo and told them in no uncertain terms not to buy the business. None of this was ever proven. The cash filled Lynch and Hussain's war chests for the continuing legal battle – and for when the British judge decided how much they had to pay HP in compensation.

IN SAN FRANCISCO, on 22 May, Jonathan Bloomer testified. The former chair of Autonomy's audit committee (albeit only for a short time until Autonomy was sold) was a very credible defence witness, with an impeccable City of London pedigree. By now, he had become the chairman of Morgan Stanley International, the UK-based subsidiary of the US bank.

He was one of the few figures who had not wavered in their support for Lynch over the years. Several of the bankers and lawyers who had been involved in the HP deal refused to fly out to the US to help him, either because they felt that they were being used for their status or because they had been warned off the whole affair by their firms. After all, the judgement in the UK civil trial was categorical and it seemed like a lost cause.

But Bloomer always felt he had done absolutely everything by the book, and he was not going to see his reputation dragged through the mud. He stuck by his arguments, as he had before. Lynch was not fussed about the accounting, he said, and the hardware sales were not significant enough to disclose to the market. He lent authority to Lynch's narrative and stayed on for a few days of the trial, sitting in the courtroom to listen.

One of the strangest and most dramatic moments of the trial came very shortly before Lynch testified, when a witness called Harriet Slack, a senior Clifford Chance associate, took the stand. She was meant to be giving straightforward testimony about the evidence behind some of the charts, documents and data that the Lynch team was putting before the jury.

Unexpectedly, the prosecution started ripping her apart, asking her off-kilter questions about how much money she earnt, the length of time she'd worked on the Lynch case, and combing through her professional biography. Post-it notes flew around the defence counsel table as they sat wide-eyed, wondering what on earth was happening. Slack could see the notes being passed between them out of the corner of her eye and started to look panicked. In the small hours of the morning, Lynch's team tried and failed to rule for a mistrial. It was worth a shot.

The next morning, Breyer was furious. In no uncertain terms, he told the jury that the government's cross-examination had been improper, and that there was nothing to suggest that Slack had exercised her duties in anything but a professional manner. In addition, Lynch's wealth should not be held against him. 'If you think Dr Lynch has considerable resources, you ought to think what the United States government has,' he said.

THEN CAME THE moment when Chris Morvillo and Lynch raised the stakes and went all in.

With the press bench full to capacity, and as Angela watched from the first row of the gallery, Lynch himself took the stand and raised his right hand, taking the traditional oath to tell the truth, the whole truth and nothing but the truth. Relaxed and smiling as ever, this was his moment. Clad in a dark suit, white shirt and blue tie, he delivered the performance of his lifetime as the everyman. The self-deprecating British charm was dialled up to full blast.

His co-star Morvillo, in the role of supporting actor, led him through the first few days of those well-rehearsed theatrics. The two men began with an easy icebreaker. Morvillo asked Lynch to confirm that they had met 'a lot'. Lynch agreed. 'You're probably sick of me at this point?' Morvillo flicked back. 'It's a bit like we're married sometimes.' Lynch chuckled. Morvillo grinned back at him and the court laughed. Putting Lynch in the firing line like this was risky, but it quickly became apparent that the strategy was going to pay off.

They both knew their lines off by heart. Morvillo asked Lynch to reflect on what he'd heard at the trial from the various witnesses. 'Surreal,' came his response. This was all new to him, there were people on the stand he'd never met, or had just shaken hands with in passing. He was the boss! People met him all the time, he could not remember them all! The description of the company that the jury had heard across the previous ten weeks of the trial did not bear any relation to the realities of the Autonomy he had run back in the UK.

He played up his Britishness for the jury, dropping in silly Anglicisms like 'bean counter' and 'good bloke'. Lynch was off to the races.

He compared running Autonomy to being a record producer; there were lots of failures, but that's OK if you have one hit. Life is nuanced and it is messy. If you take a microscope into any kitchen, you'll always find some bacteria somewhere, he said. Autonomy was like any big company in that regard. How could anyone manage a big business without *some* mistakes being made?

That particular metaphor – the bacteria in the kitchen – had taken some time to perfect, and it paid off, landing well with the tech-friendly, business-minded jury.

Lynch went for broke with his life story. The character depicted on the stand was 'just Mike', the working-class kid done good, with Irish parents, real salt-of-the-earth types. His mother ran the nursing station at the emergency department of a London hospital.

He painted a rich, emotional picture of his past. He shared memories of childhood experiments dismantling alarm clocks, and long commutes to school at Bancroft's, of mopping hospital wards when he spent summers working with his mother. With the odds stacked against him, Lynch had won a place at Cambridge, and from his research there went on to found a business that became a crucial part of his nation's technology economy.

There were stories of his startup days, of a handful of people in a dingy office who wanted to change the world. As for his right-hand man, Hussain? He was not a school friend, only a 'third level out' acquaintance at Cambridge. Yes, Lynch had been at Hussain's wedding, but that was with all his other Cambridge friends. Not a big deal. Was Autonomy's CFO good at his job? Yes, 'I think he was', Lynch responded.

All in all, it was an utterly charming portrait of a truly special person who had a lovely, wholesome life which he'd built from nothing. A man with a caring family, with clever daughters with normal teenage concerns. A man with the will to succeed, who had done just that and now cultivated rare-breed cattle at his home in Suffolk. A quirky expert in agricultural matters, such as the dangers of over-breeding farm animals and 'frankencows', a deprecating term for a genetically modified animal.

Lynch sold the jury his own version of the American Dream, with a twist of British modesty and humour. And Judge Breyer sardonically called it out at one point. We didn't get to the strawberry fields, he noted, nor the clotted cream nor the cheddar. Morvillo replied that those bits had been edited out for time.

The rest of Lynch's time on the stand was less evocative than his descriptions of cattle and holiday jobs making tea for the elderly. There may have been no mention of cheddar or strawberries, but there was a lot of talk of procedure, of emails, of meetings, deals and strategy. One thing he would have done differently at Autonomy, Lynch said, was to have knocked Hussain's involvement with the sales team on the head.

Then his wingman, the affable Morvillo, stepped back from the spotlight. It was time for Lynch to go it alone – time for Adam Reeves, for the prosecution, to tear his story apart. Yet just as Rabinowitz had found out four years beforehand in London, Lynch was a very cool customer in the witness stand, measured and reasonable. Reeves barely laid a glove on him.

There was even an unfortunate comic moment when Reeves tried to pin Lynch down on the Autonomy culture. He displayed a *Times* article entitled 'Swimming Fast in Piranha-Filled Waters', accompanied by a photograph of Lynch standing in front of a fish tank. Reeves asked Lynch if they were piranhas, confident of painting his choice of the predators as emblematic of his wider attitude towards the company's culture. But zooming in, it was clear that the fish were not piranhas. Instead, the tank 'was full of peaceful, loving, harmonious fish,' Lynch retorted.

He would retell this anecdote to everyone after the trial. It was one of his favourite moments.

As for Chamberlain, his lawyers decided against putting him through the pain of being on the stand. They had utter confidence in their client's honesty and clarity, but he did not remember many of the transactions which were being discussed, which was problematic and may have made him look shifty.

The trial dragged on, the drama in the courtroom a foil to the more mundane routine going on outside it. Chamberlain ran around and around the city to clear his mind, Lynch was forced back to the Pacific Heights house every night for his curfew, and the shadow jury reported into Jonathan Baum every day.

On Tuesday 4 June, it came to an end with the closing arguments.

Lincenberg's tactic was to present Chamberlain as the honest and trustworthy admin man, not the one who made any important decisions or knew about any side agreements on sales deals. For Heberlig, there was 'magic in Mike'. He was just a successful, driven man, the mathematics whizz kid who got to Cambridge through his brainpower and determination.

For the prosecution, Bob Leach said there *was* a conspiracy at Autonomy, that everyone had a job to play in it. Hussain and Egan cooked up the deals, Chamberlain blew them past the auditors and Lynch flew the plane, all the while deceiving the stock market. Lynch was utterly in control and domineering, he said, ably supported by Andy Kanter and Pete Menell.

Leach complimented the jurors for their long service and for not falling asleep – 12,000 exhibits and 80 witnesses would challenge any human's willpower and attention. And with that, it was over.

The watchful panel retired to decide Chamberlain's and Lynch's fates.

THE DEFENDANTS AND their families could only wait, sick with feelings of fear and anticipation, willing time to accelerate. They retired to the Breyer lounge on the eighteenth floor of the courthouse, nervously playing cards, reading, fidgeting with their phones and pacing up and down. It'll be a while, Morvillo said, as the jurors peppered the lawyers with questions.

The groups settled in for the long haul. But then, late in the morning of Thursday 6 June, the lawyers were working on satisfying some jurors' requests when, out of the blue, a note appeared. The jury had reached a decision. All hearts in the room stopped.

Lincenberg went over to Karen and her husband: 'Come on, we have to go to the courtroom now.' Chamberlain wasn't even in his suit and frantically began to strip off in the office, re-dressing in a shirt and jacket, trying to assemble himself for whatever came next. 'We have to go NOW, Steve,' his lawyers and wife urged. Adrenaline surging through their bodies, they rushed to the courtroom.

Morvillo went to get a glass of water to calm his nerves ahead of the verdict. He was far from convinced that it would go their way. His hands were shaking as he filled the cup, and most of the water ended up on the ground. He took a breath, but his hands were still trembling. Lynch turned to Angela, kissing her on the forehead as they entered the court.

Judge Breyer was already in position. Lynch sat, as usual, in the middle seat at his legal table, with Morvillo to his left and Heberlig at the head. Morvillo murmured a few words of encouragement to Lynch: 'However this turns out, we're going to be there for you, and we'll get through it together.'

They heard the jury congregating outside the little door to the courtroom, as they always did before they came in. Then, there was an unusual sound from the room where the jurors had been deliberating: a laugh. It was strange, Morvillo thought, and his heart started to lift.

As the jury filed in, everyone sensed that something was different. The atmosphere was lighter. There were a couple of smiles from the jurors, and one of them even looked Chamberlain in the eye. It was another good sign.

As breaths were held all around the still courtroom, Breyer was handed the verdict sheet. He took his time reading it, flipping through it. Then he handed it back to his courtroom deputy to read.

Gripping the hand of one of the female lawyers from Lynch's team was Karen Chamberlain. On the other side was Rolo Igno, holding Angela's hands tightly in his.

'Count one: Not Guilty.'

A collective exhale of breath was accompanied by cheers, grins and clapping. There was also a momentary sense of disbelief from some, including Lynch. Angela raced into the well of the courtroom like a greyhound out of the stands towards Lynch, and Karen followed to embrace her husband. But the verdict wasn't done yet. There were fifteen counts in total.

Just as Hildyard had done, Judge Breyer delivered the punchline quickly, except this time it was the opposite, and spared them the pain of going through each count one by one.

'With respect to counts two through fifteen: Not Guilty.'

Improbably, they had won.

There was an eruption of emotion, tears, bear hugs, whoops and high fives. Lynch stood stunned for a few moments before he and Angela embraced again. Just a week or so shy of his fifty-ninth birthday, he had been given the best of all possible gifts.

The jurors were allowed to hang back and chat to the lawyers after the verdict and ask questions. Surprisingly, none seemed to have done any sneaky research. The biggest question was, of course, what had happened to Hussain? They were surprised to hear the answer. Another juror asked Morvillo how many pairs of reading glasses he had, and everyone collapsed into giggles.

Around the world, WhatsApp groups of aggrieved former Autonomy staffers lit up in shock. 'He's got away with it,' one said, 'I cannot believe it, he has landed on his feet again.' 'How?' another asked, 'this is not right,' it is 'classic Mike to dodge prison, when it is absolutely where he should be.'

The heart-pounding panic which had hounded Lynch, Chamberlain and their families constantly for an entire decade had been instantly turned into a shaky, almost disbelieving relief. The marathon was finally over.

It was a scramble to find a venue that could accommodate the entire extended team at such short notice, but a dinner to celebrate was hastily arranged. Where the men had once felt terror, now they felt the trembling emotion of its extraordinarily unexpected release. 'I can't even begin to unwrap what just happened,' Lynch said, 'because if I do, I'll fall apart.'

The day after, still punch drunk from the night before, Karen filmed Chamberlain sitting in front of the window of his rented apartment, lit up by the sunshine streaming in behind him. Holding a beer in one hand, he sang loudly and joyfully to the skies, to the world beneath him, and to the love of his life: 'Innocent Man' by Billy Joel.

THIRTY-FOUR

The Aftermath

Now you have a second life – the question is, what do you want to do with it?

– *Mike Lynch,* The Sunday Times, *27 July 2024*

Lynch woke up after the victory party and, for the first time in a decade, the world did not come crashing down. He felt lighter, but fully emerging from this kind of lengthy traumatic experience would not happen overnight.

Flying out of San Francisco, it was not until the rugged landscape of the West Coast grew wilder beneath him that he started to relax. He wasn't able to completely let himself go until Seattle became Vancouver and the mountains grew higher and snow-capped, even in the warm sun. You never know what tricks the US government might have up its sleeve, he thought to himself. But looking out of the plane window, leaving US airspace behind, it was finally time to sink into the seat and exhale.

This leg of the journey was a hell of a lot more comfortable than the last one had been.

Once he was back at home, his two daughters served as a stark reminder of the passage of time, of how life had continued while he had been away. They were both now all grown up and ready to fly the nest, onwards towards their next adventures. The stigma and stress of the trial had haunted their childhoods and their teenage years. Hannah, having just completed her A levels, had won a place at Oxford to study English. The Dreaming Spires were obviously inferior to Cambridge, Lynch joked, and she was not tackling a more valuable scientific subject, but he was hugely proud of his accomplished youngest.

Mike and Hannah Lynch.

He really did love his alma mater, though, and had been irate when his eldest daughter Esme's application to his old college, Christ's in Cambridge, was rejected a few years before – especially given his hefty donations to the institution. He had even been named a Lady Margaret Beaufort Fellow years earlier, an accolade reserved for a select cohort who show their 'commitment' to the college.

This twinge of resentment against those he perceived as the disloyal dons, happy to take his money but not his daughter, had now somewhat passed. Esme was studying engineering at London's illustrious Imperial College, globally renowned for its leading position in the sciences, and she was excelling academically, earning her father's deep admiration. She was always very much her father's child.

As well as his family, Lynch had his tight group of friends to catch up with and thank for their belief in him and support of the family while he was away. David Robbie, a long-standing friend from his BBC days, wanted to plan a small homecoming dinner for a few selected guests in Suffolk after the summer. Lynch acquiesced but wanted to make sure there were not going to be any bossy speeches or fuss and bother.

In a tear-jerking interview with Danny Fortson of *The Sunday Times*, Lynch said it felt as though he'd been given the gift of a new life and that now he had the chance to consider what he truly wanted to do with it.

This was true, to an extent. But there was another roaring tiger in his path to deal with first, which could kybosh this 'gift': HP. While Lynch was more than ecstatic to be safely home on British soil, his victory was bittersweet. He had not returned to a totally clean slate nor a completely fresh start: in Britain, he and Hussain had been found categorically guilty of fraud two years earlier.

He had thrown off the shackles of the prison threat and he had the most important thing, his liberty, but he still faced a hefty payment to HP for their victory in the British civil trial, of an amount still to be decided. Even the hundreds of millions of dollars he had earnt from the sale of Darktrace, plus whatever was left from the original sale of Autonomy to HP, would not stretch to the $4 billion the American giant was seeking.

Lynch had to decide whether it was worth now trying to settle the case, given the damning detailed judgement against him, or whether he wanted to keep on fighting, buoyed up by the criminal verdict. He had spent several fortunes on lawyers by this point. Did he really want to spend any more, heading into another unpredictable situation?

THAT SUMMER'S NEWSPAPER headlines concentrated on the verdict in the US, telling the story of the plucky, determined Lynch slaying the dragon that is the US legal system despite its crushing might. He was treated relatively favourably by the normally snarky British press.

Lynch, single-mindedly promoting his recent Not Guilty status, proclaimed to the world that he was picking up the sword of justice on their behalf. In a widely shared interview, he told the BBC's Evan Davis vehemently that he was only back in the UK because he was innocent, but also because he had enough cash to fight his case. Now he wanted to use his freedom to fight against the unfairness of effective access to legal representation and the US–UK extradition treaty.

It was simply wrong, Lynch proclaimed to the world, that the arm of the US law could reach the UK in this manner; that US prosecutors could have more power over a Brit than the local policeman. He wanted to champion the wrongfully accused as a free man. Painting himself as one of them, as a victim of a miscarriage of justice who had won redemption, he planned to put some serious financial and legal muscle behind it.

Lynch approached Reid Weingarten to come and work with him on a new justice organization, telling one of the world's top lawyers, in a very Lynch way, that it was time to stop messing around with his high-profile corporate work. He wanted to create a UK version of the

US Innocence Project, which works to free those wrongly convicted of crimes and fights to overturn death sentences.

There were other matters that kept him busy, including a new business. For years, Lynch had avoided restaurants that played background music of any kind, as it made deciphering his companion's speech incredibly difficult for him as a hearing-aid user. This had always bothered him, to the point that he did something about it. His brain whirring as always, he had come up with an idea to solve the problem a few years earlier, and it was now starting to take shape.

It was called Hearable. It was a hearing aid that could pinpoint individual voices rather than letting in an unfiltered cacophony of noise. An alternative to noise-cancelling devices, which try to block out the background noise completely, Lynch's idea was to identify the speaker's voice and turn it into a clearer, computer-generated voice, either female or male with different pitches. This could allow the aid wearer to have a discussion with multiple speakers and flick between different people (sometimes called the cocktail party effect: the ability to focus on a specific sound or conversation, e.g. listening to one person in a noisy environment like a crowded party, while filtering out other background noise).

Deafness, Lynch felt, should not preclude people from visiting a pub and having a conversation, just like anyone else. While he had been in San Francisco, a research and development team based in the St John's Innovation Centre, the crucible of Autonomy, had started doing the work.

Between media interviews, Hearable and his legal crusade, Lynch was quickly back into the swing of things. He went to meet Patrick Vallance, the government's former chief scientific advisor, now a minister, to talk about companies' access to finance. And after years of not speaking with her due to the ongoing case, he was finally reunited with Nicole Eagan for a quick drink in the Lanesborough Hotel. At one point, he went to meet Sushovan Hussain for a curry in Chelsea. Toasting their freedom with a Cinzano, they talked about the possibility of trying to settle with HP, and of moving on from the debacle that continued to blight their lives.

Back in Loudham in Suffolk, his comforting spot of nowhere on the road to nowhere, he was welcomed by a delighted staff who had waited anxiously for his return, desperate for any information from America. He walked around the grounds and checked in on the livestock. His pack of dogs now had an extra member, Faucet, who retained some special privileges he had earnt in the US, such as sleeping on the pillow next to Lynch. It was good to see his fleet of cars: the SS Jaguar and the silver Aston Martin, which was incredibly uncomfortable for more than one person but a joy to drive.

He went to his beloved Ashe Abbey mill and turned the wheel. There was a 'welcome back' text message from Jeff Parish, the retired estate manager, expert carpenter and joiner who had restored the mill with such care over a decade. 'It is wonderful to be home,' Lynch replied, telling Parish that his wheel was working beautifully – he had been away when it was finished, so it was the first time he'd had a chance to see it in its final, fully repaired condition. There was a kind of symmetry in the timing; the mill-wheel restoration had started just as the first lawsuit was kicking off.

Shortly after his return, the Lynches held their usual summer party on the lawn of Loudham Hall. Caterers dashed around placing canapés and nibbles on trays, while glasses were filled and arranged in neat rows on trestle tables. With Lynch at home, the 2024 summer party would be the one to end all summer parties. Locals and friends were invited, along with all the staff at Loudham and their families.

There was no dramatic recounting of recent events, but Lynch was on ebullient form. Mark Gilbert, the Loudham Hall stock-keeper, still weak from his long, life-threatening illness, joined the party along with his extended family. He wouldn't have missed it for the world, given the Lynches' extraordinary generosity and kindness towards him at the worst moment of his life. He had not expected to ever leave hospital, just as Lynch had not expected to ever leave San Francisco.

When he arrived, Gilbert reached out to shake his boss by the hand. Lynch shook his head at him. 'I'm not shaking your hand today,' he said, and he pulled Gilbert in for an enormous bear hug. Then he stood back: 'I never thought I'd see the day that you were standing here and walking about in this garden,' Lynch marvelled at him with a smile. 'It's good to have you back, Mike,' Gilbert said, grinning cheekily. 'I hope you enjoyed your holiday in San Francisco.' Lynch wrapped his arms around him once more, and told him: 'We've both fought our battles this year, and we've both won.'

RETURNING TO A warm Cambridgeshire summer, Stephen Chamberlain was finally reunited with his son and daughter. He got stuck into life back home with his trademark practicality, volunteering to help a struggling local business sort out their accounts, continuing with his habit of going on long runs and starting to do a little business consulting here and there. He was nervous about his job prospects, but work was trickling in.

He never tried to hide his experience of the trial, describing his time spent in the dock as a career break, although there was no gap in his CV. He set out how he had worked tirelessly as a full-time member of his own legal team, striving to prove his innocence.

Proud of his mental resilience and the way he'd coped with the trial, Karen was delighted to have her husband back, not least because they had an unfinished house and he had a lot of jobs to be getting on with. Finally, they could settle back into the steady, safely mundane rhythm of an ordinary life, free from the shadows of the past decade. In a sign of how stressed he had become, Chamberlain had all but stopped posting the pictures and routes of his runs on Strava towards the end of April that year, but they soon picked up again when he got home.

On 11 June, he completed his first run back in England. It was a slower 10 km than he would have liked, because he was a bit out of shape and had enjoyed the large American food portions a little too much. He quickly ramped up his regime. In July, he tackled one of those crazy endurance tests he had become so addicted to, running in the boggy, high slopes of Snowdonia in Wales, then took on yet another later that month in the Lake District.

Running could not shake the one lingering source of anxiety which still haunted the Chamberlains, a dark cloud which would not go away: their debt from the residual legal fees. What began as a nagging worry soon settled into something heavier, souring into dread. The funds that Lynch had personally allocated for Chamberlain's lawyers had run out before the trial had even begun. Not wanting to abandon him, the firm had continued working throughout the period, but now there was an enormous bill, with a sum printed on it that the British couple was entirely unable to pay.

As a result, Chamberlain experienced far more sleepless nights after the trial was over than he had done in the run-up to the event itself. Lynch suggested that the lawyers should take the win itself as payment; after all, he said, their stunning victory in such a high-profile trial was utterly unique and you couldn't put a price on that kind of marketing and publicity.

He was right about one thing: the trial did win plenty of awards and coverage. In the end, the Chamberlains paid what they could, but it remained an awkward, unfinished business.

Lynch and Chamberlain didn't see one another after San Francisco. Their lives had been untangled by the verdict and they both had a lot to do, seeing their own friends and family, trying to get their lives back on track. Despite their shared experience, they did not speak very much nor meet for a big victory lunch. Instead, they planned to go for a low-key beer after the summer was over.

JONATHAN BLOOMER, WHOSE support for Lynch was so deeply appreciated, had been home for a while, back with his wife Judy, a devoted trustee for a women's health charity, and a former psychotherapist and teacher. The energetic couple had been married for five decades, had three grown children and were just a few weeks away from welcoming two new grandchildren.

Aged seventy, the Bloomers were the type of people who were always busy, attending their local church in Kent on Sundays when they could. Jonathan was an enthusiastic sailor, and rugby fan in his spare time. The Lynch family invited them on holiday later that summer, to thank Bloomer for his unwavering backing and the effort he had made in testifying yet again.

ACROSS THE ATLANTIC, worn out after his victory, Chris Morvillo had returned to New York a conquering hero. The thrill he felt at the career highlight of winning the case – incredibly, he had spent a third of his working life on it by the end – was matched only by his joy at being reunited with his family. I am so glad to be home, he declared with feeling to his friends, adding that none of this would have been possible without his wife, Neda.

Morvillo and three of his brothers had all followed their father Robert into the legal profession, and with so many attorneys around, the success was never going to be allowed to go to his head, although they teased him that they were never going to hear the end of this newfound fame. Neda Morvillo, who had been with Chris since his postgraduate days, could also poke fun at him. When someone called him a perfect husband, she replied, 'Why, because he's away so much?' Morvillo's phone was abuzz with tempting offers from law firms wanting to poach him from Clifford Chance. He was the toast of the town, the darling of the white-collar crime scene.

Looking back at the past decade and its triumphant, improbable conclusion in a rare public social media post, Morvillo thanked everyone involved in the trial and his family for their support, ending his message like any other fairy tale: 'And they all lived happily ever after . . .'

THIRTY-FIVE

The *Bayesian*

Wealth doesn't make any difference. It doesn't matter what the next number is, but it is a great enabler.

– *Mike Lynch*, Management Today, *1 June 2000*

In 2014, not long before he turned fifty, Lynch had treated himself to an early birthday present: a £27-million yacht called *Salute*. He did not have any romantic hankering for a life at sea, nor any innate passion for it, but the yacht allowed him complete seclusion. She was a status symbol where he could do as he pleased without interruption.

With a bow to the man that he outwardly feted as the source of all his wealth and success, Lynch renamed her *Bayesian*, after Thomas Bayes. This change flew in the face of maritime superstition, which holds that renaming a vessel brings bad luck. But for Lynch, with his love of probability, the yacht had to have 'Bayesian' emblazoned across the stern, along with another important word: 'London'. Ever the patriot, she would sail under the British ensign rather than a flag of convenience.

At fifty-six metres long, *Bayesian* was classed as a superyacht by length and was just five metres short of counting as a megayacht, the next size up. She was designed by Perini Navi, an Italian shipyard with a long heritage, known for its skills at blending beautiful aesthetics with technology. Length, though, was not the appeal. It was the height that mattered. The *Bayesian* had a striking feature: a single seventy-two metre aluminium mast, one of the tallest in the world, built at the behest of its previous owner in 2008.

Lynch was exceedingly proud of this feat of engineering; it was one of the first things he would point out to guests. As if they could miss it. While most yachts with such elevation had a double mast, the *Bayesian*'s rarefied single feature meant there was more space on deck for the children to play, the family boasted. Although that kind of statement mast wasn't without its issues – one guest recalled it had collapsed once while the yacht was at sea, when Lynch was not on board – images of the *Bayesian* show her cutting elegantly through the waves, with her large white sails taut in the wind, her gunwales almost touching the water.

Another standout feature was her retracting keel. This allowed the draught – how deep the bottom of the boat sits in the water – to be reduced from ten metres to four metres, and meant she could be moored in shallower waters for easier access to the shore.

On board, there was a timeless grace to the yacht's finish, with teak decks (a lighter wood than many boats use) sunk low towards the sea. The air-conditioned interior, in its neutral tones, had won design awards, and nodded to a pared-back Japanese elegance. There were cushions, leather banquettes, glassware, vases with flowers, coffee-table books, lamps . . . it was like being in a floating hotel.

She was also surprisingly spacious, with six cabins which could sleep up to twelve guests. Friends who were lucky enough to be invited to a holiday on board gasped at the size of the rooms, which were set further back in the boat than the narrower crew quarters towards the front. The master suite was especially generous, with its own dressing room. There was a room with bunk beds for younger guests to snuggle into.

Beneath the surface, every detail on board was micromanaged, every minor feature was considered. During the yacht's refurbishment, Lynch had called in Jeff Parish, his trusted estate manager and carpenter, and urged him to get on a plane to Mallorca where the *Bayesian* was being worked on. There was something not quite right, Lynch stressed. It was the toilet seats. Parish duly agreed to go, chuckling to his wife as he packed his bag to spend a week working on the bespoke teak seats in a dry dock.

When Lynch bought the yacht, it was just two years after HP had made its fraud allegations, so the *Bayesian* was acquired in the name of Revtom Ltd, a company owned by Angela which was based offshore in the Isle of Man. This followed a pattern for Lynch of keeping assets in her name, such as the majority of the family's Darktrace shares and Loudham Hall, which was transferred to her in 2020. It was the safest thing to do, given the legal threats. Latterly, holidays had been just her, the children and assorted guests anyway. As soon as the threat of extradition reared its head, Lynch was unable to travel because the US could have started its proceedings from anywhere, so he stayed firmly put.

Unlike other prestige assets like a private jet, a convenient way to get from a to b, a superyacht depreciates in value, sits idle most of the year and is astonishingly expensive to run. Basic annual maintenance and operational costs can be around 10 per cent of the original purchase price. A good crew is essential, and salaries can be high. Captains, engineers and chefs can each command thousands of pounds a week and the *Bayesian* could have up to ten crew members on board at any one time.

All of this meant a lot of work, and so, as is typical for a superyacht, the management of the *Bayesian* was outsourced to an experienced yachting company, Camper and Nicholsons.

WITH THE LOGISTICS taken care of, *Bayesian* soon became the unrivalled centrepiece of the Lynch family's social calendar. A trip on the yacht was, friends breathlessly recalled, like being dropped into the glossy pages of luxury magazine *Condé Nast Traveler*. It was a world of quiet opulence, that most people can only glimpse from the shore and only a fortunate few can ever truly call their own. Some would joke, however, that while it was nice to be asked, the last thing they wanted was to be stuck on a yacht with Lynch for a week.

Friends who accepted the invitations were whisked by private jet to lovely parts of the world, such as Antigua or Italy. Once there, the crew, dressed in a uniform of matching polo shirts, would line up to welcome them on board. Every whim would be taken care of, cabins tidied and beds remade, while they enjoyed a day's snorkelling, relaxing on deck, exploring historic sites and beautiful towns. Just like a hotel, there were stacks of pillows and cushions on the bed and, if guests tried to get rid of them, they would insistently keep reappearing.

Angela in particular enjoyed planning the holidays and assumed responsibility for much of the entertainment. The Italian shipyard Perini Navi holds an annual regatta, and the Lynch family went all out in preparation for it. For most owners, the regatta means an immaculate uniform of chinos and blue blazers. Aboard the *Bayesian*, however, one year featured a much more flamboyant Studio 54 theme, with a host of friends in platform shoes and frilly shirts. Angela was adamant everyone should go full-on glam and dress to the nines.

Each holiday, she treated her guests to schedules of cultural tours and activities, rather than spending the week simply lounging about, cocktails in hand. There was a little dinghy with a sail on the *Bayesian*, and the retractable hatch at the stern had steps down to the sea, where people could climb down for a swim. Sometimes the crew would set up a rope so guests could swing off the side of the boat and jump in.

Food on the yacht was cooked by its chef, Recaldo Thomas, known as Rick, a self-taught Canadian based in Antigua with an infectious smile and a knack for making the kinds of meals people really want to eat. He was popular with the crew and guests, not just for the food he created, but for his handsome smile and his calm presence.

Thomas had been crewing yachts for years and was looking forward to retiring from the charter life. He had a vegetable garden and a beautiful home back in the Caribbean to look after, and he was beginning to tire of life below deck, as fun and well-paid as it could be. He had a bad back, and so, despite his love of the job, he felt like his yachting days were almost over.

Over time, some of the crew of *Bayesian* had become close to the Lynch family, especially chief stewardess Sasha Murray, whose boyfriend was also on the staff rota. The Lynch family treated the crew with respect and warmth. The younger members of the crew were not that much older than Hannah and Esme and were often greeted as their friends, swimming with them and accompanying them on nights out. This last bit was important. If the crew members went to party with the girls, they were not there for fun – instead they were expected to keep a close eye on the teenagers for their parents. It let the kids loose, with supervision.

In the summer of 2024, as soon as the verdict was announced, Lynch started making plans to once again host parties on *Bayesian* and, this time, the holidays would be for all of those who had helped him win the case. It was an important time for him and Angela, who had been a more united front during the trial than they had been for a long time. The summer was a fresh start, as they looked to a future together. It was understood by their friends that they were 'trying again'.

There were a few different trips planned over July and August. The core legal team and supportive friends and associates were all invited. Some couldn't make it, of course. Brian Heberlig was chaperoning his son, who was spending time in Cameroon. He would not be allowed to escape the 2025 holiday, Lynch told him. Reid Weingarten was still too unwell to travel. But many others were to be treated to a much-deserved week away around the Italian coast, including Jonathan Baum and his wife.

Flying to Italy to board the yacht for the first trip, Lynch was arrested on arrival. The red notice on his file – an international request issued to law enforcement agencies worldwide to locate and provisionally arrest a person pending extradition – had not been removed.

The error was resolved with a phone call to the US authorities, but it caused a few heart-stopping moments. Lynch was detained for about an hour and made a call to Morvillo, who woke with a panic in the small hours of the morning back in New York, as if from a bad dream in which his former client was still officially regarded as a wanted man.

Lynch saw the funny side.

One week, Rolo Igno and his family were on the yacht's guest list, having just spent time in Chelsea and Loudham at the invitation of Lynch. Igno's youngest daughter idolized Hannah, in the way that younger girls look up to the 'big girl' in a group, especially one so accomplished. She followed her around all week, and Hannah was kind to her in return, patiently tolerating the adoration. It was a truly special holiday for the Igno family, who were now being invited to move to London to work for the Lynch family full-time.

Capri, Positano, Amalfi. Angela arranged tours and visits onshore, dinners and walks, making sure guests got the most out of the history and the richness of the treasures of Italy. Everywhere they went on the yacht, there would be stares, phones out, videos, TikToks, Instagrams. One hot afternoon on a trip to Ravello, the group toured a church. It was another beautiful day.

Lynch and Igno walked a little way beyond the others and stopped by a lookout tower next to steep-sided cliffs which fell away into the blue below. The *Bayesian* was anchored in view. They leant across the ledge, looking out to sea, and Lynch told his bodyguard about the moment he received a phone call to say he was to be extradited. It was in that exact spot, he told Igno, and the police were waiting

Mike Lynch and Rolo Igno.

below to take him away. Angela snapped a picture at that moment of the two men.

Shedding the stress of the trial was like peeling an onion. At one point, Igno turned to him and asked, 'Are you there yet?' and he said, 'You know, Rolo, I think I'm almost there.'

IN NEW YORK, ahead of a flight to Italy where he in turn would join the assembly of Lynch's guests aboard the *Bayesian*, Chris Morvillo was looking forward to some time with his family after spending so long away from them working on the trial.

Neda needed some convincing to go on the yacht. It didn't seem the most tempting prospect to spend a week with Lynch and some work colleagues, especially as she'd only just got her husband back from San Francisco. But they came up with a plan to meet their daughters Sabrina and Sophia the day after the Italian yacht break and have a family holiday in Greece.

Now the children were grown up, it was to be a precious occasion.

THIRTY-SIX

Unforeseen Events

The investigation has established that, in the assumed loss condition, wind speeds in excess of 63.4 knots on the beam were sufficient to knock Bayesian over.

– British Marine Accident Investigation Branch, preliminary report, 15 May 2025

On a warm Friday evening, sitting out in their Cambridgeshire garden, the Chamberlain family were having drinks and chatting about the future. The children, Teddy and Ella, were now in their early twenties – it felt like they were all experiencing some kind of new beginning.

In front of a bonfire, Steve Chamberlain became quite philosophical. The family talked about life and death and his wishes for his funeral when the time came. The conversation took Karen off-guard, and she teased her husband for his unusual sentimentality that evening, even though they had just celebrated their twenty-fifth wedding anniversary. He kissed his family on their heads and told them he loved them, before heading to bed.

First thing the next morning, on Saturday 17 August, he went out for one of his long runs. The tiny, charming city of Ely was just starting to bustle and stir as he ran through, passing its famous cathedral in the centre and then its train station until finally he was out in the open, in Cambridgeshire's famously flat countryside. He ran steadily along the picturesque trail next to the Great Ouse River, which meanders out peacefully from the conurbation, encountering only the ponderous barges on its waters and the occasional silent, solitary fishermen on its banks.

He had been going for just over an hour when, at 10.10, he emerged on the narrow footpath from the river trail onto the Newmarket Road, a single carriageway outside the small village of Stretham. He hopped over the low barrier to cross the road to pick up the trail again. At that moment, a blue Vauxhall Corsa came down the road, crested over the humpback bridge crossing the river and careered into him.

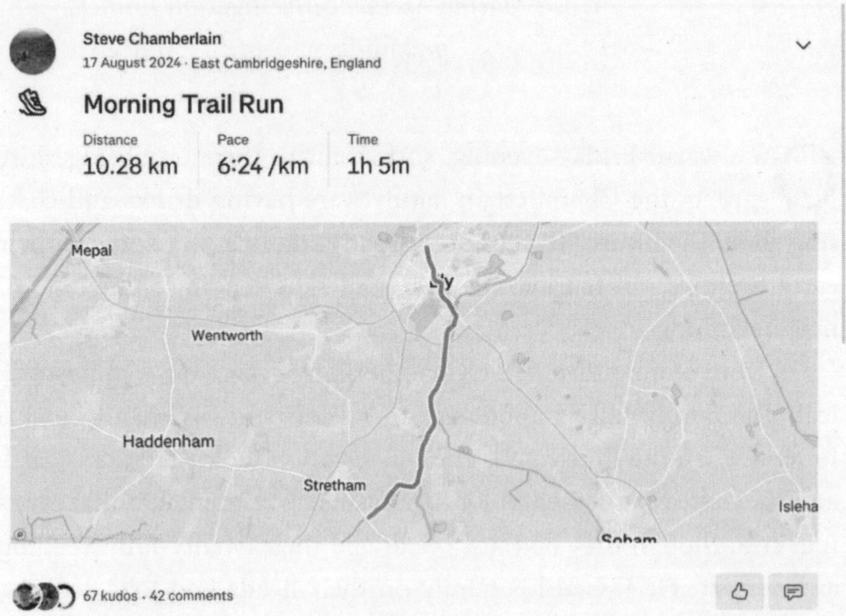

Stephen Chamberlain's final Strava entry.

The little orange line which traces Chamberlain's final Strava route ends abruptly here.

The driver of the car, a forty-nine-year-old woman from a local village called Haddenham, remained at the scene to help. Chamberlain was seriously injured and taken to Addenbrooke's Hospital in Cambridge.

ABOARD THE *BAYESIAN*, the crew sailed around Lipari, Salina and Vulcano islands on Sicily's northern side.

The Bloomers, Jonathan and Judy, had joined the yacht, alongside Chris and Neda Morvillo and Charlotte Golunski – an employee from the Autonomy and Invoke days – her husband James Emslie and their baby. There was another Clifford Chance lawyer, Ayla Ronald, and her partner Matthew Fletcher. Hannah Lynch was there too, having had friends staying on board at various points over the summer.

It was Sunday 18 August. Exactly thirteen years since the hot London day when Autonomy was sold to HP. More importantly for those on board the yacht, it was the day before the holidaymakers were due to fly home. James Cutfield, *Bayesian*'s captain, was choosing a sheltered place to drop anchor for the evening. They would be glad to leave. The mood was sombre as everyone had been plunged into gloom at painful news from England: Steve Chamberlain had been hit by a car while running, and his life was hanging in the balance. With horror, Morvillo texted his fellow lawyers from the trial to let them know. The joyous spell of the previous week had been broken.

The weather was uncomfortably hot and stuffy, so they all moved into the air-conditioned living area below deck, trying to process the news.

*

ON THE SAME stretch of water, about 150 metres away, was Captain Karsten Borner, the owner of the forty-two-metre *Sir Robert Baden Powell*, who was also looking for a suitable place to settle his yacht and passengers for the night.

Some of his guests were leaving a day earlier than the others and, being an organized and thoughtful soul, Borner decided the best place to stop would be somewhere close to Palermo, the chaotic Sicilian capital. By dropping anchor there, the departing guests would easily make their early flight the next morning but would still enjoy the last day of their holiday along a charming bit of coast.

Borner checked the weather and chose to anchor off the small fishing village of Porticello. Once he was happy with his chosen position in the bay, he checked the forecast again. There was a thunderstorm on the way, with winds due to get up later that night. It wasn't a weather warning but it looked a bit dicey. Even so, Borner was confident that the yacht would be protected from any waves outside Porticello, and that he was in the right spot to face the headwind.

That evening, at about 9.30, Borner's guests gawped as the *Bayesian* dropped anchor nearby. They pointed at the unusually large mast, taking photos of the stunning vessel. Cutfield had had the same idea as Borner regarding the location. *Bayesian* had been moored at Cefalù on the northern coast, but had motored the 25 nautical miles west, given the impending weather. She anchored with the centreboard raised and sails tucked away.

Captain Borner is a fit, globe-trotting salty sea dog who looks younger than his years, with sun-bleached white hair and a rugged, weather-worn face. He is an experienced sailor, having spent over forty years crossing the seas from Sudan to Sardinia and St Lucia. He had converted the *Sir Robert Baden Powell* (named for the founder of the Boy Scouts) from an icebreaker thirty years before, when he had first started work with his trusted Egyptian first mate, Gamal. He had seen a lot in his time and was well aware of the dangers of the water. He once had to rescue a diver and a yacht drifting towards a reef in the Red Sea. On another occasion, he saw a forty-metre yacht on fire. He had weathered many storms, both metaphorical and literal.

That Sunday, however, he cast his mind back to an incident exactly two years earlier, off the coast of Corsica, when he had encountered a waterspout – essentially, a water tornado. It was unlike anything he had ever experienced before. The phenomenon arrives as quickly as it leaves and is a fierce force of nature.

Rising sea temperatures have made spouts more of a risk. For several years, Europe has consistently been getting hotter and hotter in the summer months. The water in that part of the Mediterranean is now around 32°C in summertime – thirty years ago, that was the average water temperature in the Red Sea off Sudan. Borner knew it was getting to be too warm back when he had experienced that first waterspout. It was going to happen again, he and Gamal agreed.

At 9.45 p.m., Borner picked up his guests from their onshore dinner. They begged him to do a loop of the superyacht in the dinghy. He chuckled and did just that. Phones out, the guests snapped away and chatted excitedly as they returned to their lodgings on their sailing yacht next to the larger, grander *Bayesian*. It was nice to look at, Borner remarked, but he wouldn't want to sail across the ocean in it.

ON BOARD THE *Bayesian*, with the news of Chamberlain's critical condition, no one was in the mood for celebrating, so they had gone to bed early and sober. The last guest turned in about 12.30 a.m. In the early hours of 19 August, Matthew Griffiths, the deckhand, was keeping watch. His job was to record the weather, wind speed and location – on the hour, every hour. At 3 a.m., the wind speed was 8 knots. Looking out over the sea, he saw a storm in the distance, flashes of lightning dancing dramatically through the skies. The thunder and clouds seemed to be getting closer. He took a video at 3.55 a.m., posting it to Instagram, a film which shows the *Bayesian*'s flags flapping in the wind. The rain started and he went about closing the hatches.

Everything felt normal, until it didn't.

A couple of minutes later, the wind kicked up radically, reaching about 30 knots, and Griffiths felt the anchor was dragging. At 4 a.m., he went to wake up Cutfield, the captain. Together, they went to the flying bridge and the crew started getting up and heading out of their accommodation.

Recaldo Thomas, the yacht's popular chef, headed to the galley, where he stowed away cutlery, pots and pans. He greeted his busy colleagues with a cheerful 'Good morning!' in his usual good-humoured way. Tim Parker Eaton, the chief engineer, experienced in storm conditions, got up and headed to the engine control room to prepare the yacht to move, making sure all the generators were running.

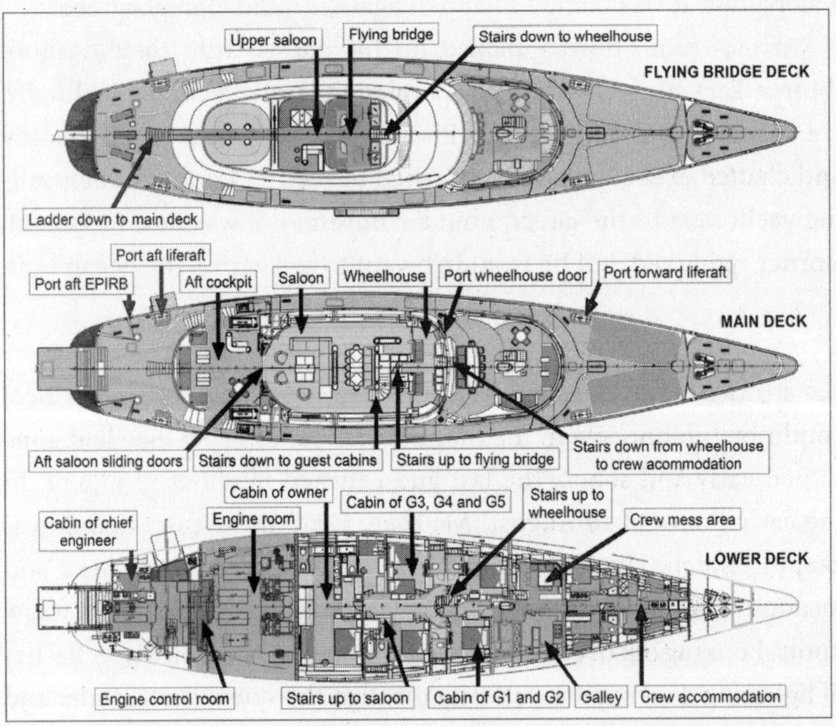

Layout of the *Bayesian* (Source: Marine Accident Investigation Branch report 2025).

Sasha Murray went on deck and began to do all the normal things, like bring in the cushions and plants, anything that might fly around outside. The windows and hatches were closed.

Angela, awoken by all the motion and commotion, went on deck to see whether the morning's taxis would still come at 8 a.m. as planned, to take the guests to their onward destinations. But events had gone far beyond this level of administration. Golunski, Emslie and their baby got up and headed to the saloon, just as a rain-soaked Murray entered.

Suddenly, conditions on board became impossible. Cutfield prepared to move the yacht to face the wind, when it raged above 70 knots, far beyond hurricane force. The awning above the flying bridge ripped from port to starboard.

At 4.06 a.m., in a heart-stopping moment, the storm overwhelmed the yacht, and in less than fifteen seconds the *Bayesian* tipped over 90 degrees onto her starboard side. People and objects were hurled across the deck like rag dolls. Furniture skidded, toppled and smashed with splintering force. Anything unsecured became airborne, slicing through the chaos like shrapnel. Then, with a gut-punching jolt, the generators died. Darkness swallowed everything until the emergency lights blazed to life, stark and unnatural, throwing the scene into a theatre of shadows and fear.

Cutfield and Angela were among the injured. Griffiths was thrown into the sea. Below deck, two other crew members hauled themselves up stairwells into the engine room. Ayla Ronald and her partner Matthew Fletcher used furniture drawers as a ladder to climb the walls of the corridor towards the saloon. A wall of seawater surged over the starboard rail, crashing onto the deck with a roar. In an instant, it found the open stairwells, pouring down in unstoppable torrents. Water tore through cabins and corridors, swallowing everything in its path with terrifying speed.

Tijs Koopmans, the chief officer and second-in-command, found Angela and pushed her through the cascading water to the captain on the flying bridge, along with Golunski, Emslie and their baby. Griffiths climbed back aboard and into the wheelhouse with the bosun, before lifting Ronald and Fletcher onto the flying bridge and inside. They found themselves in an air pocket by the closed door on the front left side of the wheelhouse, and with help from someone outside, they were able to get to the door and escape. Koopmans, who had been swept to the back of the saloon and into another air pocket, dived down to open the sliding doors at the back and managed to swim clear of the vessel.

These survivors were treading water in the open sea, hanging on to cushions to stay afloat – even the baby was put on a floating cushion. They used a phone torch to search for others.

Cutfield swam back to the yacht, trying and failing to release a life raft, until finally, on the other side, Koopmans managed to free one from the sinking wreck. It was inflated at 4.24 a.m. and they fired a flare ten minutes later. Chief Engineer Tim Parker Eaton used his torch to signal a distress call to a hotel on the cliffs above them.

From the life raft, Murray saw the bow of *Bayesian* rise up and then slip beneath the surface. It sank in fifty metres of water. Parker Eaton managed to fire a flare at 4.34 a.m. but it blew sideways in the strong winds. He fired another at 4.43 a.m. This one was spotted.

ABOARD THE *SIR Robert Baden Powell*, guests tried to get some rest on deck. It was far too hot to sleep below in the cabins.

At midnight, a weather warning was issued for strong winds.

The passengers were captivated by the thunderstorms picking up, and the lightning flashes which illuminated the horizon. Looking out to sea, sometimes the *Bayesian* would be lit up dramatically by a forked crackle of light, before a roll of thunder.

A couple of guests were worried about getting onshore to catch their morning flight. At 3 a.m., midway through a sleepless night, they asked Borner if he'd take them earlier than the planned 6 a.m.

start. He agreed and prepared to launch the tender. But the weather suddenly intensified and, by the time the passengers had gathered their belongings, the thunderstorm was getting closer and closer.

Borner could see the storm moving on the radar. The wind was starting to worry him. He decided to act. 'Let's start the engine!' he told the first mate – he needed to keep the boat in position. He started the engine and battled three times to keep it running. It was at full power, but still Borner physically struggled to keep *Sir Robert Baden Powell* steady.

It was all just a warm-up act. Shortly before 4 a.m., the storm really got going.

The rain fell in torrents. *Bayesian* was drifting one way, then another, seemingly dragging its anchor. The wind came in fast from the north-west, and the terrible, vast surface of the ocean became white in a foamy and urgent rage.

The rain drenching Borner's face made it hard to see anything at all. It felt like tons and tons of water were being dumped on him. He'd never experienced anything this severe in all his years at sea. His crew and some passengers had rushed about a little earlier to close the hatches, the portholes, the skylight and the entrances. They braced themselves for the onslaught of water.

Winds were now at over 60 knots, 70 miles per hour, almost touching tornado speeds. The *Sir Robert Baden Powell* was keeling (leaning over) at quite a tilt. Borner still wasn't worried about his yacht; he didn't think there was a real danger of his ship sinking as long as he held it steady. But he was concerned that if they drifted onto *Bayesian*, there could be a serious problem.

The ship still tilting, Borner and Gamal looked around frequently to check where the *Bayesian* was positioned. Suddenly, all was black. The lights on the yacht had gone out.

'It must have sunk,' the first mate called over.

'Are you crazy?' Borner replied. 'Something that big couldn't have sunk so fast.'

He turned to look and, as a flash of lightning briefly brightened the dark skies, he could make out a vast black triangle above the horizon, right where the *Bayesian* had just been.

With dread and fear, he realized it was the bow of the ship.

Borner turned back, struggling once more to keep his own yacht in position against the storm. No more than twenty minutes had elapsed from the start of the onslaught to that moment.

When the wind dropped suddenly a few minutes later, the *Bayesian* was no longer on the ship's radar at all. Borner and his first mate checked and checked again – it was not there. 'It must have drifted!' someone called out, in panic. But surely it couldn't have! Not so far and not so quickly.

Then, a shout came from a passenger who was scanning the blackness of the horizon to try to see what was going on: 'A red flare!' Borner saw a second flare and, in what he later described as a split-second decision, he and Gamal jumped from the deck into the tender.

In moments, they reached the spot where *Bayesian* had been anchored.

It was gone.

THERE WAS NO sound but the cry of a baby, the noise drifting eerily over inky blackness. The water was flat and gentle. There was nothing to see as Borner and Gamal looked over the surface. It was like a millpond, calm and deathly serene.

Then, cushions and chairs, floating gently. The debris confirmed what they feared.

Suddenly, they saw the torchlight, and the baby's crying became louder, and soon a raft came into view. They had found, finally, the people they were looking for.

The raft held the survivors, some in their night clothes or underwear, having had no time to dress themselves. Some were visibly wounded, and in shock. Only the baby continued to make a sound.

Trying and failing to tow the raft, Borner decided to get all fifteen people into the small tender and transfer them to the *Sir Robert Baden Powell*. The *Bayesian* crew had managed to perform some first aid in the raft, but it was clear that they all needed to go to hospital.

A woman, who was bleeding from her head, spoke to Borner urgently in Spanish: 'Please keep searching,' she said. 'There are more people inside.'

He told her that they needed to go back to the ship and that they'd continue the search after that. In the event, Gamal continued scanning the water for several more hours, alongside Captain James Cutfield, who had survived, and an engineer and a guest from the *Sir Robert Baden Powell*.

Borner rushed to call the coastguard while his passengers and crew took care of the survivors. They found clothes, blankets, towels. Borner instructed a crew member to take names and document the injuries. It was daylight by now, and more boats were combing the water for survivors, but Borner didn't hold much hope. Another half an hour passed. It was now almost two hours since the initial rescue.

Finally, a coastguard boat came into view around the corner of the cove, and a commander came aboard the *Sir Robert Baden Powell*. The boat started to transfer the wounded to shore.

One of the rescued party did not want to go, clinging on to the improbable hope that the tender would return with more survivors. She refused to move.

Borner recognized the woman who had spoken to him in Spanish. He was worried about her, and pleaded with the coastguard to take her. She needed medical attention, fast. She had a cut above her eye, there was a lot of blood, and she was nearly incoherent in her speech.

It was only when a crew member told him quietly that she had just lost her daughter and her husband that it became clear why she was so reluctant to leave – why she did not want to give up hope. It was Angela.

THIRTY-SEVEN

Funerals

There was a child very much alive in the man. There was a constant playfulness in his demeanour. There was a free-ranging artistic sensibility coalescing, in rare and original form, with the rigour of a formidable intellect. Here was a man propelled by an innate curiosity to ponder and revel in the possibilities of life.

– Albert Read, eulogy for Mike Lynch

When his phone rang at six in the morning on Monday 19 August, Greg Morvillo immediately knew that something was wrong.

It was a colleague from his brother's law firm, telling him that the *Bayesian* had sunk and that there were passengers still unaccounted for, including his brother Chris and his sister-in-law Neda. At that point, they'd been missing for about eight hours.

Greg knew in his heart to prepare for the worst. His first task was to get in touch with Sabrina and Sophia, Chris and Neda's daughters, who had been about to fly to Greece to meet their parents after a short stop in London. He hastily arranged for them to return to New York, concerned for their privacy given the media interest in the Lynch saga. He spent all day breaking the news to their loved ones. It was torment.

After twenty-four hours, he got the call from the consulate. It was so much worse than he thought it would be, even though he knew it was coming.

THE *BAYESIAN* LAY intact on the seabed. The search and rescue operation was intense, watched by the world's media, who descended on the small village of Porticello in their droves, capturing every moment, questioning anyone they could, beaming live footage around the world as the hope of finding any survivors slowly faded.

It appeared that the yacht had veered wildly as the storm intensified. The angle at which water could theoretically begin to flood into *Bayesian*, once it keeled, was forty-two degrees. When that was breached, it could take on a ton of water every second. It seemed as if she had flipped onto her side before sinking backwards, keel first. It baffled experts, who said that the yacht should have been able to withstand the storm and certainly not sink so quickly.

Recaldo Thomas's body was discovered first. Days later, the bodies of those still missing – Judy and Jonathan Bloomer, Neda and Chris Morvillo and Mike Lynch – were found on the boat. The last to be recovered was Hannah, found alone in a cabin next to the others.

Rescuers suspected they had been looking for air pockets.

Some friends found out from WhatsApp groups, others saw the news of the sinking on television and pieced it all together. There was disbelief, vain hope, and then horror.

Andy Kanter and Richard Gaunt flew out to Italy to support Angela, who was still bearing the wounds of the accident.

Back in England, in Worcestershire, Jonathan Bloomer's twin brother Jeremy was doorstepped by the local BBC radio station. Calmly and kindly, the retired dentist explained that his nephew, one of the Bloomers' grown-up sons, was in Sicily trying to establish more information and deal with the officials there. He said, voice calm but at times quaking: 'He was my older brother by half an hour, it means a lot when you lose your twin.'

In Antigua and in the global yacht-crewing community, tributes started to pour in for Recaldo Thomas. He was an inspiration to many, friends said, credited with introducing espresso martinis to Antigua's iconic Skullduggery cafe. Crew who had worked with him on other yachts talked of his reliable sense of calm, of how encouraging he was of others, and of his infectious smile.

While the families were trying to grieve, the world's press continued its feeding frenzy. The Lynches' media representative, Salamander Davoudi, was dealing with an avalanche of enquiries for information and comment. There were reports of journalists trying to climb into ambulances with the injured to get a scoop. With Angela still in Italy, Mike's Suffolk friend Lord Deben stepped up to do some interviews and to speak for Lynch's legacy.

Rolo Igno sent Angela a personal tribute to Lynch, his new friend and the person who had completely changed the course of his life over the previous year. He'd written it after staying up until the small hours, distressed by the news of the *Bayesian*. It was widely quoted in the international media, and he woke up to a flood of messages on LinkedIn and other social media platforms.

KAREN CHAMBERLAIN WAS quietly sitting on the bus, en route to Addenbrooke's Hospital in Cambridge where Steve lay in a critical condition, when she got the text telling her the news about the tragedy in Sicily.

It was layer upon layer of shock. She could not believe it. No one could. Then came the unthinkable. In the early hours of 20 August, her husband's life support machine was turned off.

*

AFTER THE HORRORS of late August 2024 had unfolded, the surviving parties faced the unenviable task of organizing funerals.

Tributes were paid to Jonathan and Judy Bloomer, touching LinkedIn posts about kindness and support. Their children released a statement saying:

> *Our parents were incredible people and an inspiration to many, but first and foremost they were focused on and loved their family and spending time with their new grandchildren. Together for five decades, our only comfort is that they are still together now. This is an unimaginable grief to shoulder.*

They had a private funeral.

There was an outpouring of love for Steve Chamberlain from friends and colleagues. He was a person who was genuinely valued by those around him, and it showed. Billy Joel's 'Innocent Man' played at his funeral.

In New York, hundreds squeezed into a memorial service for Chris Morvillo. Brian Heberlig could not say enough good things about him. Reid Weingarten simply said he missed him.

In London, the Lynch family held a moving double funeral for father and daughter at St James's Church on Piccadilly. The six pallbearers for Lynch included his cousin and close friend Gerard Morris, Rolo Igno, Richard Gaunt and Sushovan Hussain. Those for Hannah were young men. It was a painful sight, a smaller coffin held on the shoulders of teenagers. There were over 400 mourners present, each of whom was given a booklet which was filled with Hannah's poetry. At the heart of the sad event, Esme and Angela brought some of the family's dogs, too, including Faucet.

Igno was handed small bags of their favourite sweets – one with Mike's favourite, Haribo Goldbears, and two of Hannah's beloved M&S Percy Pigs. He pinned the packets onto Lynch's pall, which displayed a beautiful picture of his beloved Loudham estate. He recalled with overwhelming emotion just how many times he had snuck those gummy bears to Lynch behind Angela's back in San Francisco. It felt like their private joke, but one he would never get to truly share again.

Music was always important to Lynch; this double funeral featured 'Just Like Heaven' by the Cure and 'Forever Young' by Alphaville. There were eulogies from family friend Albert Read, who spoke of Lynch slaying the dragon of the US justice system, but also of him at home, relaxed with his family, displaying his wry sense of humour. Sir Paul Nurse, president-elect of the Royal Society and a Nobel Prize winner, said Lynch was always 'reassuringly ordinary' despite his very many achievements and railed against what he called 'the biased, asymmetrical extradition agreement between the UK and the US'. Hannah's English teacher paid tribute to her talents and called her the best student he ever taught.

It was a gathering that no one had expected, that no one wanted, and a most shocking end to a remarkably improbable series of events.

Epilogue

I'd like to think that when people look back, one of the things I did was produce one of the world's first true AI companies. I hope that the impact I've had on the UK has played a role in creating this incredibly vibrant technology scene we have here now. I'd like to think that I've had a good role in getting the Government to understand the importance of science and technology in the UK economy.

– *Mike Lynch,* Archives IT, *31 January 2017*

What are the chances that these two men, Lynch and Chamberlain, who had just won their blighted lives back in an interminable, almost impossible legal victory, would lose them over the course of the same weekend?

About four in a billion.

This is the number that Abid Hussain, head of insurance at the City firm Panmure Liberum and a friend of Jonathan Bloomer, calculated for me at the time. It's an estimate of probability that may have made Lynch chuckle morbidly and, over the course of writing this book, I have often wondered what figure he would have come up with.

The entire affair was so extraordinarily unlikely that conspiracy theorists went into overdrive. There were stories of assassinations; of a plan by a government, HP or an unknown power to somehow create the storm and send it to the *Bayesian*. Misguided connections were drawn between Darktrace, the secret services and Mike Lynch. Many reported that the *Bayesian* contained safes that held hard drives stuffed with state secrets that someone would murder for.

There was indeed a safe on board. But a friend of the Lynches remarked later that it was far more likely that it contained sweets and Jaffa Cakes which Mike was hiding from Angela, rather than anything that could threaten national security. Even so, the theory attracted enough attention to become an ongoing question.

There were accusations in comment sections of newspapers directed at the crew, questions over their actions, and whether all had been done that should have been. Both the Lynch and Chamberlain families had already had their fair share of official scrutiny over the years, but it only intensified. Even as this book went to press, the deluge was not over.

The vacuum of information around the case was quickly filled by internet gossip. It was a distraction from what really happened and, away from the rumourmongering, there were attempts to find more concrete answers as official probes were started into the circumstances surrounding the deaths.

On 15 March 2025, representatives of those who lost their lives in the *Bayesian* tragedy gathered for the first hearing into their deaths at Suffolk Coroner's Court in Ipswich, a bland grey building on the outskirts of the busy town. Those who could not be there in person listened remotely on a conference call. It was only a short pre-inquest. The full inquiry is ongoing at time of writing.

There are several inquiries into what happened to the *Bayesian*, undertaken by marine investigators, including criminal investigations. The UK's Maritime and Coastguard Agency is looking into potential breaches of maritime legislation, while the Italian authorities are considering charges equivalent to manslaughter. After the surreal events of 2024, which had flashed by in a blur, everything now felt as if it was moving extremely slowly. The Suffolk coroner remarked that these investigations would have a bearing on his final report, once he had heard the evidence.

At the end of April 2025, the long process of bringing up the yacht's 510-tonne wreckage from 49 metres below sea level, where she had lain for more than eight months, began. The insurance company hired two specialist Dutch salvaging companies to do the £20 million of work. The unique mast had to be cut off and removed by an underwater robot with a saw, while the heavy body of the yacht, containing 18,000 litres of diesel, was picked up in its entirety by a crane, backed up by inflatable balloons. There was another tragedy. During the preliminary operations, one of the diving crew died, a thirty-nine-year-old Dutchman named Rob Huijben. The salvage was temporarily halted. Observers remarked that the yacht was cursed.

An examination of the vessel, it is hoped, will provide some longed-for answers for all concerned. A preliminary report by the UK's Marine Accident Investigation Branch, published in May 2025, found the sinking was caused by design 'vulnerabilities'. At anchor, with its retracting centreboard raised and its sails lowered, the yacht was more vulnerable to extreme weather, but the crew and owner were unaware of this as it was not mentioned in the yacht's stability information booklet, the investigators said.

*

TEDDY AND ELLA, Steve Chamberlain's children, started running in tribute to their father and, on an emotional day in April 2025, alongside reams of his friends and family, completed the route that he never got to finish.

In May, a coroner concluded that Chamberlain died as a result of a road traffic collision. The inquest heard that the driver was within the 60-mph speed limit. Her statement said Chamberlain had emerged into the road from nowhere. She had braked hard, but he was too close. A motorbike rider who witnessed the collision saw him tossed 15 feet into the air, and said that the entire incident took a matter of seconds.

MANY OF THE characters in this book are doing their best to forget their association with Autonomy and to cast off the memories of an utterly miserable period, but some threads of the story have been tied up in happier bows.

Daud Khan and Paul Morland still meet up occasionally, with others from the City, to talk about Autonomy. Recently, Morland asked Khan why on earth they had spent so much time over the years on it all, speaking to investigators and travelling back and forth to the US to testify against Lynch and Hussain. Khan shrugged with a sigh, and said that it was 'just the right thing to do'.

Stouffer Egan went on to work for Oracle and, later, a Silicon Valley success story called Flexport, which souped up the technology behind the global freight industry. In 2022, he co-founded a company called Rally Reader, an educational technology business which helps to improve kids' reading skills.

Nicole Eagan remains at Darktrace, where she is Strategic Advisor.

Andy Kanter sits on the board of Luminance, among other companies. He divides his time between London and Spain.

On 10 October 2024, Poppy Gustafsson was asked by the new Labour government to be the Minister for Investment, to act as an ambassador for UK companies and to bring funds from abroad into

UK tech (she would step down in September 2025). She was made a member of the House of Lords and is now formally known as Baroness Gustafsson of Chesterton OBE.

Sushovan Hussain plans to write a book about his extraordinary experiences in prison, and has set up a business called Liberatus to help ex-convicts join the workforce. He has also taken charge of Hearable, Lynch's hearing aid business, trying to build a working product with the clever cohort of Cambridge engineers in the St John's Innovation Centre. He still believes he was unfairly prosecuted. Those close to him are concerned that he hasn't got to grips with the reality of the last two decades. He finally settled with HP in May 2025 for £77 million, which has, it is understood, still left him with a sizeable percentage of his assets to see out his days.

IN CONTRAST, DESPITE talks, the Lynch side failed to come to a settlement with HP. On 22 July 2025, the familiar array of lawyers representing HP and the Lynch estate once again convened upstairs in the Rolls Building to hear Mr Justice Hildyard deliver his final say on the financial loss the US company had suffered.

Representing the Lynch estate was Jeremy Sandelson, the ebullient Clifford Chance lawyer who had worked with Lynch over many years. He had been brought out of retirement to take a role that others were reluctant to fulfil, given the ongoing legal proceedings. Back in court, he recalled the sound of Lynch's voice, his charm, his extraordinary intelligence and breadth of knowledge.

Hildyard, wearing black robes with red tabs at his neck, mumbled a few choice phrases about what a difficult and awkward situation it was and paid his condolences to the families of the deceased. He swept out of the room again, and copies of the judgement were left at the front.

Sandelson pulled a fistful of ten pound notes from his pocket as he departed and, as he walked past the opposition, joked that he was going to settle the case. Journalists rushed to the front to grab one of the few copies, skimming through to find the number. Had it known Autonomy's true financial position, HP would have paid £23 per share rather than £25.50, the judge found, reflecting the outcome of a hypothetical negotiation and taking into account factors like HP's urgent need for the acquisition, the value of anticipated synergies, and the negotiating positions of both parties. More than £700 million (over $900 million) was the loss suffered by HP, Hildyard found, far less than the $4 billion HP had sought, which he described as a 'wild overstatement', but far more than the value of the Lynch estate, estimated at £500 million. Lynch 'in his mind, and given HP's urgent need, in fact, held "all the cards"', Hildyard said. The lawyers were summoned to yet another hearing in November 2025, when the final damages would be awarded. As they include interest over fourteen years, they are expected to be substantially more. The judge added a rare, moving postscript. 'No words from me will be of any comfort to his wife and family. But I wish to express my sorrow at this devastating turn of events, and my sympathy and deepest condolences, having come to know and admire Dr Lynch (notwithstanding my findings against him) over the course of a very long trial.'

At the time of writing, Lynch's estate was considering an appeal.

On top of this looming financial blow, Angela, as the legal owner of *Bayesian*, could face being pursued for compensation by the relatives of some of those on board.

WHATEVER YOU MIGHT say about Mike Lynch – whatever you feel about his relationship with the truth, how he ran his businesses, treated people, and made his way to the top – it is undeniable that he had rare gifts. He created extraordinary technology, employed hundreds and generated great wealth, much of which he redistributed into other enterprises or to those who he loved.

He has left an indelible stamp on the British business world, clear in the companies he backed, some of which realized their potential only after his death. At the end of 2024, Visa announced it was buying Featurespace in a deal reportedly worth $700 million. The same year, the $5 billion Darktrace sale officially went through. Both notably followed the trend of British tech being sold into American hands. In 2025, Luminance raised $75 million, surfing the wave of interest in legal tech, as generative AI made good on its promise to change the world. Hearable, his hearing aid company, is getting off the ground. There would undoubtedly have been others, but the 'what next?' for Lynch was cruelly taken away.

He did, though, live to see his criminal acquittal, and he took enormous pride in having fought and beaten the US system which he believed was unjust. His noisy extradition fight raised awareness of the imbalances in the US–UK treaty, and is a cause that others are still championing in his name.

Lynch was a fighter. In everything he did, he wanted to come out on top. He was controversial. It is, as Mr Justice Hildyard said, a tragedy that Autonomy will forever be associated with fraud. And rather a mystery why, when it did not have to be this way.

For those he clashed with – and they were many – the scars have still not entirely healed. But his legacy will surely never fade. If there is one certainty to emerge from this very unlikely story, it is that we will never see the like of Mike Lynch again.

Acknowledgements

Writing a book of this magnitude is a group effort.

Sarah Treanor, who worked tirelessly on the project, has been a journalist for twenty years, fourteen of those at the BBC, starting in business news output editing live programmes and business and economics coverage for *Today* on Radio 4. Sarah joined the BBC World Service after that, finding a passion for long-form narrative journalism, documentaries, script-writing, features and creative sound-editing. She's hunted down passport dealers in Vanuatu, covered the migrant crisis on the Texas–Mexico border, and reported on femicide in Argentina and the diabetes epidemic in the Pacific island nation of Tonga.

George Pliotis, a Cambridge PhD classicist, worked as a dedicated researcher on the book over a period of several months. More used to investigating the world of several millennia ago, he proved the concept of 'transferrable skills' admirably. He had unending enthusiasm, tenacity and a deep understanding of how to put together long, complex submissions for information to so many organizations, including the FBI.

I am forever grateful to **Jonathan Conway**, my agent, for picking up the story when no one else was interested. I feel lucky to have had **Ause Abdelhaq** as an editor for most of the writing of this book, both for his bottomless enthusiasm and humour and his clever ideas about how to structure the narrative. Thanks to **Kate Walsh** at Pan Macmillan for picking up the baton from him so quickly and to **Fraser Crichton** for his deft copy-editing.

This book is based on almost a hundred interviews, including with Lynch's friends, enemies, advisors, former Autonomy employees and associates, along with mountains of evidence and transcripts of cross examinations from three trials. At points this felt overwhelming.

To the many people who spoke in confidence and who for understandable reasons did not want their names to appear, and to those who helped to proofread the book – you know who you are. It was not easy to dredge up old and often painful ground. As one who declined to be interviewed put it, 'many of us have spent more than a decade strung up in the furore around Mike and co . . . and nothing good comes of it.' No one had to speak, but plenty did.

There are a huge number of personal thank yous which need to be made.

To the Lynch family and their close circle for the kind introductions to key people in his life to make sure he was fairly represented. It was a horrific time for a project like this to get underway and I am grateful for their help during this sensitive period. Thanks to Salamander Davoudi, representing Lynch through the trial and then through the shock of the subsequent tragedy.

To Karen Chamberlain and the Chamberlain family for sharing extracts of Steve's diaries and to those close to him for sharing their memories of his life.

To Greg Morvillo and the Morvillo family, it was striking that no one had a bad word to say about Chris; he was a deeply loved man in his professional and personal life.

To my father, Jeremy Prescott, for his time and forensic work on the various company prospectuses, accounts and remuneration. Having a retired M&A banker and trained chartered accountant in the tent has been very helpful, to say the least. Others who helped by reading the manuscript included Simon Freeman and Tim Steer, who provided invaluable feedback, along with David Treanor for his proofreading and guidance from the outset.

My boss Richard Fletcher, *The Times* business editor, and everyone at *The Times*, the newspaper I'm lucky to call home. I'll never forget that you did not bat an eyelid at giving me time off to write this but merely asked: 'How can we help?'. Thank you Rebekah Brooks, Tony Gallagher, Chris Longcroft and Edward Roussel for your backing.

Everyone on *The Times* Business Desk. A small, perfectly formed group of brilliant people who work extraordinarily hard to produce top-quality articles, six days a week – no mean feat.

To the many, many experts who were happy to answer questions, including Stephen Robertson, Professor Emeritus, City University, London for his mathematical advice throughout. And to Adam MacVeigh, as ever, for his Bayes and AI expertise.

To the many journalists who shared their memories: Tony Quested, Rory Cellan-Jones, Gareth Corfield and Jonathan Margolis among them, along with Ian Gilby and Paul Wiffen who knew Lynch from his music tech days.

Professions feature heavily in this book . . . and I would like to thank all of the lawyers and accountants involved for their time, expertise and willingness to cast a critical eye on their own kind from time to time.

The new cohort of City tech analysts who helped me sense-check various things along the way, including Joshua Hughes at Deutsche Numis and Alasdair Young at Shore Capital. Then to the analysts from the 1990s and 2000s who so generously went back through their mental and physical archives.

A special thanks needs to go to two US tech companies. LinkedIn, an incredible journalistic resource which allowed us to find and speak to many, many of the people involved in this story in a startlingly short timescale. To Google for the use of NotebookLM, which allowed me to interrogate eye-watering volumes of material. Generative AI made it feel less overwhelming.

Captain Karsten Bohner for providing Sarah with such an accurate blow-by-blow account of the Bayesian's final minutes.

On a personal note, I would like to thank Miles Morland for the loan of Bugles where the book was born.

My wonderful mother Jackie Prescott for all her support and love through this process and my two daughters, Tilly and Carys for being so patient throughout. My grandmother, Kay Kirk, who turned 101 during the book's writing and whom I did not see as much as I would have liked while it was going on.

Last but not least, my love to Will Roe who held it all together and has pledged to flee the country next time I write a book.

Index

Image Credits

p. 26 Blues Patrol: *The Bancroftian*, Bancroft's school magazine

p. 51 Sound on Sound: Courtesy of Ian Gilby

p. 97 Autonomy share price: Source: London Stock Exchange

p. 388 Hannah and Mike Lynch: Courtesy of the Lynch family

p. 403 Mike Lynch and Rolo Igno: Courtesy of Rolo Igno